IMAGES
of America

AROUND SANGER

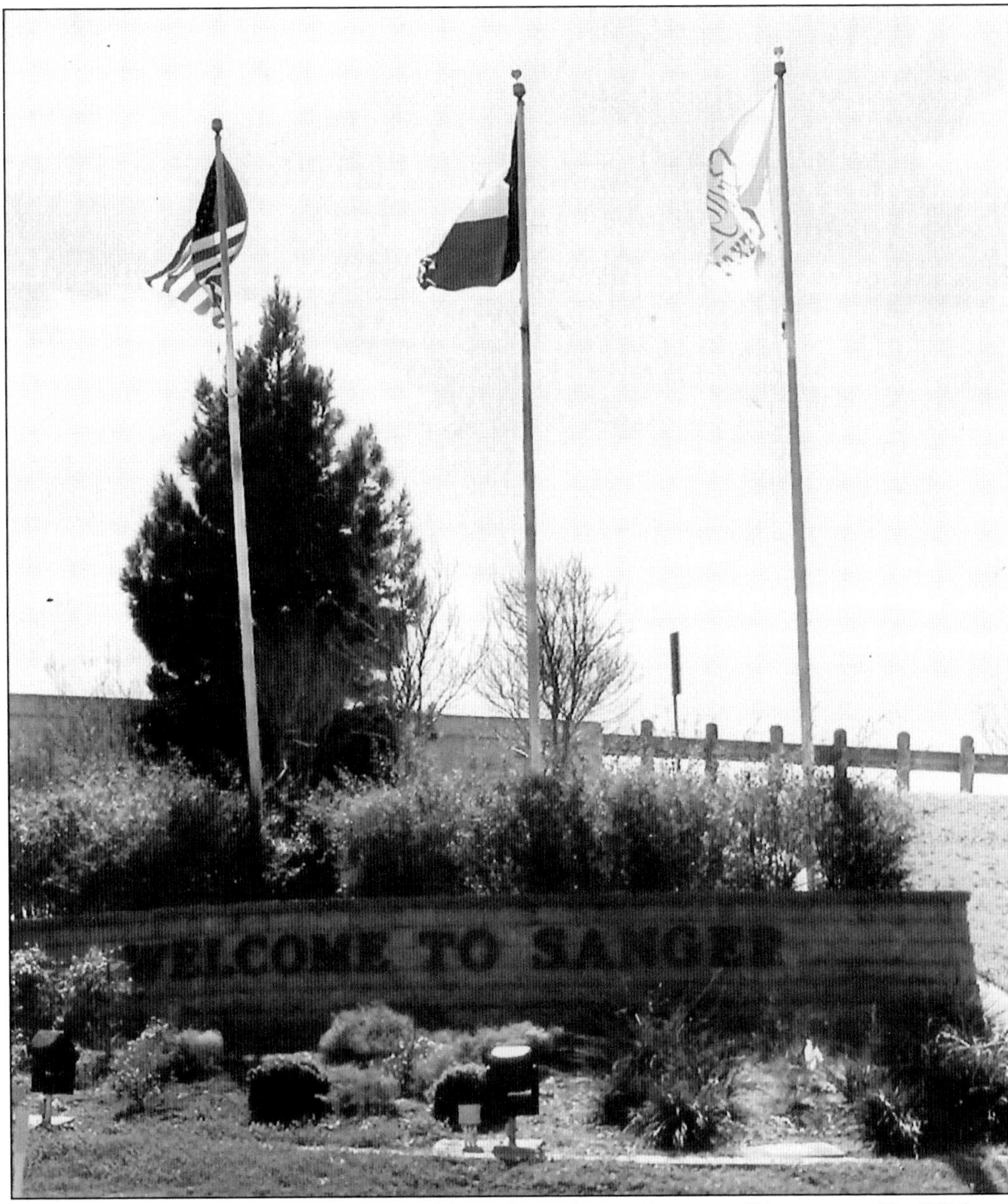

Gateway to Sanger. Northbound or southbound travelers on Interstate 35 are greeted by "Welcome to Sanger" signs posted by the Keep Sanger Beautiful committee. This organization is appointed by the city council to implement litter prevention, beautification and community improvement, and waste reduction programs. It is winner of the Governor's Community Achievement Award receiving funds from the Texas Department of Transportation for landscaping in 2001, 2004, and 2007. (Photograph by Cindy (Mays) Bounds.)

On the Cover: Kline Ice Company, 1934. With refrigerators not yet typical household appliances, ice businesses provided ice to the citizens. This image of Kline Ice Company, located on Fifth Street between Elm and Pecan Streets, shows employee Ross Mundy with a block of ice over his shoulder ready for delivery, and Jim Kline (right), business owner. Ice was 10¢ for 20 pounds or 40¢ for 100 pounds. (Courtesy of Bill Mundy.)

IMAGES
of America

AROUND SANGER

Helen (Seely) Bounds
Tona (Batis) Payne
Nancy (Campbell) Smith
and
Sanger Area Historical Society

ARCADIA
PUBLISHING

ISBN 978-0-7385-8505-5

Published by Arcadia Publishing
Charleston, South Carolina

Printed in the United States of America

Library of Congress Control Number: 2011923772

For all general information, please contact Arcadia Publishing:
Telephone 843-853-2070
Fax 843-853-0044
E-mail sales@arcadiapublishing.com
For customer service and orders:
Toll-Free 1-888-313-2665

Visit us on the Internet at www.arcadiapublishing.com

In recognition of Sanger's 125th year (1886–2011), we dedicate this book to the residents of our community— past, present, and future.

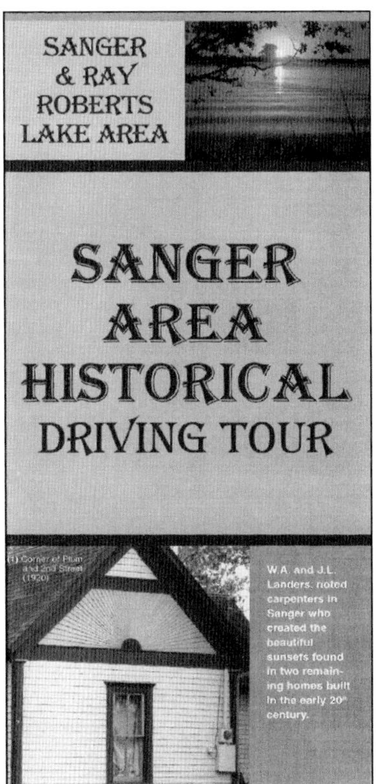

SANGER AREA HISTORICAL DRIVING TOUR. A four-page brochure outlining historic homes, churches, ranches, farms, businesses, landmarks, people, and a street map was published in 2002 by the Sanger Area Historical Society and distributed by the chamber of commerce and throughout Texas to promote the city and its historical sites. (SAHS.)

CONTENTS

ACKNOWLEDGMENTS

We thank the staff from Arcadia Publishing with whom we have worked: Luke Cunningham, Winnie Rodgers, Simone Monet-Williams, and Kristie Kelly.

Our thanks and appreciation also go to Georgia Caraway and Kim Culpit from the Denton County Courthouse-on-the Square Museum for their guidance in organizing and help in acquiring pictures; to Vicky Elieson, Kandyce LeFleur, and Lynne Smiland from the Sanger Public Library for their assistance in receiving photographs and providing a place for us to work; to Laurie (Smith) McClish and Oscar Shelton for lending a hand with scanning; to Cindy (Mays) Bounds and Millard Smith for their photography help; to Les Cockrell with the *Denton Record-Chronicle* and Blake and Lee Ann Lemons with the *Sanger Courier* for assistance with publicity; to Kimberly Johnson from the TWU library and Kathy Strauss from the Denton library for their help in obtaining images; and for the support of the Sanger Area Historical Society members in our efforts to memorialize the history of Sanger. We also thank our families for their support during the many months spent collecting the photographs, researching and writing, and developing the book in preparation for publication.

The images in this volume appear courtesy of these individuals: Diane (Hughes) Barentine, Jim Bolz, Helen (Seely) Bounds, Dee (Schertz) Brown, Yvonne (Yeatts) Cain, Elleece (Sullivan) Calvert, Haleigh CeBallos, John Chambers, Peggy (Ready) Crunk, Kenneth Frady, Idaleene (Scheu) Fuqua, Frances (Schertz) Gentle, Toni Gentle, Marlene Harper, Linda (Harvey) Hewlett, Wanda (Schertz) Hollingsworth, Mavis Hughes, Keta (Prater) Keith, Anna Lisa (Guillott) Lyon, Leonard Maughan, Greta (Hughes) Miller, Jenny (Campbell) Miller, Thomas Muir, Bill Mundy, Billy Ed Nance, Dorothy (Haskins) Nubine, Peggy (Vaughan) Pate, Barbara (Hachtel) Rippey, George Seals, Ken and Judy (Knowles) Selph, Oscar Shelton, Jerriann (Cooper) Shepard, Nancy (Campbell) Smith, Carol Tucker, Patti (Sullivan) Walker, Myrl (Yeary) Webb, Janis (Bailey) Wetherbee, Robert Windle, and Betty (Marshall) Wylie; and courtesy of these organizations: the Denton County Courthouse-on-the-Square Museum (DCM), Sanger Area Historical Society (SAHS), Sanger Chamber of Commerce, Sanger High School (SHS), Sanger Public Library (SPL), and the *Eunice Sullivan Gray Papers, 1863–2001* from the Woman's Collection, Texas Woman's University, Denton, Texas (TWU).

Any omissions or errors in factual data are unintentional on the part of the authors.

INTRODUCTION

Sanger originated in 1886 as a water stop for the Gulf, Colorado and Santa Fe Railroad because of its proximity to the cattle ranches and to the Chisholm Trail. The railroad built a side track with cattle pens and a depot, and the town of Sanger began to build around the railroad stop.

Elizabeth (Bullock) Huling (1820–1906) of Lampassas donated land for the town, and William Partlow, a native of Virginia, became the first mayor. John Thomas Chambers and later his son, Willie Bush Chambers, managed the Sanger Mill and Elevator Company and became leaders in the community.

In 1887, Francis M. Ready and his wife, Melissa, with their daughter Mary M., also called Molly, left Gribble Springs with their household belongings. They were caught in a snowstorm and sought refuge at the depot at milepost 392.16, which was the Gulf, Colorado and Santa Fe Railroad location for Sanger. The Ready family built a one-room log cabin, and Melissa cooked for the cowboys who drove their cattle to the railway for shipment to the stockyards. They later built a hotel just west of the cattle pens, and Francis Ready was commissioned as the first postmaster on March 15, 1887. He opened the post office in the lobby of his hotel on March 25, 1887.

A fire destroyed much of Sanger in 1890, including the railroad depot. The railroad rebuilt a much larger station that included a Western Union telegraph office and a Wells Fargo freight office. Tremendous growth ensued between 1890 and World War I, due to the expanded railroad facilities.

Sanger native James F. Hollingsworth became a lieutenant general in the US Army. Marijohn Melson Wilkin, a Nashville songwriter who grew up in Sanger, wrote many songs and was most famous for "One Day at a Time." Socialite Perle Mesta, a political hostess and US ambassador to Luxembourg (1949–1953), kept a home in Sanger. Dr. Roma Alva King Jr., distinguished professor emeritus of English at Ohio University and editor of *The Complete Works of Robert Browning, Volume XVI with Variant Reading and Annotations*, is a Sanger native and graduate of Sanger High School.

Early businesses included blacksmith shops, saloons, doctors' offices, a lumberyard, food stores, drugstores, dry goods stores, a bank, hotels, and boarding houses. There was a milling and elevator operation that became a producer of flour sold statewide. Its well-known product, Silk Finish Flour, was milled using silk for sifting the flour to a fine consistency.

Sanger's religious activity began with a Methodist church built on land donated by Elizabeth Huling. The First Baptist, Landmark Baptist, First Methodist, and Presbyterian churches were a part of the community from early days; only three of these congregations still exist today. The Presbyterian church building received a Texas Landmark Historical Plaque in 1972.

The Sanger school that burned in 1916 was rebuilt, but the separate gymnasium constructed in 1935 burned in 1948. A remodeled school structure was opened for the 1948–1949 school year. An elementary school was built and began operation in the spring of 1959 for grades one through five, with the remaining grades housed in the main school building that later burned in 1984. A new high school was built in 1977 at a different campus site, and the school system was divided into grade school, middle school, and high school. The Sanger school district now includes eight schools in its system.

Dr. Ervin Howard, who built his home in Bolivar and later erected a home in Sanger, served the citizens of Sanger after arriving in Texas after the Civil War. As the town began to grow, Dr. John C. Rice began his practice in 1890. Dr. Philemon J. Bowers arrived in Sanger in the early 1890s and also owned a drugstore. Dr. Samuel Gotcher arrived in 1897, and Dr. George D. Lain moved to Sanger from Bolivar in 1900 and also owned a drugstore. Dr. John M. Sullivan returned from medical school to his hometown to begin his medical practice, which continued until he died in 1958. Dr. J. Clyde Chapman, a native of Gainesville, Texas, arrived in Sanger in the late 1930s and continued his practice until the time of his death in 1990. Dr. J.S. Stubbs was a dentist who located his practice in the community in the mid-1920s. Sanger has always been fortunate to have good physicians available to its residents, as well as to those in the surrounding communities.

Over the past several years, the Sanger area has been recognized by the Texas Historical Commission with landmark and subject markers for special sites. These recognitions include: John Simpson Chisum Home Site (1936), Townsite of Bolivar (1970), Sanger Presbyterian Church (1972), Jacob Frederick Elsasser (1976), William E. Partlow, First Mayor of Sanger (1976), Noah C. Batis (1986), Forester Ranch (1987), Bolivar Cemetery (1998), Green Valley Schools (2001), Gribble Springs Baptist Church (2006), Galilee Missionary Baptist Church (2009), and Santa Fe Railroad (2010). The Sanger Area Historical Society has awarded historical markers to the Sullivan Senior Center building (2002), the Bolivar Masonic Lodge building (2002), the Landmark Baptist Church building (2002), and the Nance Farm (2008).

Sanger has grown from a railroad-loading site on the prairie in the late 1880s to a city of almost 8,000 residents. Many horse ranches moved into the area in recent years, and the Medieval Times' Chapel Creek Ranch, located just west of town, is where horses are trained for their entertainment facilities. Lake Ray Roberts, opened nearby in 1987, is a popular boating and fishing location. Well-liked restaurants Miguelito's and Old West Cafe originated in Sanger and now have locations in other cities as well. Several historical buildings are still located in the downtown area, with many still in use. At Exit 477 on Interstate 35, south of Sanger, there is a 520-foot-long mural commissioned by Keep Sanger Beautiful and painted by Lance Hunter in 2008, which depicts an interesting collage of Sanger past and present. This mural was included in *Mural Art Vol.2: Murals on Huge Public Surfaces Around the World* by Kiriakos Losifidis.

The Archives and Records Retention committee of the Sanger Area Historical Society meets bimonthly to catalog historical data. Their goal is to preserve the history of our community. Their collection is available to the public for research at the Sanger Public Library. They are "Preserving Our Heritage to Enhance the Future," the motto of Sanger Area Historical Society.

Sanger, Texas, continues as a thriving city that has grown as a result of the ribbon of growth beginning at the Mexico border in southern Texas, passing through Sanger, and ending at the Red River, the Oklahoma state line. Sanger's early settlers and their families continued the success of building the community, and many descendents of the early settlers are still prominent in the city today. By the late 1990s, Sanger's population had increased to over 5,000, helping it become a home rule city. As the city increases in population, it is important to capture these historical pictures to preserve for future generations.

One

THE BEGINNING

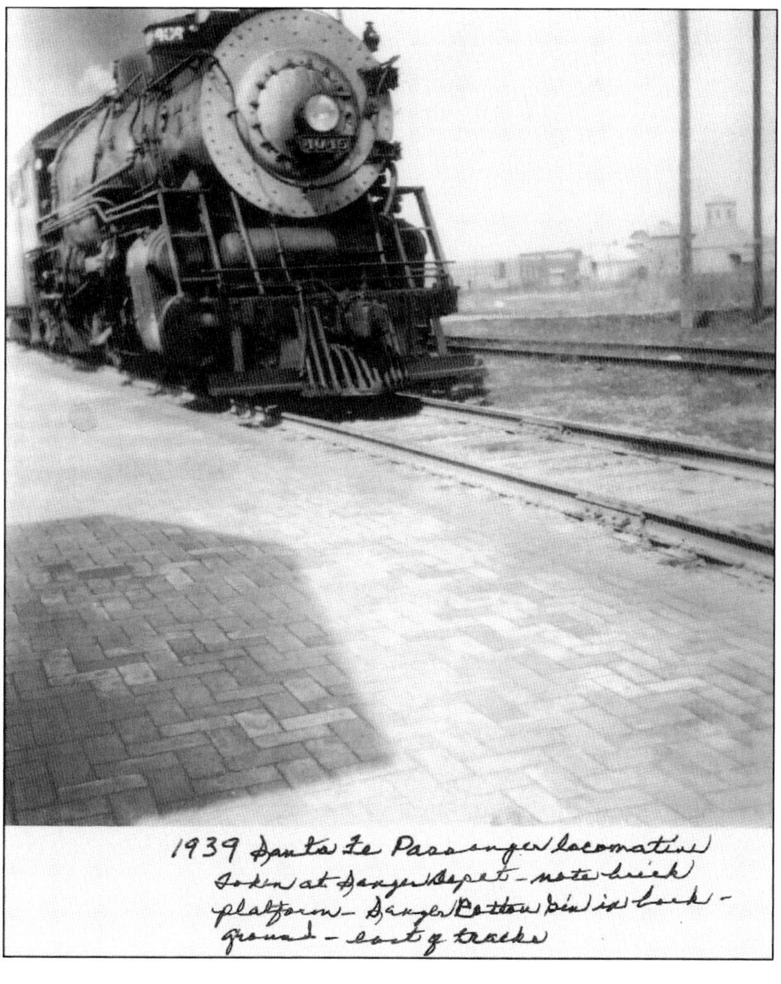

SANTA FE PASSENGER ENGINE. The Gulf, Colorado and Santa Fe Railway was instrumental in the history of Sanger. The railway, built in 1886, helped continue industry growth. In 1940, a passenger train rolled into the Sanger railway station. Hand-laid brick paving by the tracks is visible, and to the northeast of the railway tracks is one of the Sanger cotton gins. (Courtesy of Idaleene (Scheu) Fuqua.)

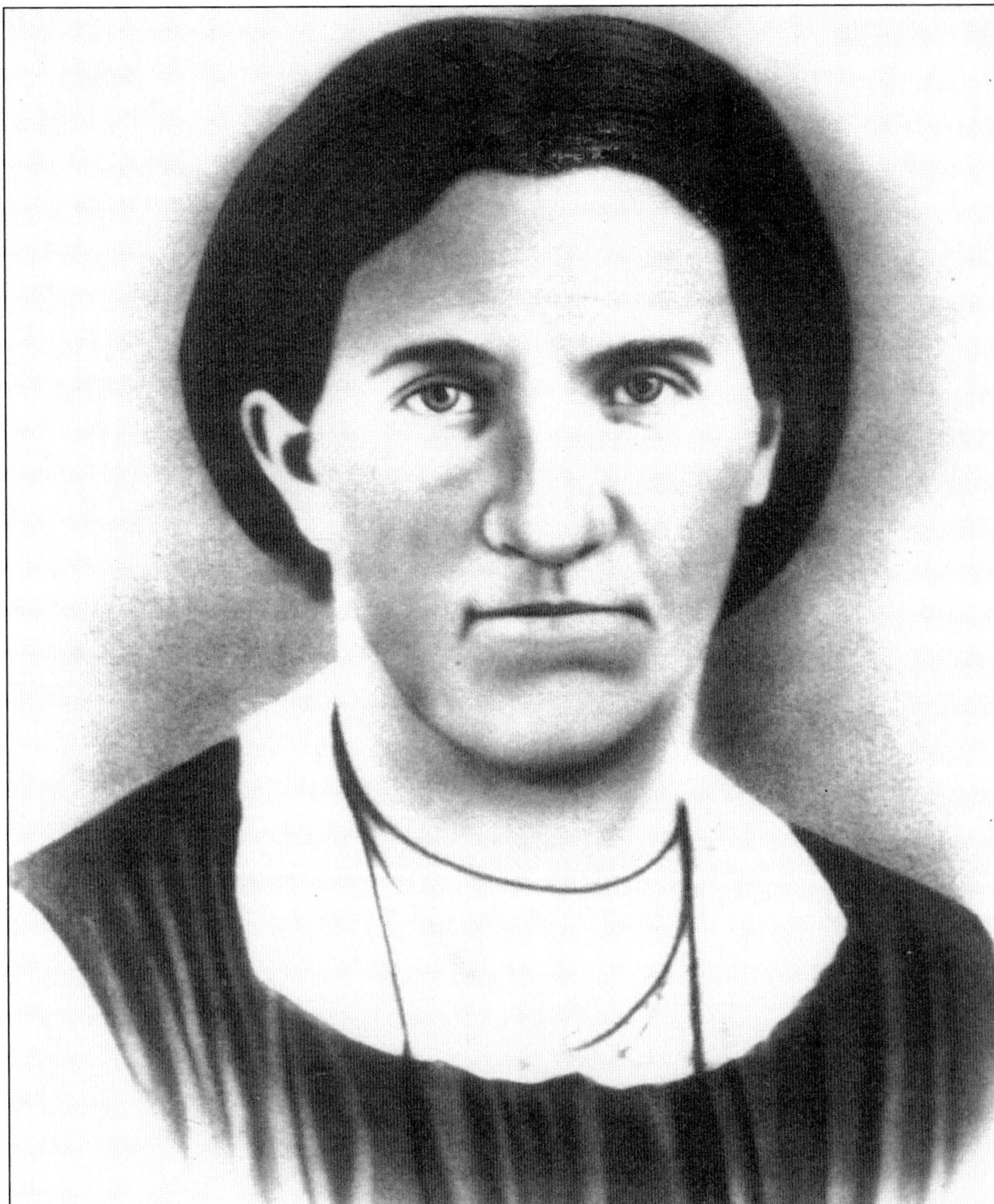

Elizabeth (Bullock) Huling. Elizabeth (Bullock) Huling, born April 12, 1820, in Bourbon County, Kentucky, was the widow of Thomas B. Huling, a veteran of the Texas Revolution who represented the Jasper District at the Fifth Congress of the Republic of Texas in 1840–1841. She sold land on June 14, 1886, recorded July 7, 1886, in Denton County. The land sold to the Gulf, Colorado and Santa Fe Railway was used for a water station at milepost 392.16 for the steam engines for the railway being built though Indian Territory (Oklahoma). Huling hired two surveyors, son-in-law J.C. Bartlett and Elijah Biggerstaff, to lay out the town and donated land for a wagon yard, well, school, town square, original cemetery site, and a Methodist church. A cornerstone on the southeast corner of the Sanger Park commemorates Huling's gifts to Sanger. Huling, a resident of Lampasas, Texas, died in 1906. (SAHS.)

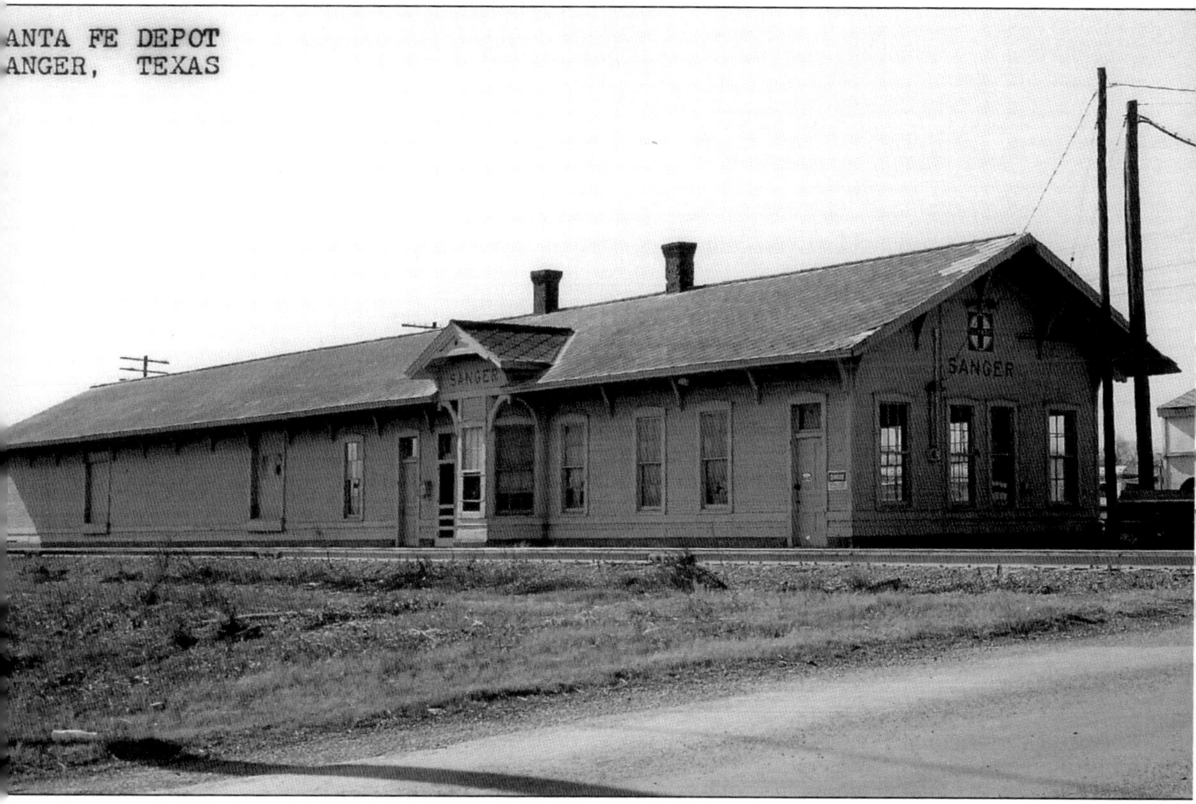

Gulf, Colorado and Santa Fe Railway Depot. The Gulf, Colorado and Santa Fe Railway became an operational line through Sanger and connected in Indian Territory (Oklahoma) in 1887. The train depot, built by the rail company, and the town of Sanger were destroyed by fire in 1890. The rail company built a larger depot with a Western Union telegraph office and a Wells Fargo freight office, which operated 24 hours a day, six days per week to accommodate the new businesses being built in the area. The Sanger Mill and Elevator Company was one of the businesses that relied on the railway for its statewide distribution of products. Famous passengers such as Eleanor Roosevelt, who dedicated the Little Chapel-in-the-Woods, and Fritz Kreisler, the famous violinist who appeared at Texas Woman's University, boarded the train in Sanger after their appearances in Denton. Passenger service eventually ended, and the railway requested the station be relocated from the railway-owned site. In 1999, the depot was relocated to a site in Tioga, Texas. (SAHS.)

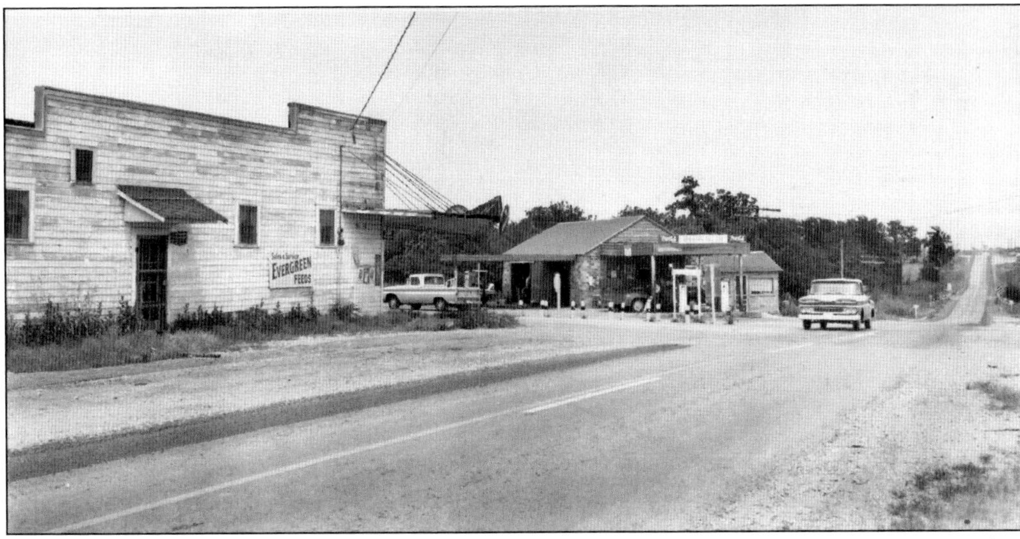

The Town of Bolivar. Bolivar began as one of six government forts in Denton County. A trading post was opened there before 1859 and people began settling in the area shortly thereafter. By 1872, there was a post office. Three schools were soon open for local children. When the railroad came through Sanger in 1886, people and businesses began moving further east, causing Bolivar to dwindle in population. (DCM.)

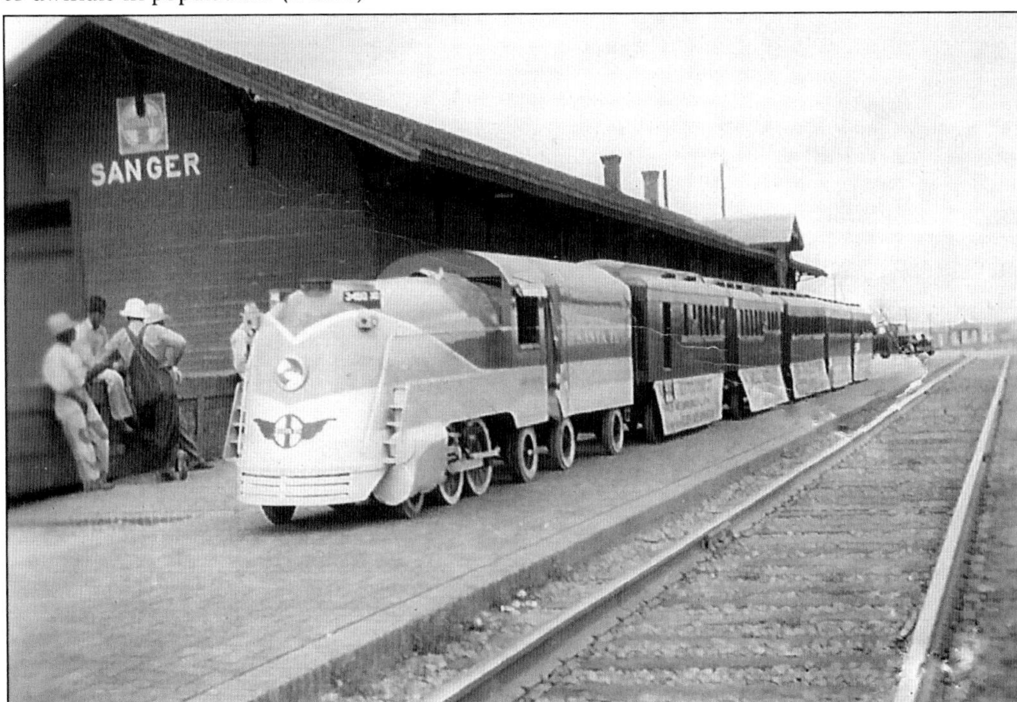

Santa Fe Miniature Train Model. The Santa Fe Railroad offloaded a miniature version of the Chief, the super-deluxe streamliner passenger train, during the fall of 1939 for display at the Denton County Fair. The miniature train was displayed at the Sanger Depot. Curious citizens at the station are seen above standing by the loading dock. Note the laid brick pavement between the tracks and the depot. (SAHS.)

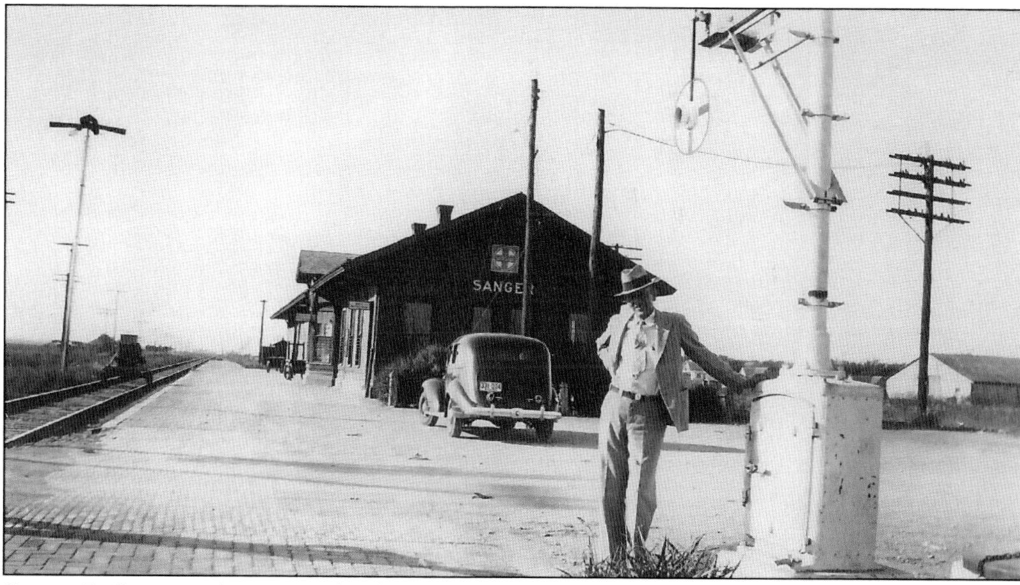

SANTA FE STATION AGENT. Fred Scheu, station agent for the Santa Fe Depot in Sanger from 1916 to 1917 and from 1930 to 1946, accommodated violinist Fritz Kreisler, arriving to board the train, by providing a meal at his home since no food service was available for later boardings. Scheu assisted Eleanor Roosevelt for her train departure after she spoke at the dedication of the Little Chapel-in-the-Woods. (Courtesy of Idaleene (Scheu) Fuqua.)

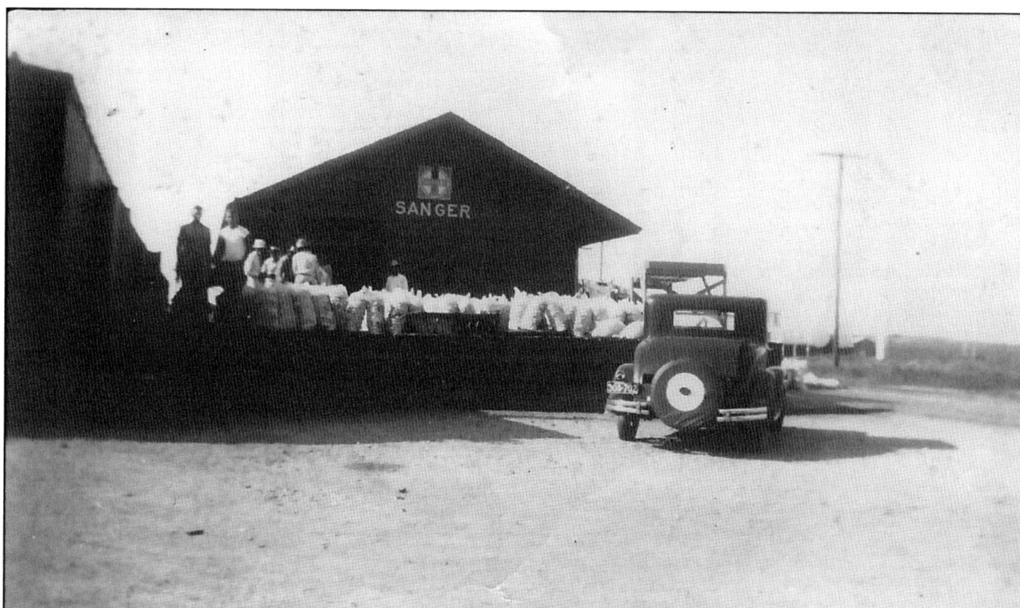

ONION CROPS AT RAILWAY DEPOT. About 1935, onion crops had been harvested, bagged, and stacked on the southern platform of the depot to be transported via rail to the markets. The railroad was instrumental in moving livestock to market, but also in the transportation of cars, farm equipment, and mail and food products. The Sanger Mill and Elevator Company used rail services for delivery of products, including Silk Finish Flour, across the state. (SAHS.)

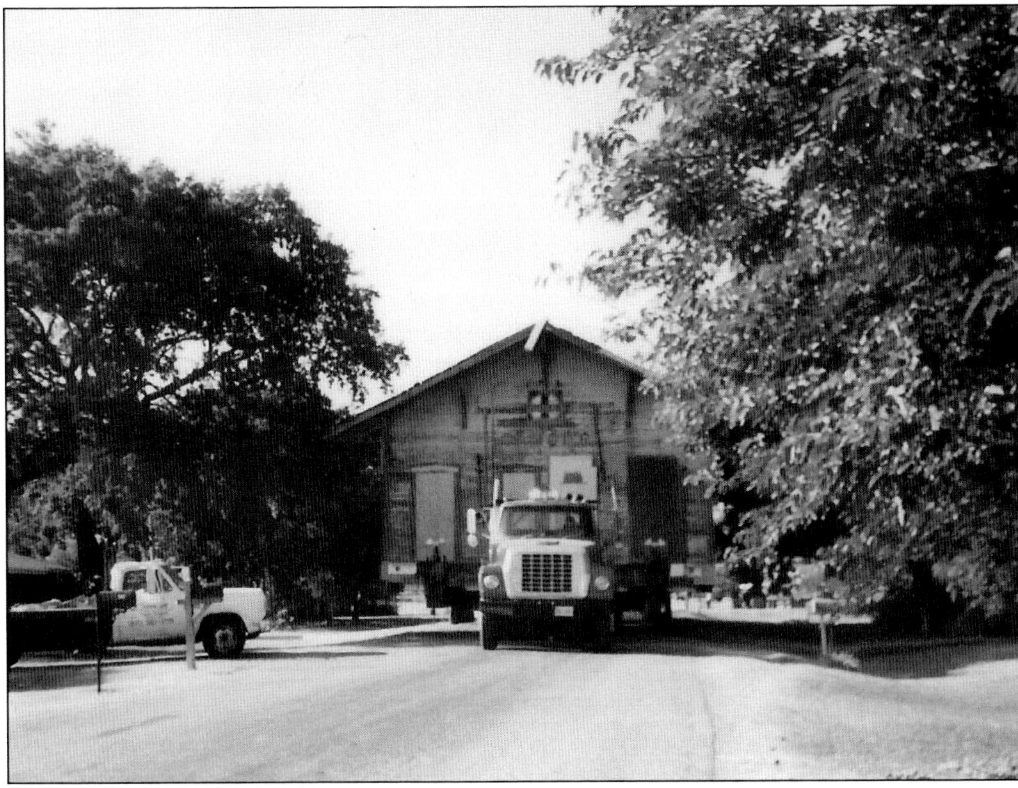

SANTA FE DEPOT. The train depot, formerly located at the southwest corner of Bolivar Street and the railway tracks, was once a thriving station for arrivals and departures since 1886. The building was eventually loaded onto a trailer, driven down Second Street, and relocated to Tioga, Texas, in 1999. It has since been converted into a commercial business on Highway 377. (SAHS.)

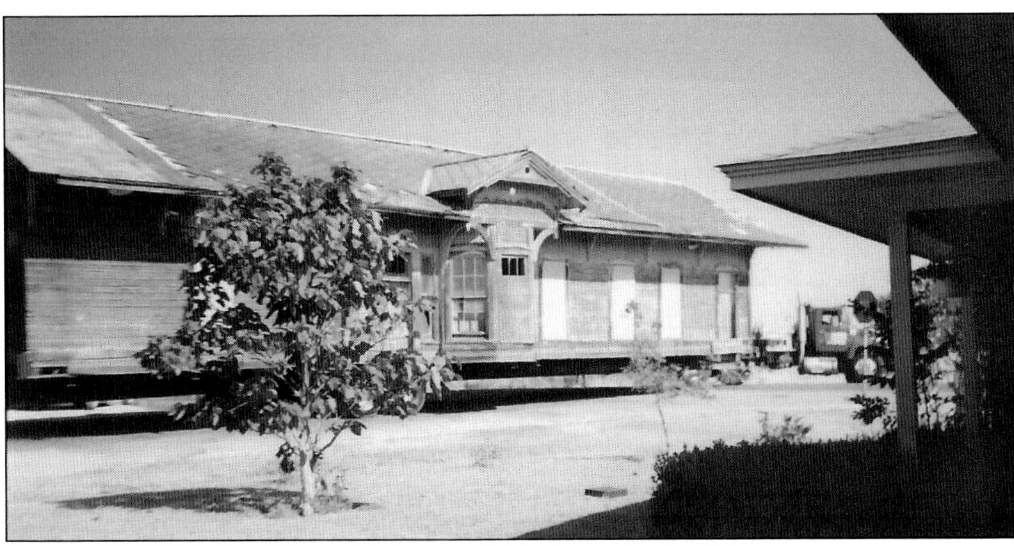

Two

The Living

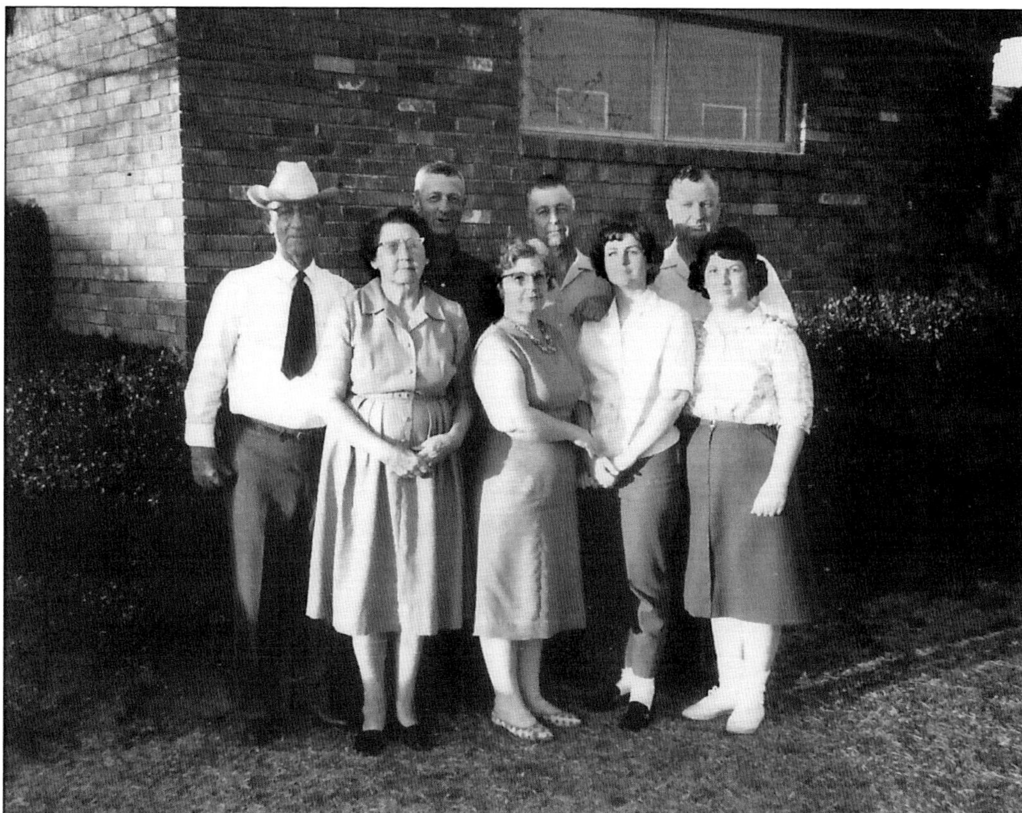

James R. Ready Family. The grandson of Francis M. Ready and son of William T. Ready is shown with his family. James Ready (far left) is with, from left to right, (first row) wife Cuba, and daughters Mary, Ethelyn, and Peggy; (second row) sons Dick, James, and Bobby. His first wife, Lena Pearl, died in 1936, and he later married Cuba (LeGear) Forrest. Francis Ready arrived in Sanger in 1887, built a hotel, and became postmaster for the town. (Courtesy of Peggy (Ready) Crunk.)

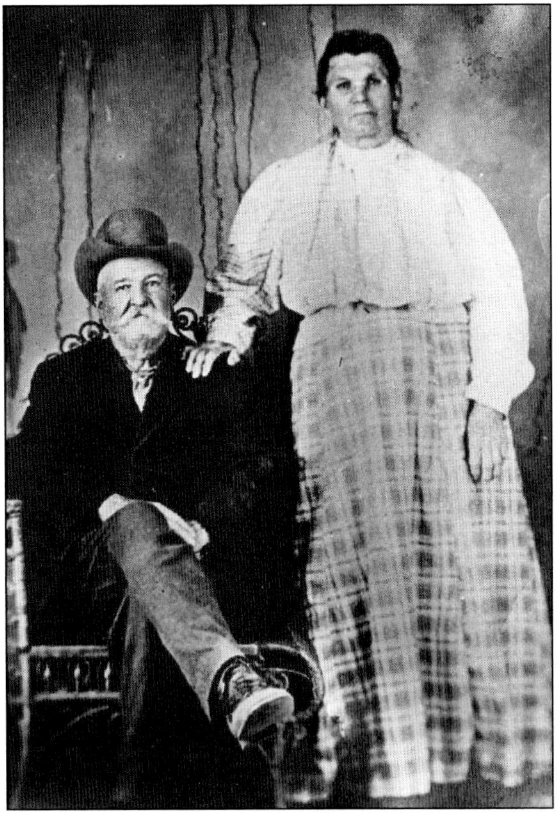

George Washington and Sarah C. Vaughan. The great grandfather of Peggy (Vaughan) Pate, George Washington Vaughan was born in 1846 in Hancock County, Tennessee. He relocated to Vaughantown, Texas, in 1905 (located at the current site of Lake Ray Roberts) after serving in the Confederate Army from October 1862 until the end of the war. He died in 1920 and wife, Sarah Caroline, died in 1922. (Courtesy of Peggy (Vaughan) Pate.)

Dan Davis, 1910. Dan Davis is seen here behind a glass case holding watches and jewelry. Davis sold and repaired watches. He was a man of many talents and was involved in a number of community activities, including co-owning the town's first water system. Davis married Lizzie (Ledbetter) Thatcher, and they lived on the southeast corner of Locust and Fourth Streets where their granddaughter Lona Joyce (Cherry) Snellgrove now resides. (SPL.)

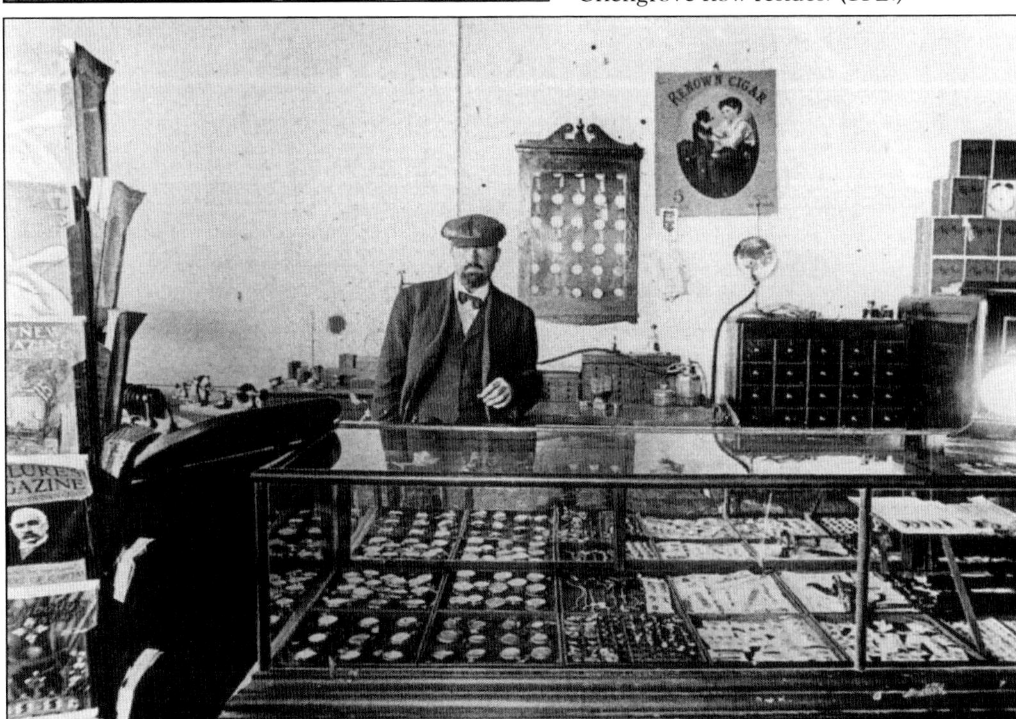

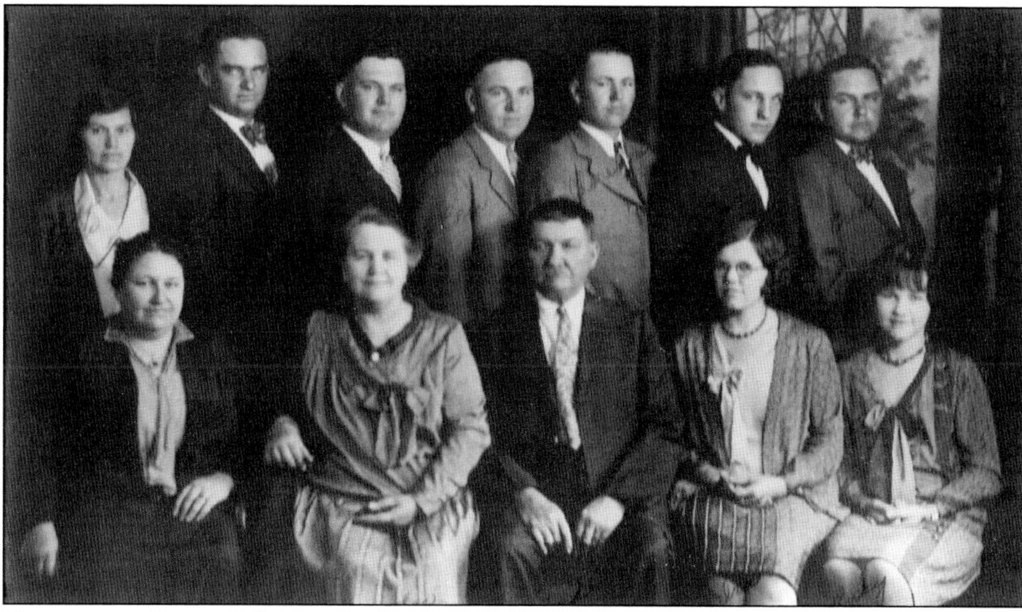

Tom Gentle Family. Thomas A. Gentle and Clarice (Rutherford) Gentle moved to Sanger in 1902. Their family included, from left to right, (first row) Mittie Belle, Clarice (mother), Thomas Alton (father), Ora Lee, and Ruby Helen; (second row) Kate Mae, Roy Egbert "Peggy," Albert Lee "Abb," Ben F., Clarence, Thomas Alton, and Bud. (Courtesy of Anna Lisa (Guillott) Lyon.)

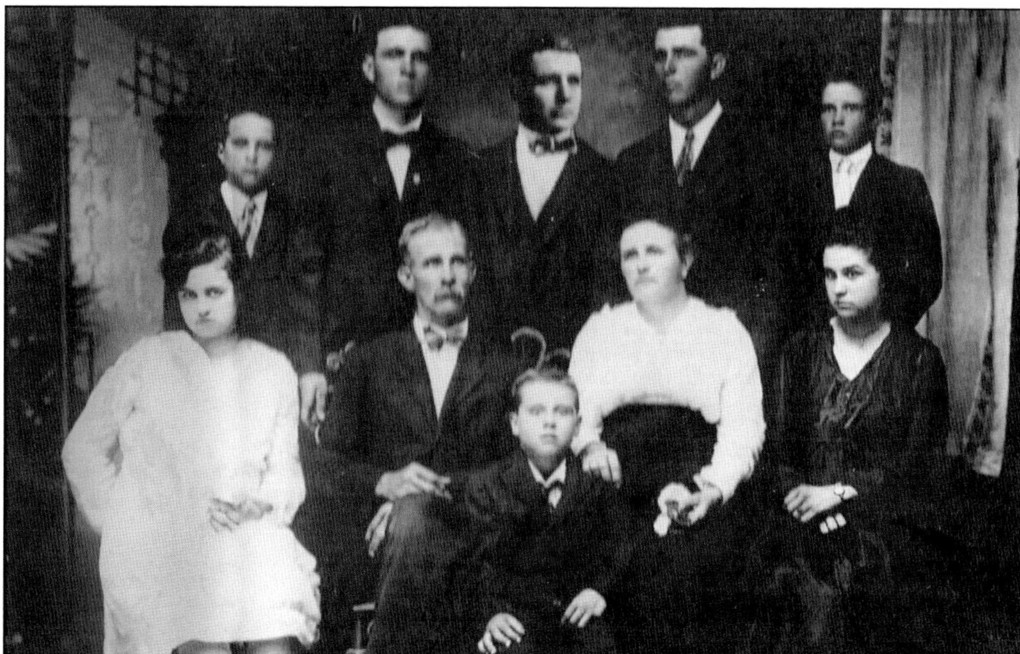

Ben Bentley Family. The Benjamin Robert and Arista M. (Nance) Bentley family of the Bolivar area included Ben and Arista with their young son (center). Other children included Clifford, Herman, Dallas, Jewel, Robert, Zada, B.R., Marshall, and Bill. Benjamin was born in 1863 and died in 1953. Wife, Arista, was born in 1872 and died in 1946. Many of the children remained in the area, and the successive generations are still a part of the community. (Courtesy of Linda (Harvey) Hewlett.)

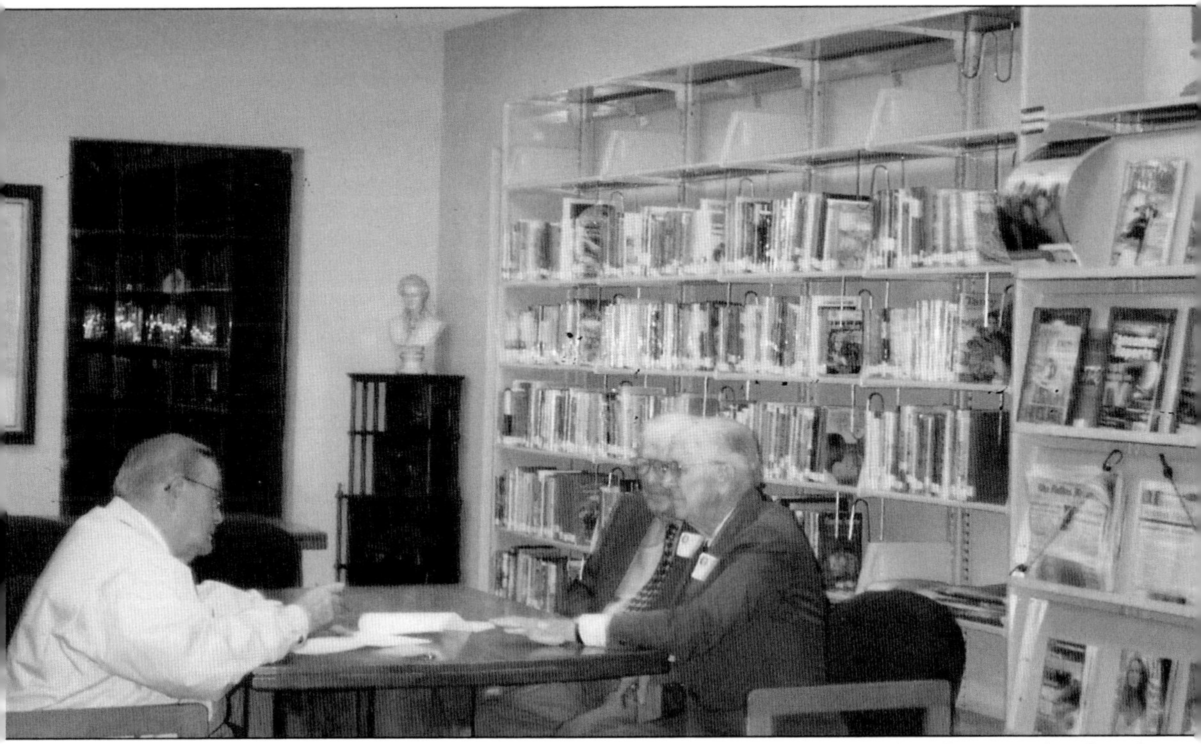

THE CHAMBERS BROTHERS. Robert and John Chambers are the sons of William Bushrod and Alma (Lain) Chambers and the grandsons of John Thomas and Anna (Griffin) Chambers and Dr. George Douglas and Martha (McCutchen) Lain. The Chambers and Lain families have played an important part in the history of Sanger. J.T. Chambers moved to Sanger in 1895 to become head of the Sanger School. He later became manager of the Sanger Mill and Elevator Company. Lain began his medical practice in Bolivar in 1892. He moved to Sanger in 1900 while he continued to care for the medical needs of people west of Sanger until his death in 1926. The land on which the library was built was purchased from a member of the Chambers family. In December 1999, the Chambers brothers signed the deed to a gift of land on Fifth Street before Mayor Tommy Kincaid for the City of Sanger. This lot is to be used for the purpose of expanding the Sanger Public Library. (SAHS.)

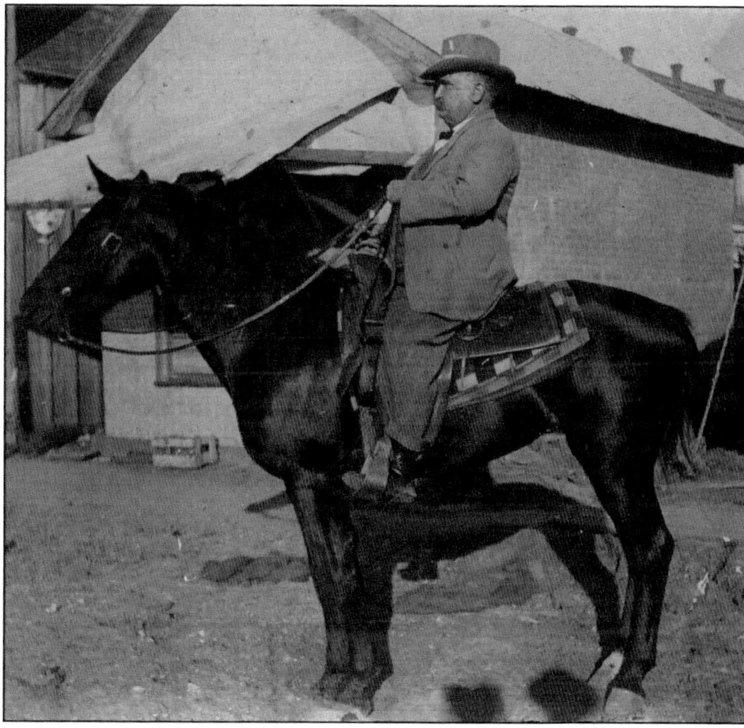

T.H. Jones, Mayor. Jones, mayor of Sanger from 1919 to 1923, sits proudly on his black horse. Jones was a grocery merchant, and his store was located on the west side of the city park. Sanger held an election to reincorporate in 1912 after earlier unincorporation. Earlier mayors prior to Jones's service were William Partlow, Andy Greene, Horace Melton, and Dr. J.C. Rice. (TWU.)

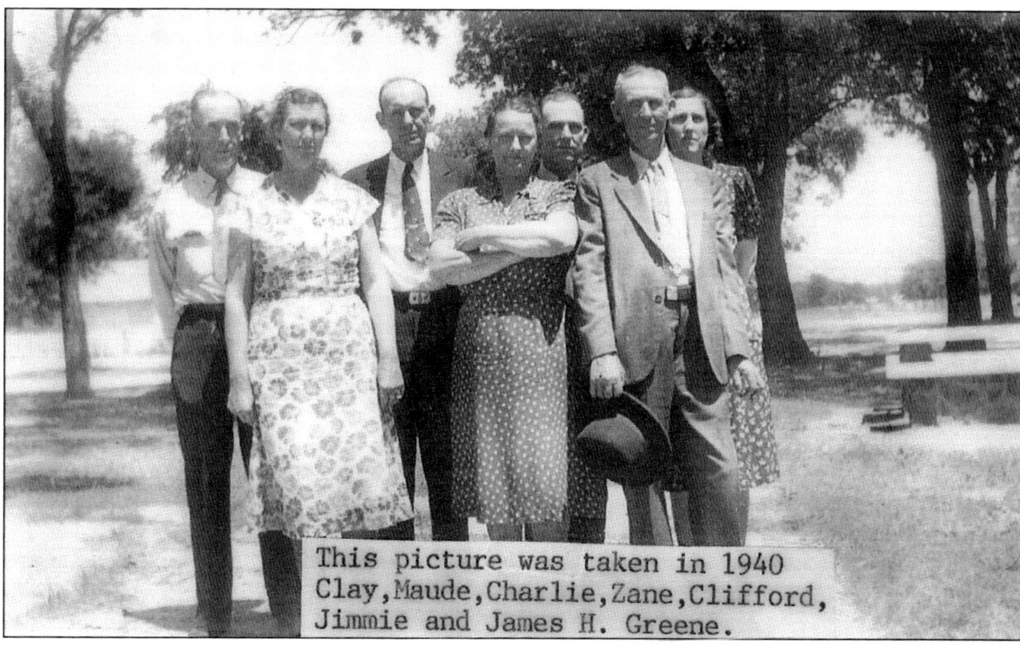

The Green Family. The family of James H. and Alice (Seal) Green are, from left to right, (first row) Maude, Zane, and James; (second row) Clay, Charlie, Clifford, and Jimmie. Clay and his wife Viola later occupied the Partlow house, home of Sanger's first mayor. Alton Lee Greene, local genealogist and historian, was a part of this family. (Courtesy of George Seals.)

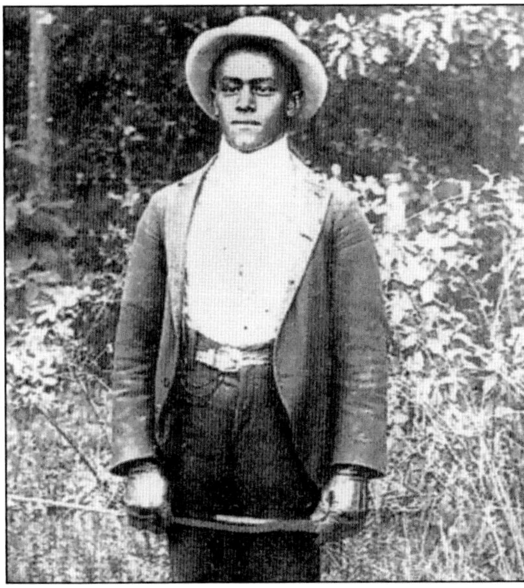
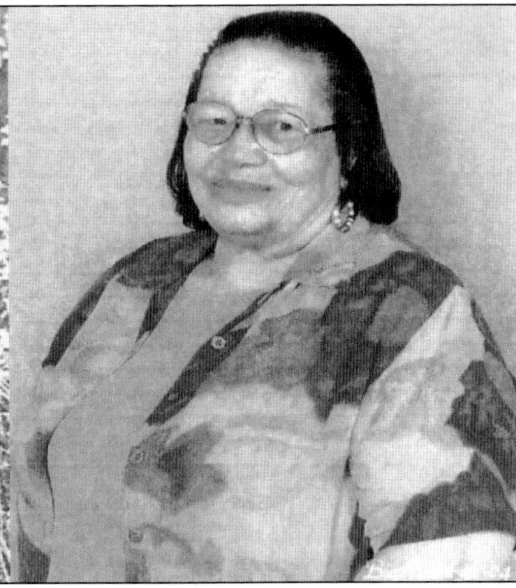

AFRICAN AMERICAN COMMUNITY. Sanger's black community included many families who have their historical roots in the city. Frank Price, (above left), pictured as a young man, is the grandfather of Dorothy (Haskins) Nubine (above right), who is the daughter of Charlie Haskins and Otlean Price. Lucille Lee Nix, (below left), taught at a school for the black community in Sanger for 18 years. When the school closed, Nix began teaching at Fred Moore in Denton, which included the black children of Sanger, until the schools were integrated in 1965 and the students began attending the Sanger School District. D.C. Turner (below right) is the father of Bessie Sims, wife of Fred Sims. (Courtesy of Dorothy (Haskins) Nubine.)

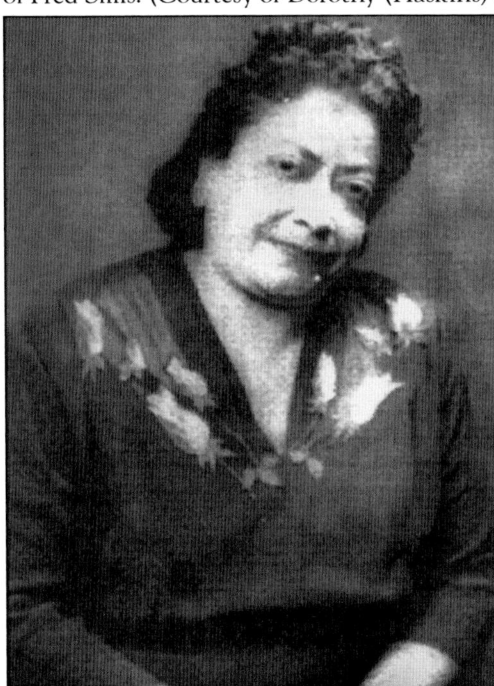
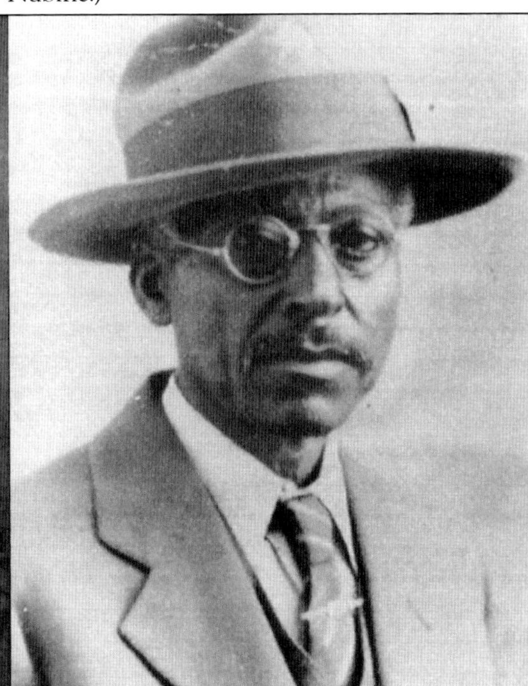

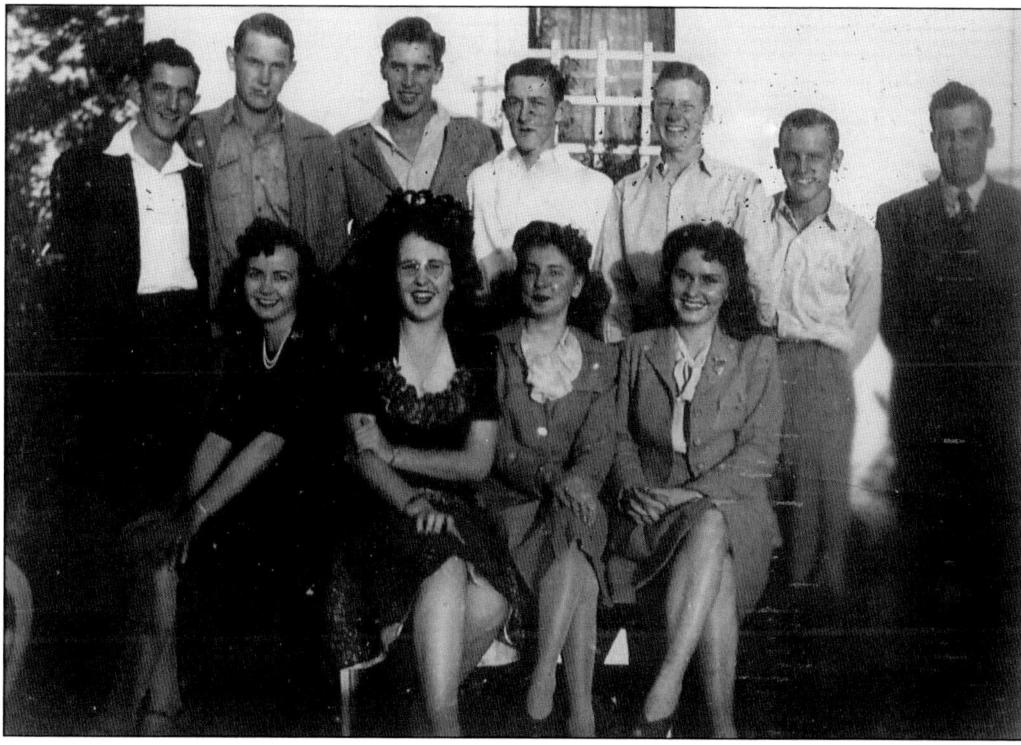

Sunday Afternoon Social, 1943. Young people entertained at the home of Fred and Ida Scheu on the northwest corner of Seventh and Peach Streets were, from left to right, (seated) Joy Morris, Peggy Vaughan, Idaleene Scheu, and Sally Ann Gentle; (standing) Johnnie Lee Richardson, J.P. Pace, Freddie Scheu, Willie Keith Pate, Bobby Joe Ready, Lloyd King, and Van Teel. (Courtesy of Idaleene (Scheu) Fuqua.)

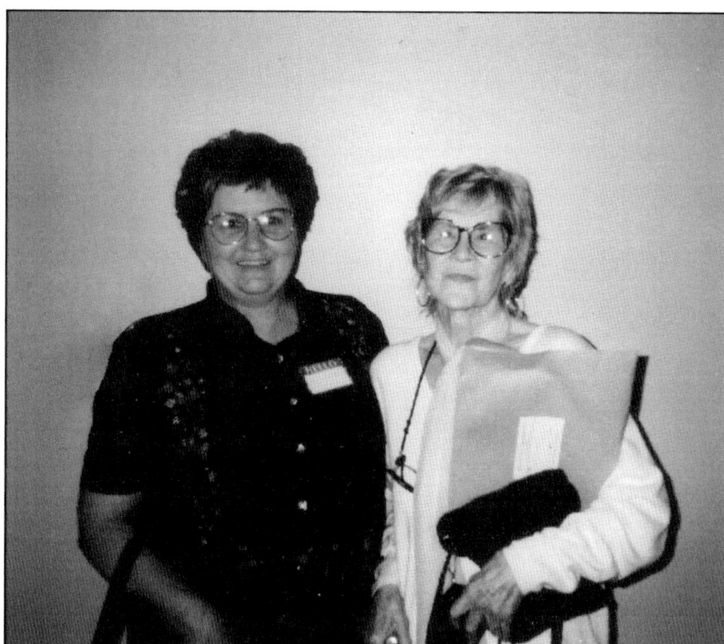

Marijohn Melson Wilkin, Songwriter. Wilkin moved to Sanger as a child in the 1920s with parents Ernest and Karla Melson. Her father established Melson's Veribest Bread Bakery at the northwest corner of Bolivar Street and Highway 77. Wilkin wrote "One Day at a Time" and "Long Black Veil," two well-known songs. Local resident Mary (Cole) Shelton met Wilkin in October 1967 while she was visiting in Sanger. (Courtesy of Oscar Shelton.)

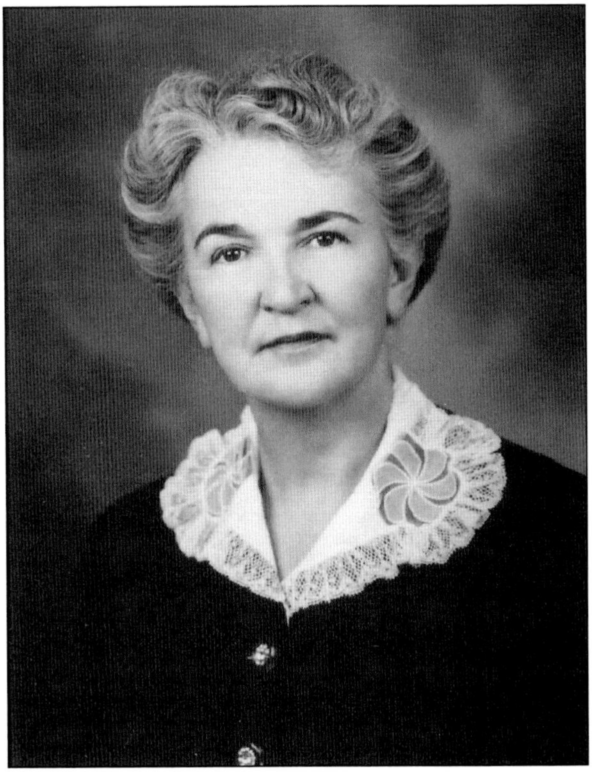

Recorders of Sanger History. Alma (Lain) Chambers (left) was known as a historian of Sanger. She wrote a history of the Wednesday Study Club from 1916 to 1948, a prize-winning story on homes of the community, and a published history of the Methodist Church, as well as many newspaper articles concerning the history of the community. She was active in many civic and school affairs. Another local historian was Eunice (Sullivan) Gray (below). For many years, she wrote a column in the *Sanger Courier* called "Now and Then." She wrote and published *The Story of Sanger, 1886–1986*, a compilation of a series originally published in the newspaper. She was instrumental in establishing the Sanger Public Library. Idaleene (Scheu) Fuqua has also contributed to writing the history of Sanger through her newspaper columns "Songs of Sanger" and "Tree of Sanger." (Left, SAHS; below, SHS.)

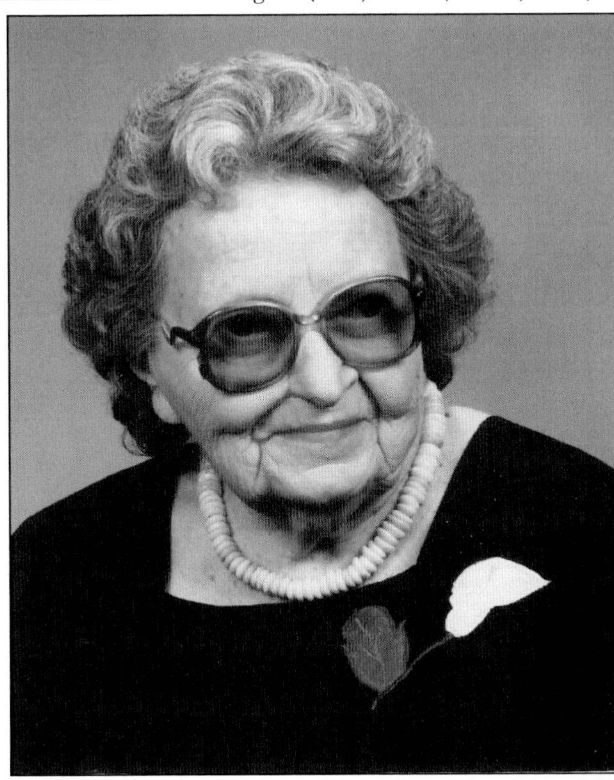

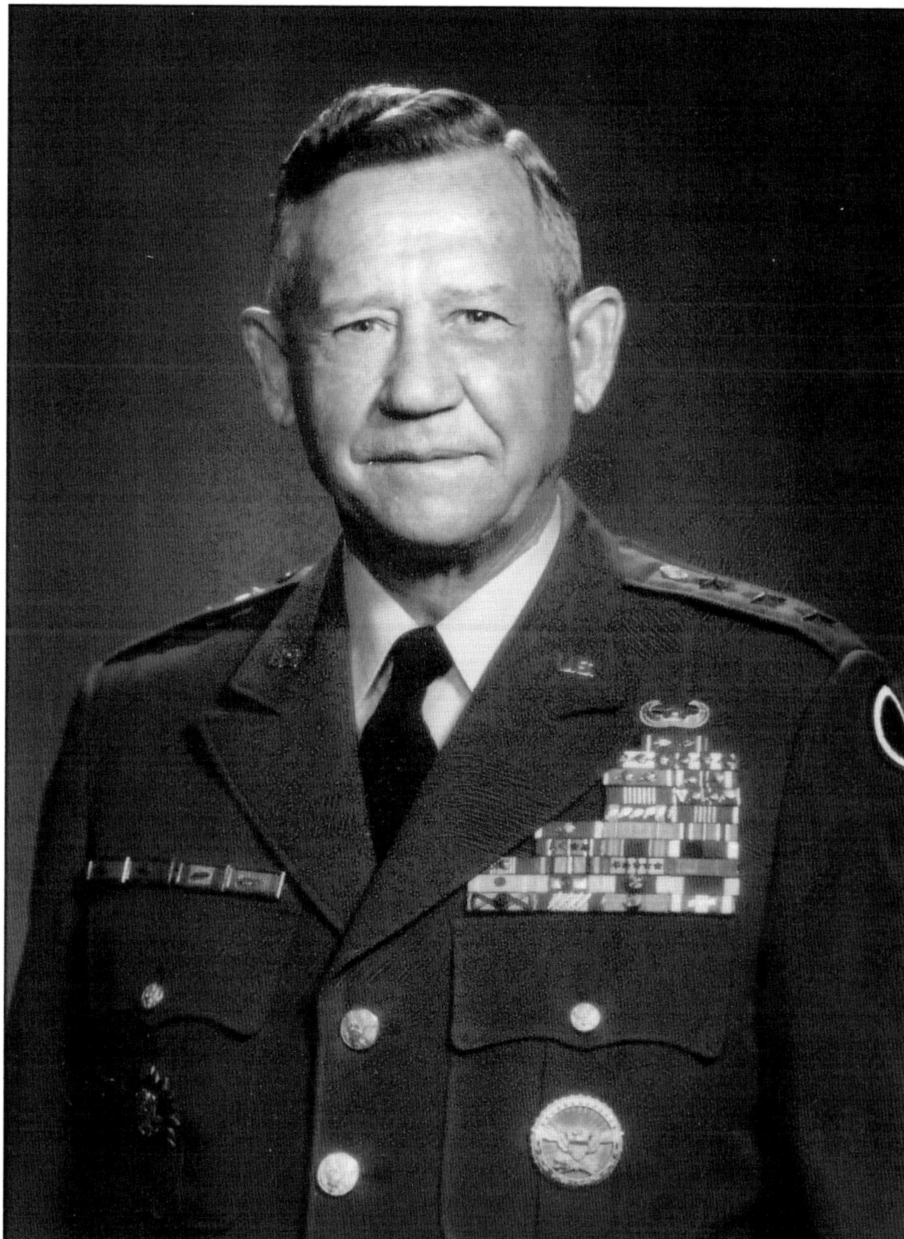

Lt. Gen. James F. Hollingsworth. James Francis Hollingsworth, born in 1918 on the family farm northeast of Sanger, was the oldest of the four sons of Jim and Mamie Hollingsworth. After graduating from Texas A&M University in 1940, he was commissioned a second lieutenant in the Army. In 1940, Hollingsworth married fellow Sangerite Katherine Elizabeth "Nickie" Nicholson, and they had one son, both of whom predeceased him. He later married Janie Harris. After a distinguished career, he retired from active duty in 1976. He was honored with the placement of a seven-foot-tall bronze statue on the campus of Texas A&M in College Station for recognition of his long and exemplary military career. A bust of Hollingsworth is on display in the Sanger Public Library. He died in 2010 and was buried at Arlington National Cemetery in Arlington, Virginia. (SHS.)

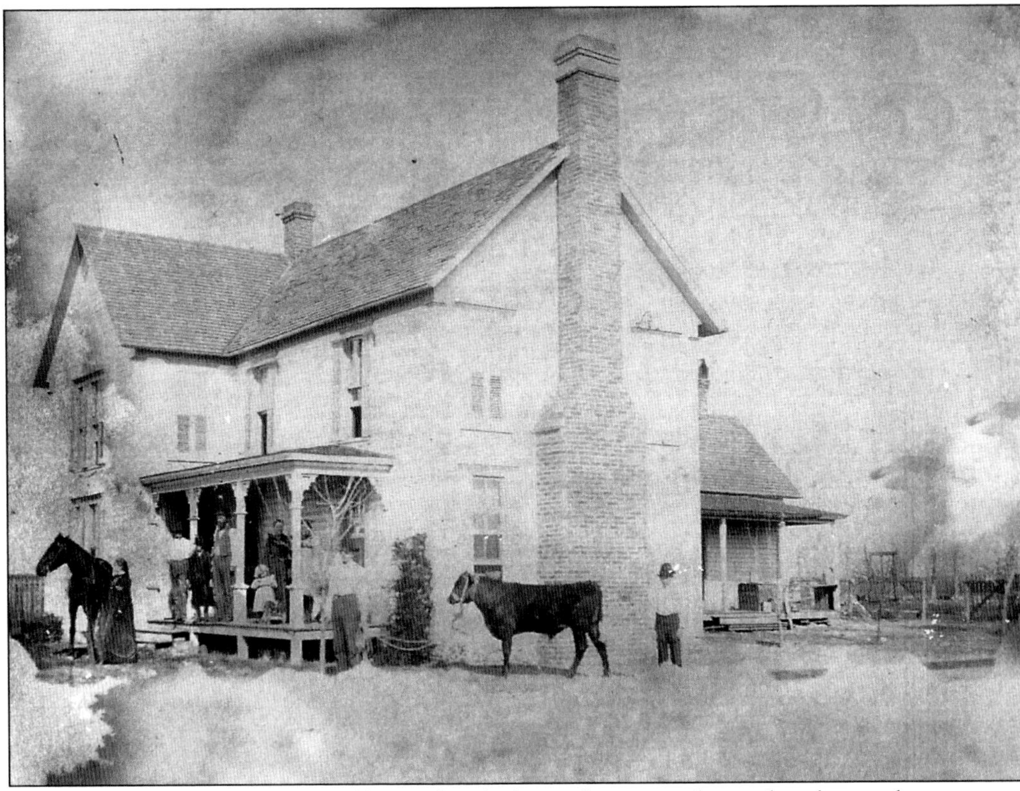

J.R. SULLIVAN HOME. Jack R. Sullivan's five-bedroom home was located at the northwest corner of Sixth and Plum Streets. He was one of the original organizers of the Sanger Mill and Elevator Company. His granddaughter Eunice (Sullivan) Gray was dedicated to preserving the history of Sanger. Although he was a Baptist, Sullivan donated the land for the Presbyterian church in 1901. (TWU.)

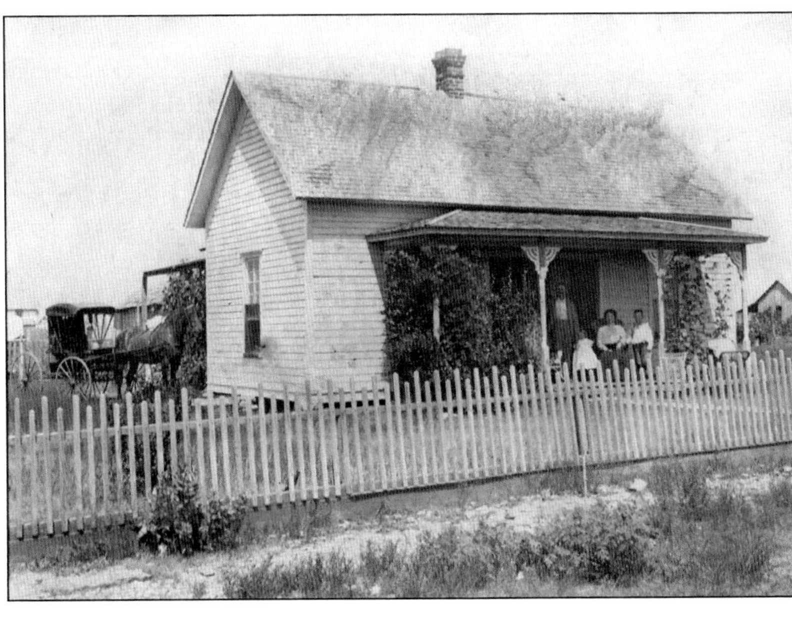

W.D. BROCKMAN HOME. The Brockman home was located in the area of the Sanger Public Library at Fifth and Bolivar Streets. Brockman owned the first dry goods store. The horse and wagon at the rear of the home appears to be waiting for its passengers as the family gathers for a photograph on the front porch. (TWU.)

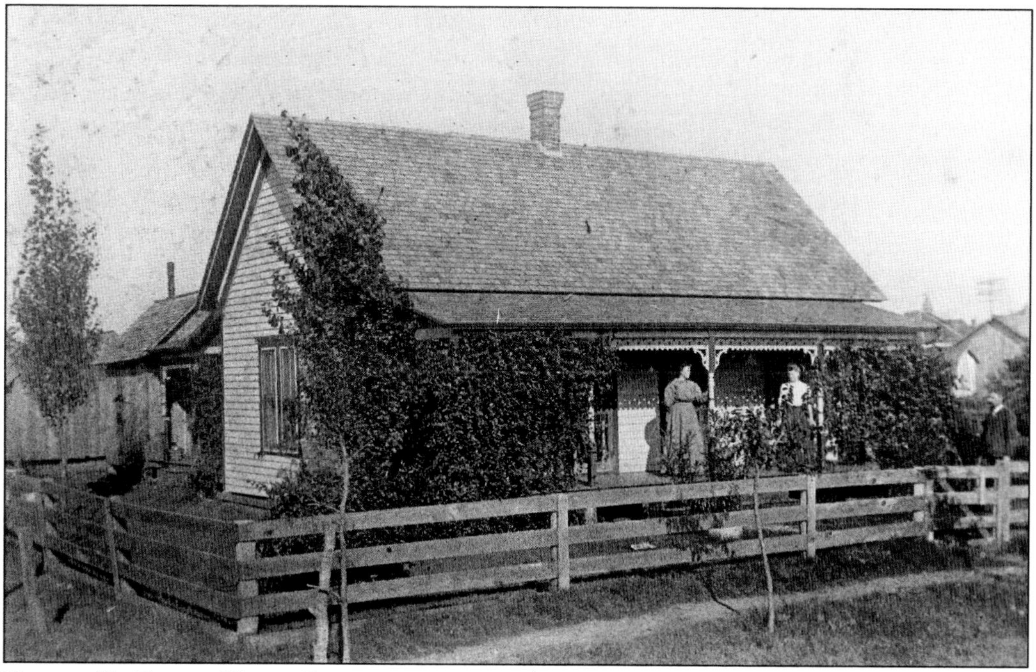

HOWELL D. GREENE HOME. Greene was appointed postmaster of Sanger in December 1899, April 1908, and December 1924 (as acting postmaster). Greene later owned and operated a grocery store. His home, once located at the northwest corner of Fourth and Cherry Streets, no longer stands. (Courtesy of Oscar Shelton.)

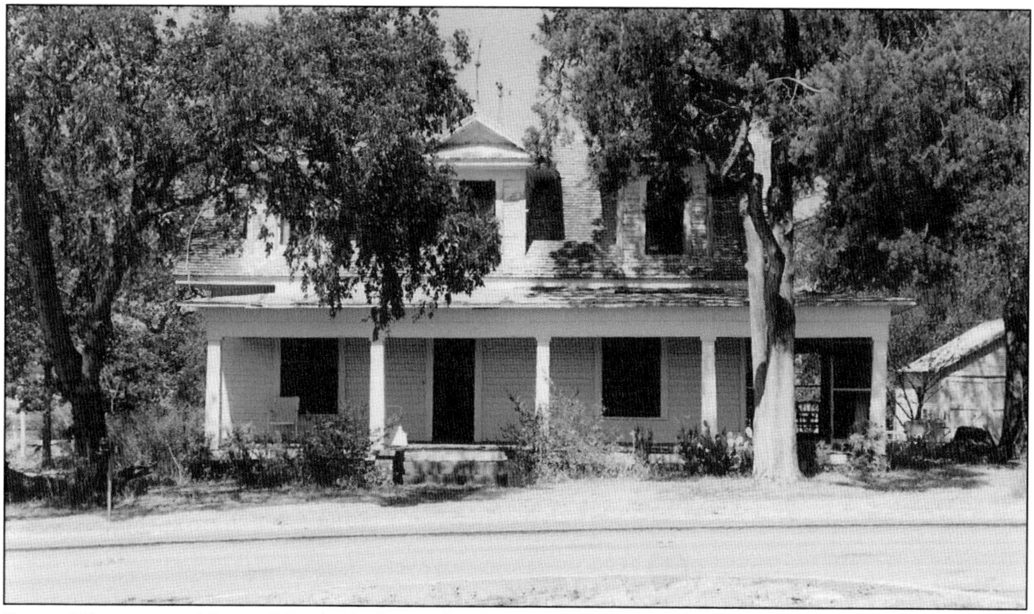

BATIS HOME AND FARM. Noah C. Batis (1860–1950) arrived in Sanger in 1889, established the Sanger Stock Farm known for fine horses and mules, and provided veterinary care for locals though he had no formal training. Batis was county commissioner for Denton County from 1919 to 1923, and his homesite was awarded a Texas Historical Marker in 1986. The site is located on Farm-to-Market Road 455, north of Chisholm Trail Elementary. (SAHS.)

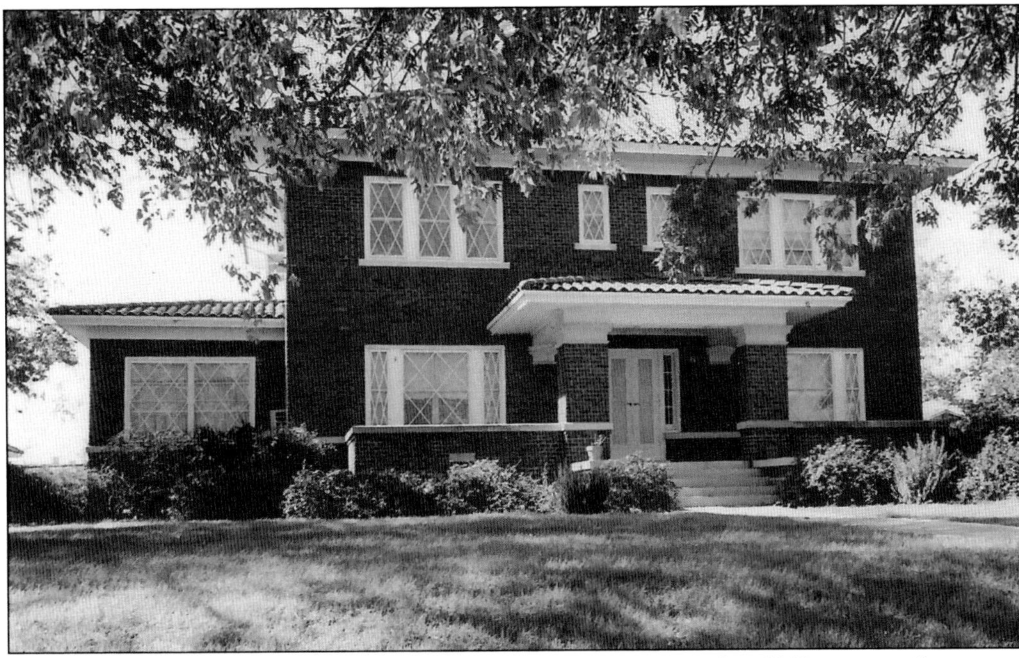

E.L. Berry Home. Berry, born in 1860, arrived in Texas in 1881, and in 1890, came to Sanger and became cashier of First National Bank and president of Sanger Mill. His home, a red brick two-story structure, is located on Interstate 35 at the west end of Bolivar Street across the interstate. This home was owned by Dr. J. Clyde Chapman for many years. (SAHS.)

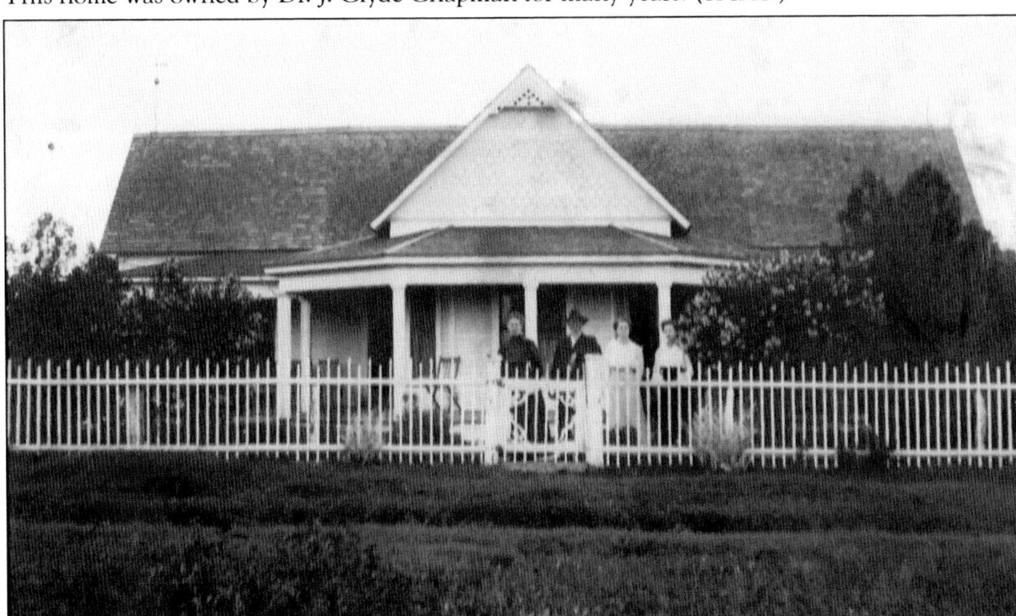

Jones Home, Early 1900s. Burl David and Paulina Jane (Dawson) Jones, seen here with two of their 14 children, are in front of their home on South Second Street before 1918. Jones was the last Confederate veteran living in the community. He farmed, served as justice of the peace, a bank vice president, and a gin manager. He and his son Watt operated a seed and feed store and livery stable. (Courtesy of Jenny (Campbell) Miller.)

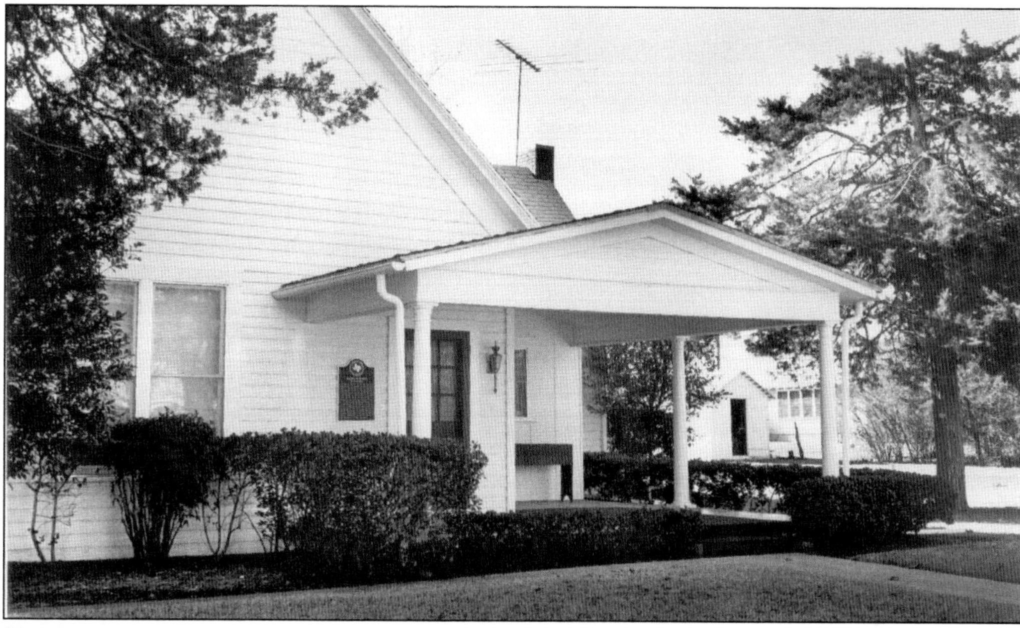

The Elsasser House. Jacob Frederick Elsasser built this residence on the northwest corner of Seventh and Peach Streets in Sanger in 1901 after his two-story farmhouse east of Sanger burned. His daughter lived in the house until 1939; the Fred Scheu family also lived there for several years. It was purchased by Willard and Helen (Seely) Bounds in 1952 and was awarded a Texas Historical Marker in 1976. (DCM.)

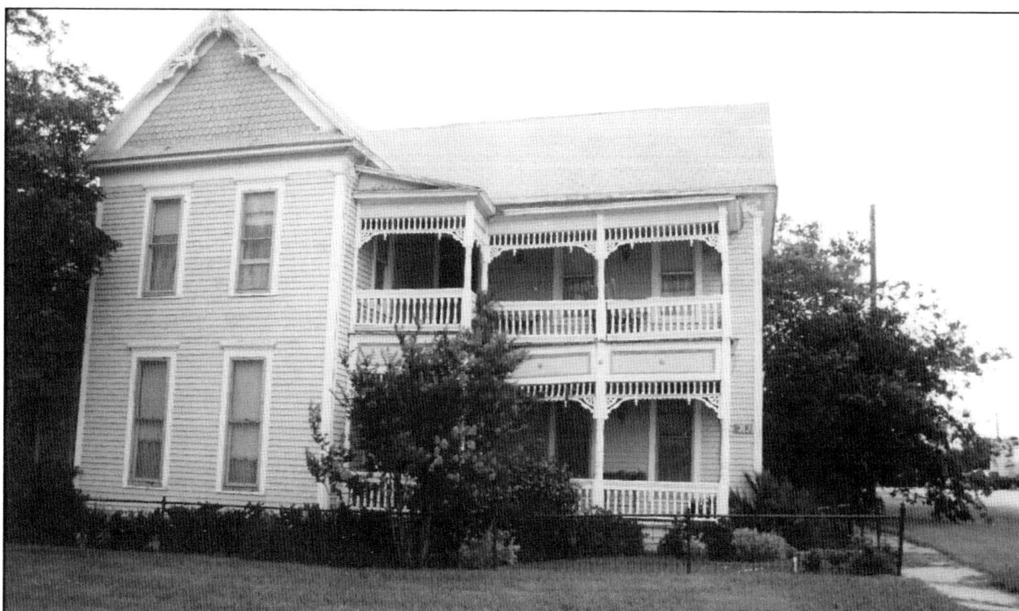

Nicholson Home. Still standing today, the John Nicholson home, located at Fourth and Elm Streets, was the family homestead. When Nicholson's sister died after caring for their widowed mother, he and his wife, Eula, spent years restoring the gingerbread-style home. Nicholson served during World War I and was later Sanger's postmaster. Their daughter Katherine "Nickie" Nicholson married Francis "Holly" Hollingsworth, who became a three-star general in the US Army. (SAHS.)

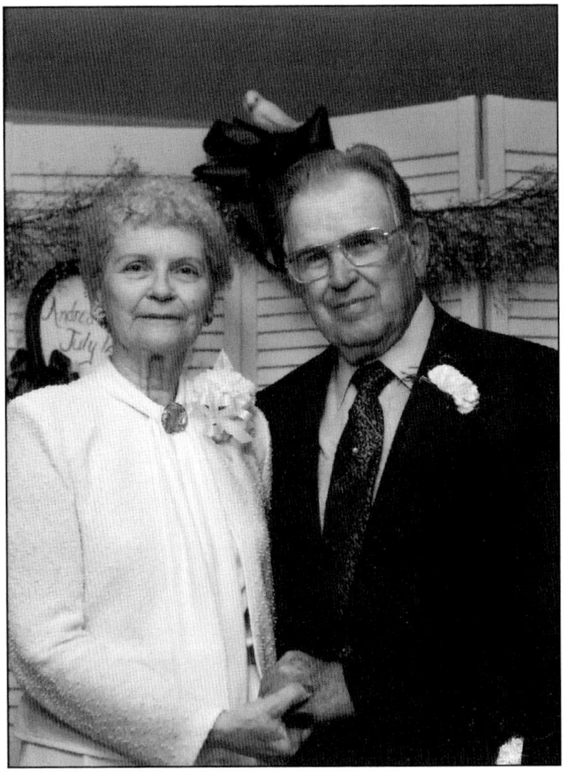

GENE HUGHES, LEADER/BUSINESSMAN. Hughes and his wife, Greta Dayton, owned and operated the local movie theater for many years. Hughes, Dr. Clyde Chapman, and Harold Easley developed and built the Sanger Manor in 1964, which housed Chapman's clinic and contained 58 nursing care rooms. Hughes was justice of the peace for 25 years. He built over 200 homes and apartments in the community. (Courtesy of Greta (Hughes) Miller and Diane (Hughes) Barentine.)

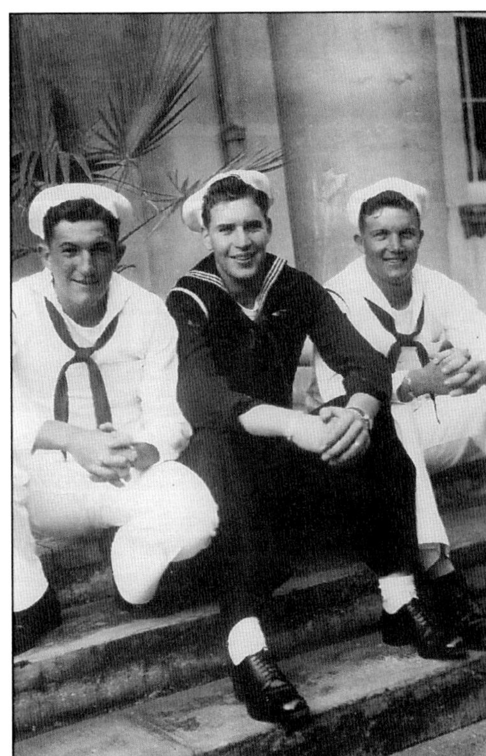

YOUNG MEN SERVING THEIR COUNTRY. Sanger boys Johnnie Richardson and Freddie Scheu, along with Bobby Williams of Borger, Texas, are shown together while serving in the US Coast Guard during World War II. Richardson went on to become postmaster at Sanger, and Scheu was in the telecommunications business. (Courtesy of Idaleene (Scheu) Fuqua.)

Three

The Healing

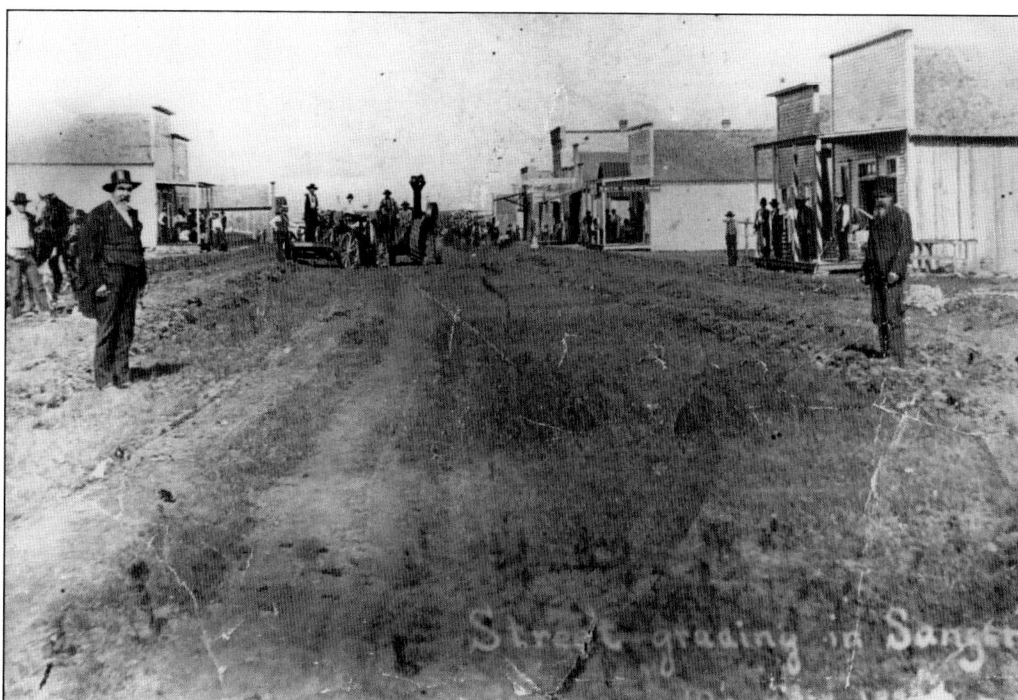

Sanger's First Doctor. The man on the left is Dr. Ervin Howard (1826–1897), Sanger's first physician; on the right is B.S. Gay, pastor of First Baptist Church. They watch alongside other interested bystanders as a steam tractor pulls a grader near the east end of Bolivar Street. Howard moved his practice from Bolivar to Sanger. The date printed on the picture is May 23, 189?. (TWU.)

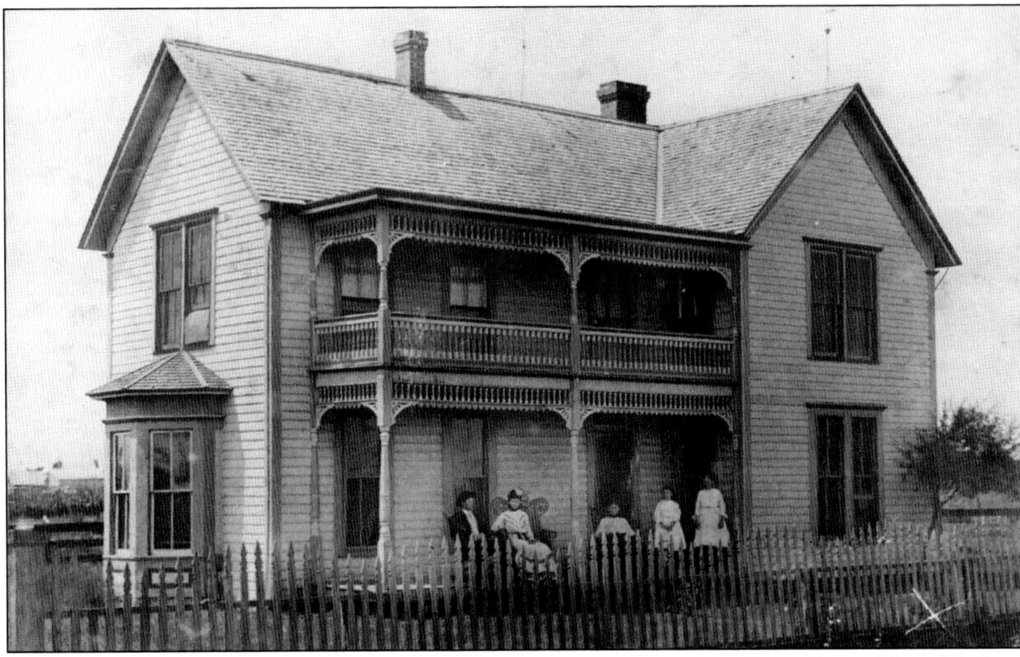

Dr. Ervin Howard Home. The home of Dr. Howard (1826–1897) was located at Fifth and Bolivar Streets, currently the location of the Denton County Government Annex. Howard originally lived in Bolivar and built a home in Sanger that remained in the family with son Eugene, granddaughter Eula (Howard) Gary, great grandchildren Lona Graham (Gary) Bryson and John D. Gary, and great-great grandson, Jerry Bryson, but it was eventually torn down. (TWU.)

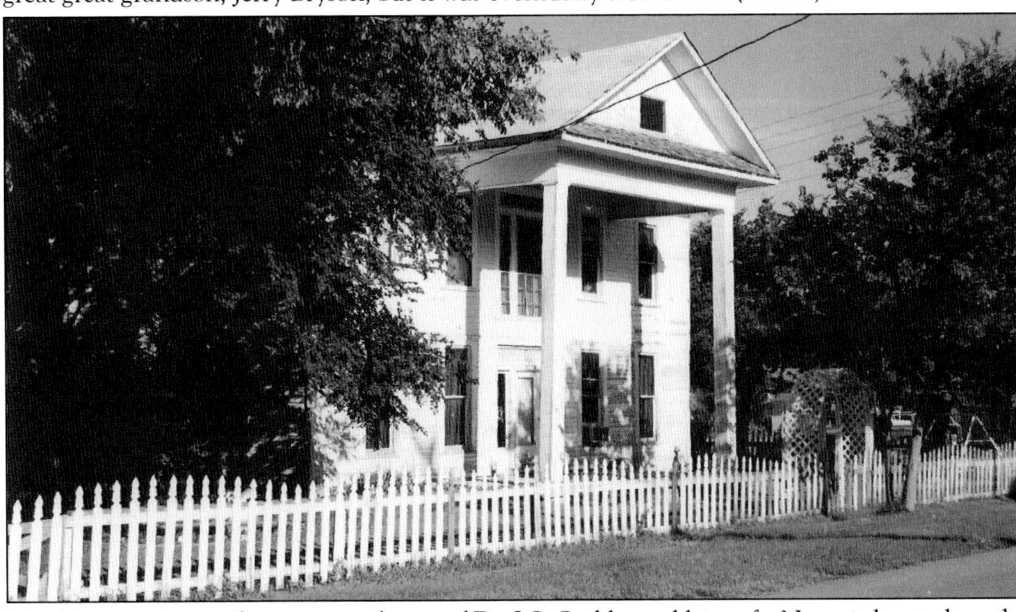

Dr. Stubbs Home. The two-story home of Dr. J.S. Stubbs and his wife, Nora, is located on the original site on the northeast corner of Fifth and Peach Streets. Dr. Stubbs opened his dental business in Sanger in the 1920s and became known for his expertise in fitting his patients for dentures. The Stubbs had three children and were active in the community. Dr. Stubbs died in 1958. (SAHS.)

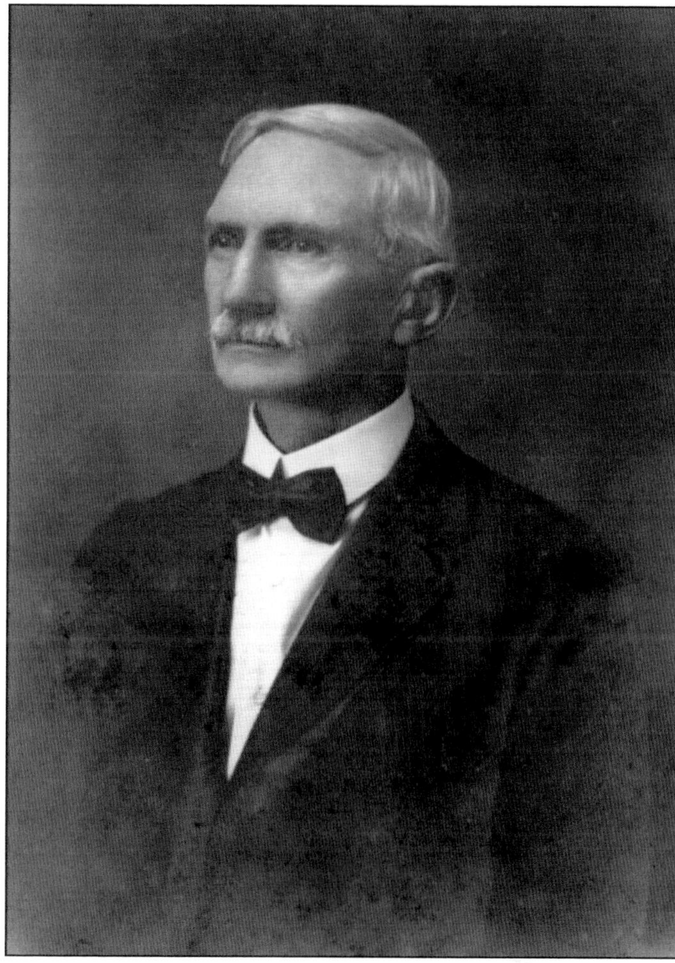

DR. JOHN CLINTON RICE. Dr. J.C. Rice, born in Tennessee, moved to Texas in 1868. He attended school in Pilot Point, and after graduating from Vanderbilt University, began practicing medicine in Sanger in 1890. He was the first in Sanger to purchase an automobile, which arrived from Chicago in 1909. Dr. Rice died in 1948 after 58 years of attending to the medical needs of the community. (DCM.)

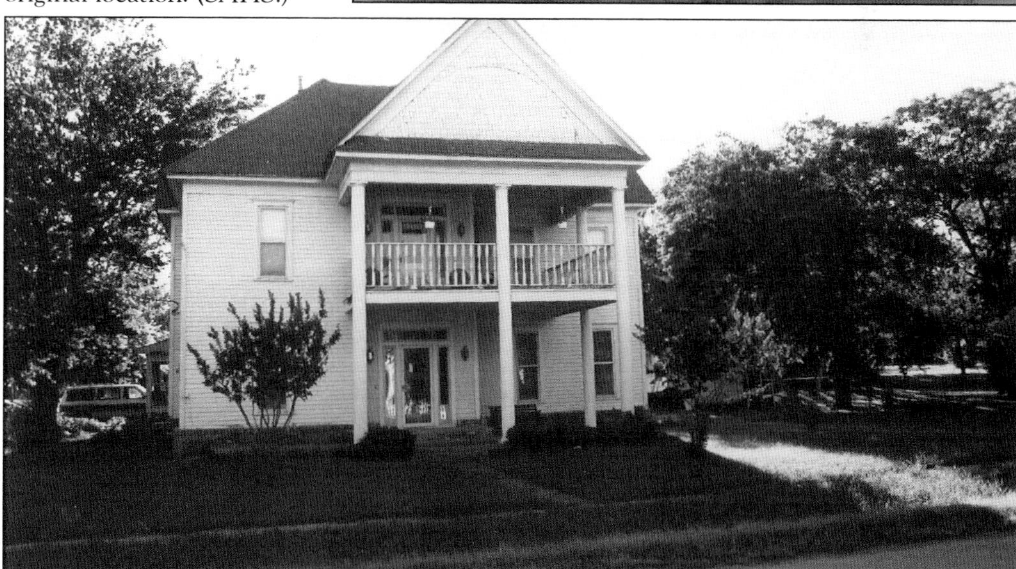

DR. JOHN C. RICE HOME. Built in 1918 by J.T. Chambers, the home located on the northwest corner of Fifth and Peach Streets was sold to Dr. John Rice three years later. Chambers built a new home a couple of blocks west for his family, as this two-story home had a steep staircase. The Rice home is still standing in its original location. (SAHS.)

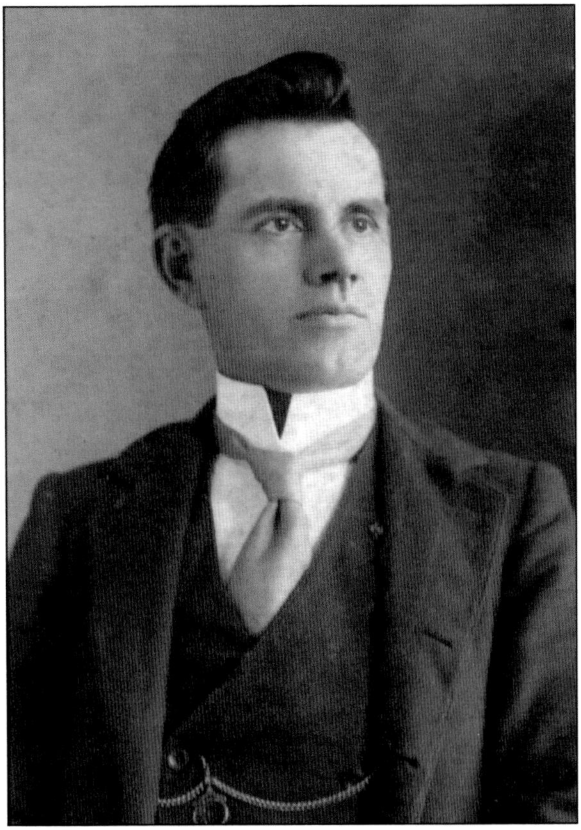

Dr. Samuel Alexander Gotcher. Dr. Samuel A. Gotcher began his medical practice in Sanger in 1897 after receiving his degree in 1895 in St. Louis, Missouri. He later developed Numotizine, a medication for the treatment of pneumonia, bronchitis, and related conditions, which was manufactured in Hobart, Oklahoma. In 1917, Gotcher became an ordained minister and continued life as a minister until his death in 1922 in Chicago. (TWU.)

Gotcher Home. The Dr. Samuel A. Gotcher home was located at the northwest corner of North Fifth and Plum Streets in the late 1800s. In the photograph below, the doctor and his wife are on the porch of their home with a child. The bicycle to the left was used by the doctor to make house calls. The home currently stands in Sanger at the original location. (TWU.)

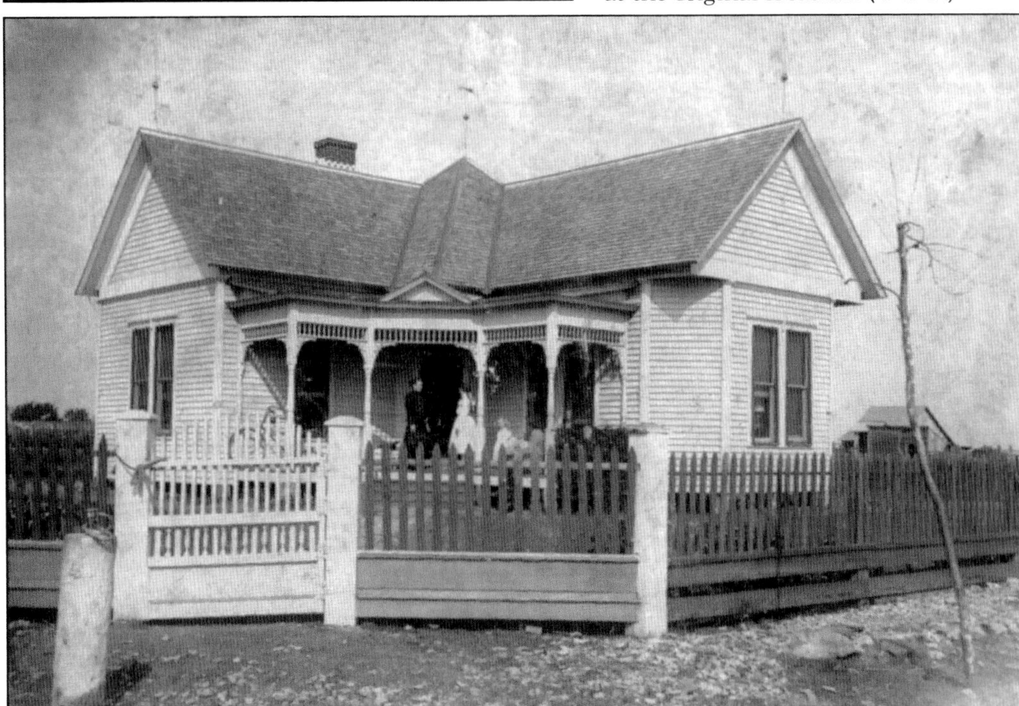

Dr. John M. Sullivan. Graduating in 1910 from Fort Worth University Medical School, Sullivan was born in 1885 before the town was founded and died in 1958. He was known for never mailing a bill for services; he understood if someone was unable to pay. In 1956, Dr. Sullivan stated he had delivered over 3,500 babies. (Courtesy of Patti Sullivan Walker)

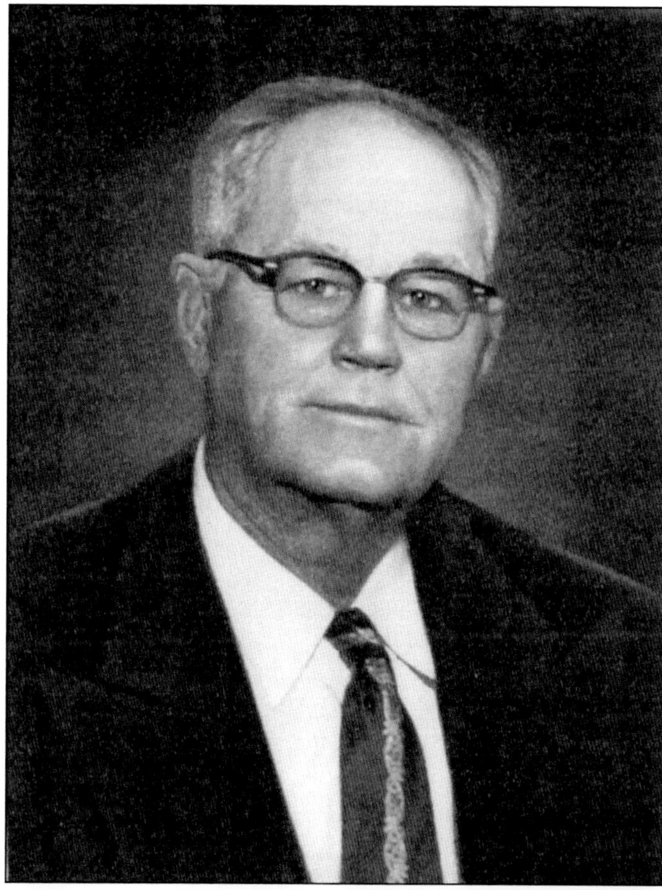

Dr. John M. Sullivan Home. The Sullivan home, located on the northeast corner of Bolivar and Eighth Streets, was home to Sullivan and his wife, the former Charlotte Gambill. Their son John Lewis was a prominent attorney in Denton County and lived in the home for many years. Patti Sullivan Walker, daughter of other son Gambill, currently resides in the home. (SAHS.)

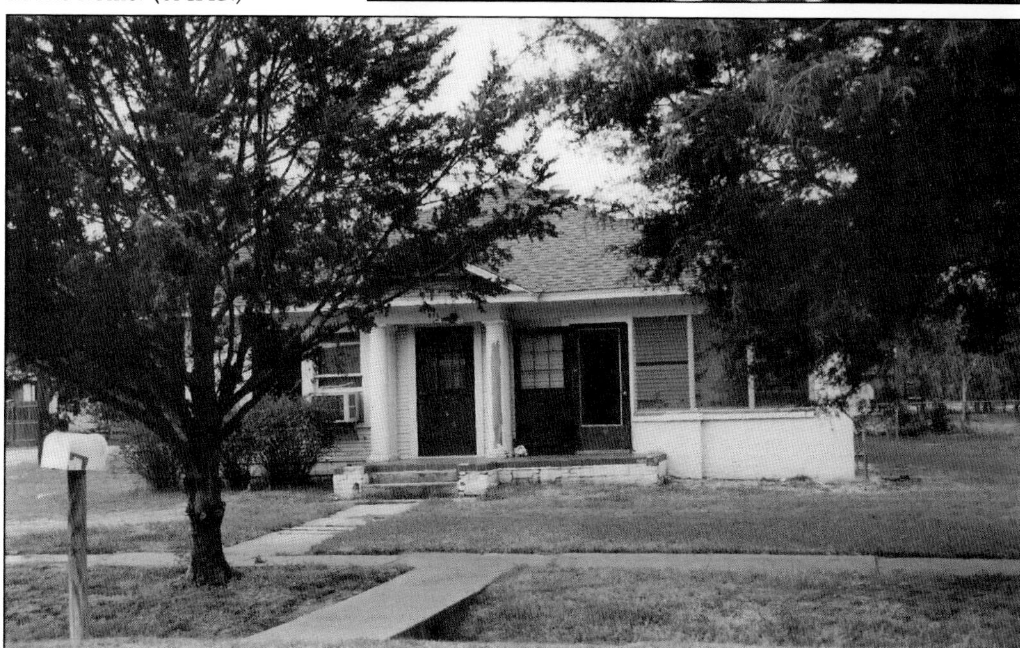

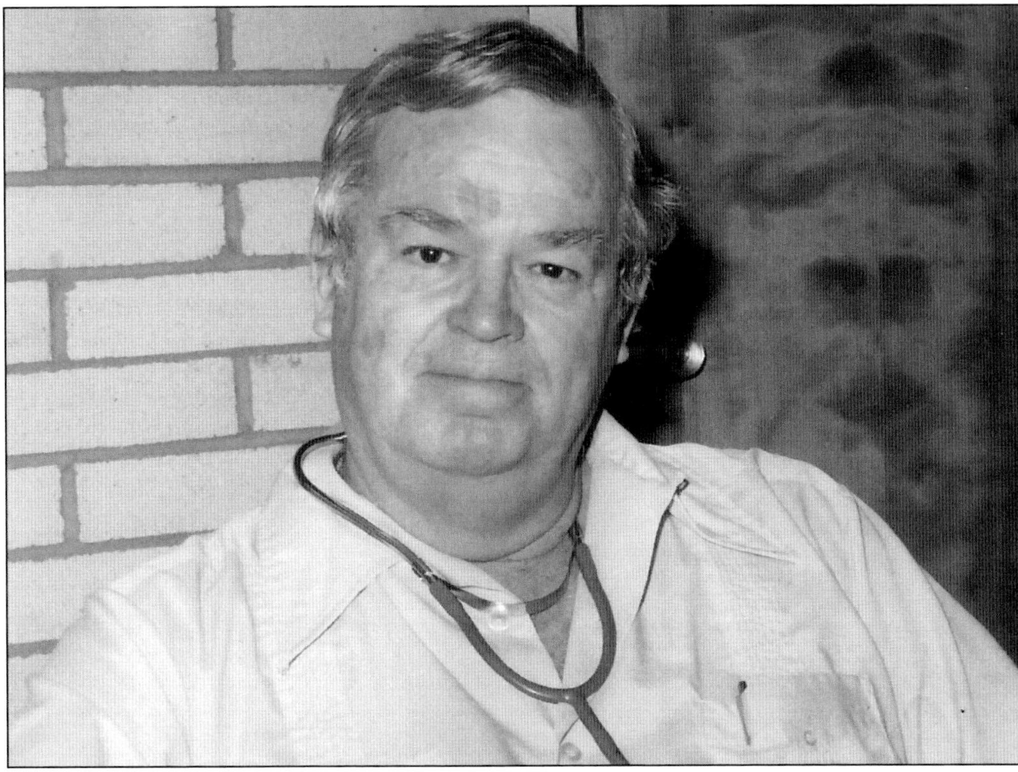

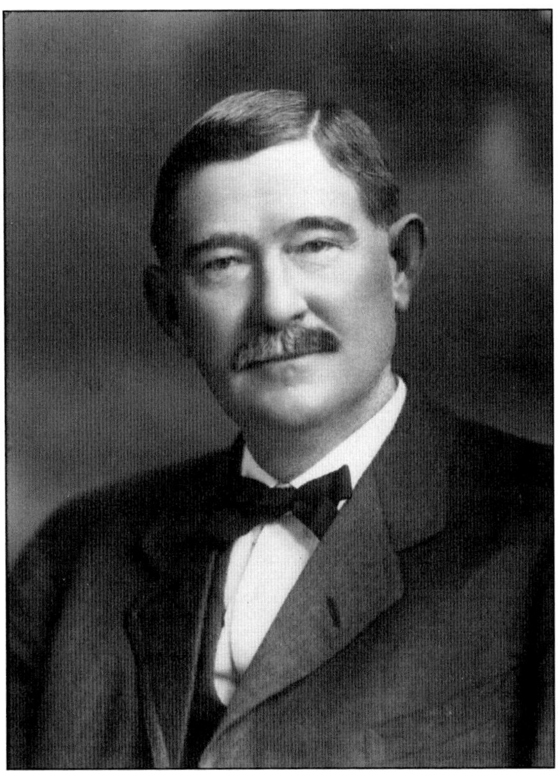

Dr. J. Clyde Chapman. Dr. Clyde Chapman served the Sanger community for over 50 years. Prior to opening the Chapman Clinic on Bolivar Street in 1941, he operated an office in the rear of Pansy Freeman's pharmacy. Dr. Chapman and wife, Frances, donated the original clinic building as the first library for the community. He was born in Gainesville, Texas, and graduated from medical school in Kirksville, Missouri, in 1937. (SAHS.)

Dr. George D. Lain, 1861–1926. After graduating medical college in Louisville, Kentucky, in March 1892, Dr. Lain began his practice in Bolivar, Texas. As the railroad passed through Sanger, Lain moved his family to Sanger in 1900 and divided coverage of the area with Dr. John C. Rice. Lain covered the west side of town and Rice covered the east. He died in 1926 at the age of 64. (Courtesy of John Chambers.)

Four

THE WORSHIPING

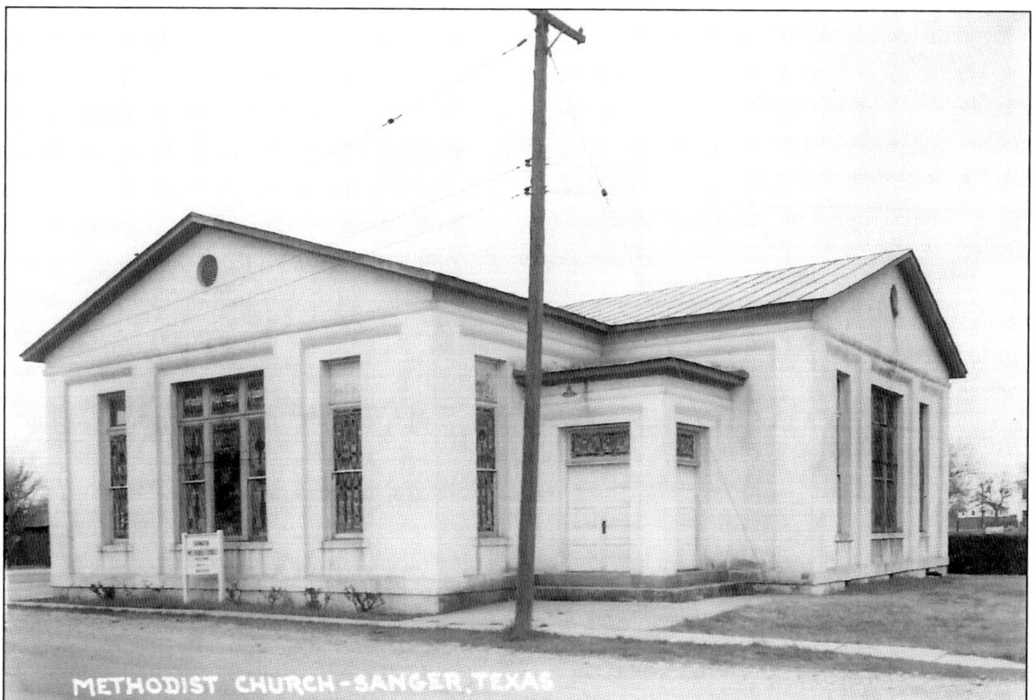

FIRST METHODIST CHURCH. Sanger's first church constructed its earliest building in 1896 on land donated by Elizabeth Huling. Newer buildings have since occupied this site on the west side of Fifth Street where the First United Methodist Church now meets. The book *Papa was a Preacher* by Alyene Porter provides interesting facts about life in Sanger from 1913 to 1915. (Courtesy of Jim Bolz.)

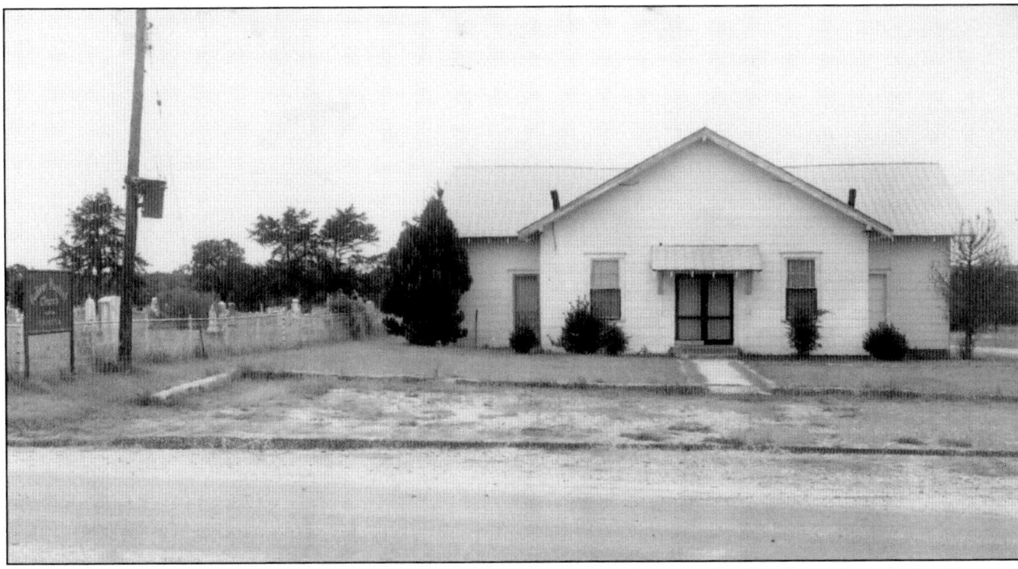

Bolivar Baptist Church, 1958. The church was organized in 1883. The first church building on this site burned in 1927. Beginning in 1928, the church met in this building next to the historical Bolivar Cemetery until a new church building opened nearby in 2003. This building is now home to the Divine Nature Church. (DCM.)

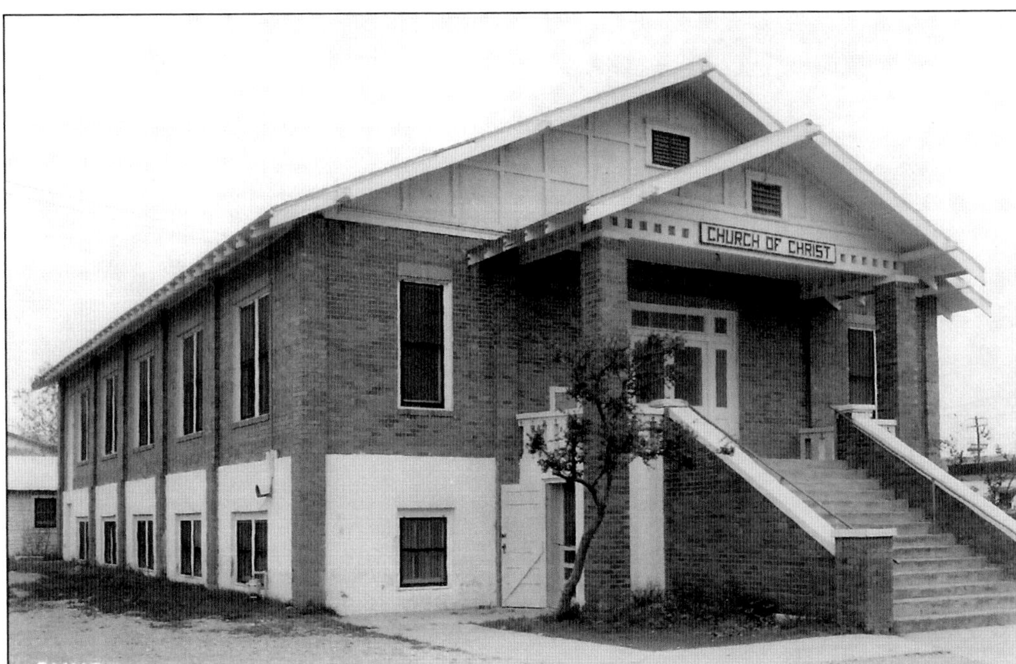

Church of Christ. Before 1903, the Church of Christ met in the Odd Fellows Hall located in the upper story of the Wilfong building. This two-story brick building was built in 1924 on the southwest corner of Fourth and Cherry Streets. The church met in it until a new building was completed in 1963. The 1963 building now houses the Sanger Bargain Depot. (Courtesy of Jim Bolz.)

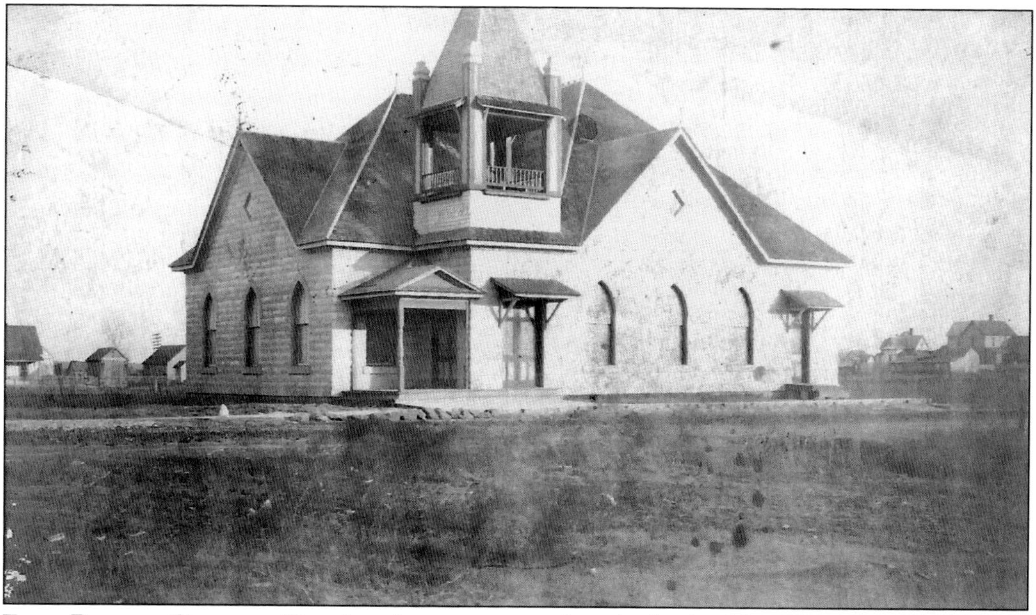

First Baptist Church. The church was organized in the back of Peter's Store in 1892. This concrete block building was built in 1905 near downtown Sanger. It served as the meeting place until 1961 when a new church building was opened on South Fifth Street. Landmark Baptist Church has occupied this building in recent years. (Courtesy of Jim Bolz.)

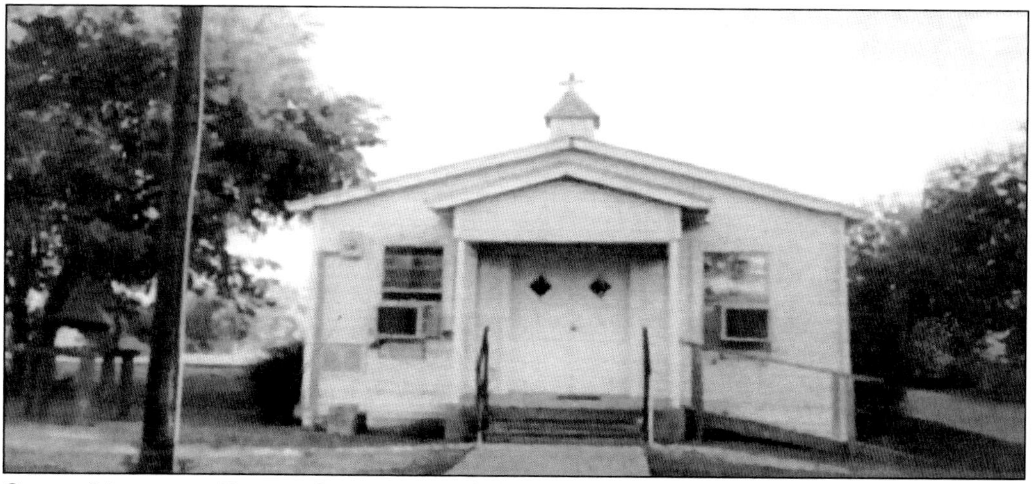

Galilee Missionary Baptist Church. Founded in 1909, the church was awarded a Texas Historical Marker in 2009. Originally located on the McCarty farm south of Sanger, it was moved for the black children to attend school in the fall of 1910. Rev. R. Curry was the first pastor, and the site was donated by the Shirley family. It was later rebuilt and is now located on Willow Street. (Courtesy of Dorothy (Haskins) Nubine.)

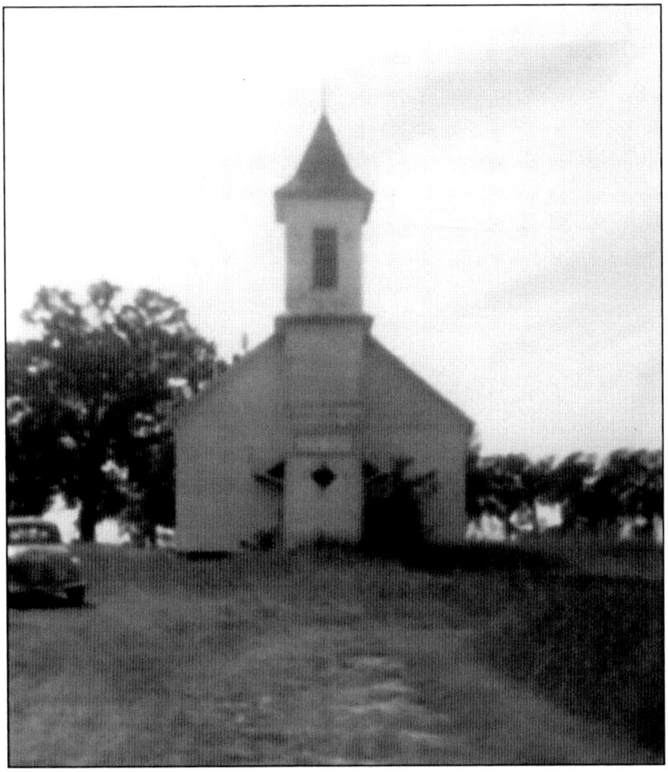

Gribble Springs Baptist Church, 1950. This building stood for approximately half a century before it was torn down in 1952 to make way for another building that was being moved from Vaughantown. A historical marker was awarded to the congregation in 2006. The community of Gribble Springs, named for the Gribble family, is located east of Sanger on Farm-to-Market Road 2164, which is also known as Missile Base Road. (Courtesy of Mavis Hughes.)

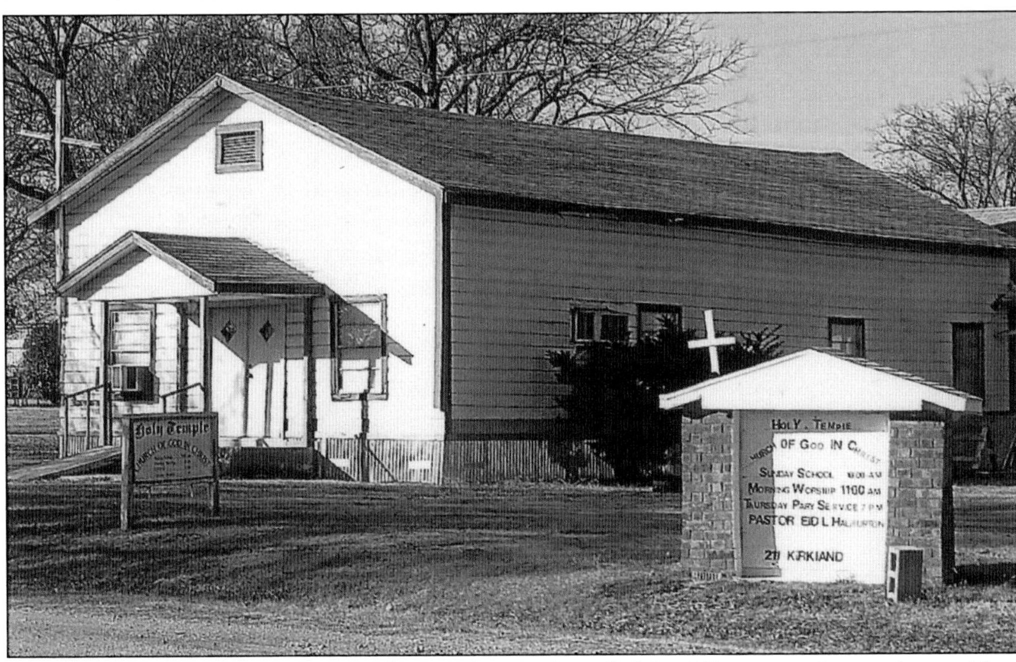

Holy Temple Church of God in Christ. Located on Kirkland Street on the southeast side of town and near the Galilee Missionary Baptist Church, the Holy Temple Church of God in Christ maintains a small congregation, including Sam Jones, who celebrated 56 years as a member of the church in 2010. Jones died May 17, 2011, at age 88. (Photograph by Cindy (Mays) Bounds.)

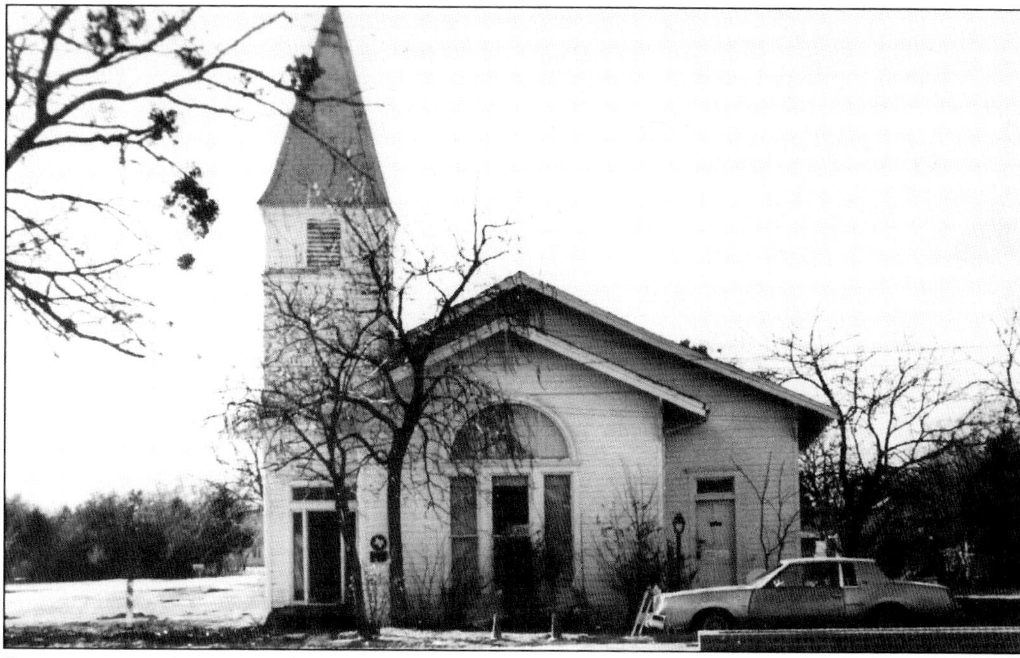

Presbyterian Church. The Presbyterian church was completed in 1902, and the final service was held in August 1971. Unique flooring was deliberately slanted toward the rostrum, and later the building was used for community gatherings. No longer serving as a place of worship, it became city property in 1987 and functioned as a library until a new library was built in 1995. It was designated a Texas Historical Landmark in 1972. (SAHS.)

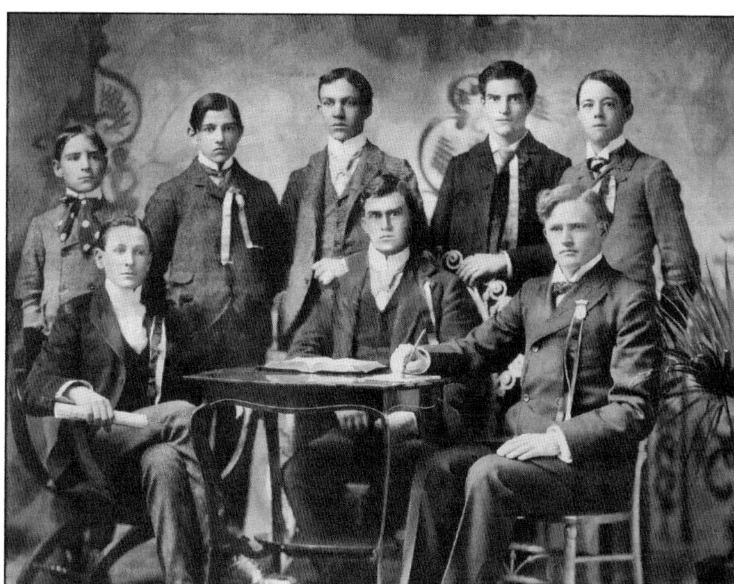

Church Mystery Picture. The old c. 1900 Presbyterian church building was being renovated in 2005 when a picture was found in the walls. It had been folded twice and came apart when it was opened because it was very brittle. The Sanger Area Historical Society had the picture digitally restored but, although much research has been done, those who are pictured and the occasion are still a mystery. (SAHS.)

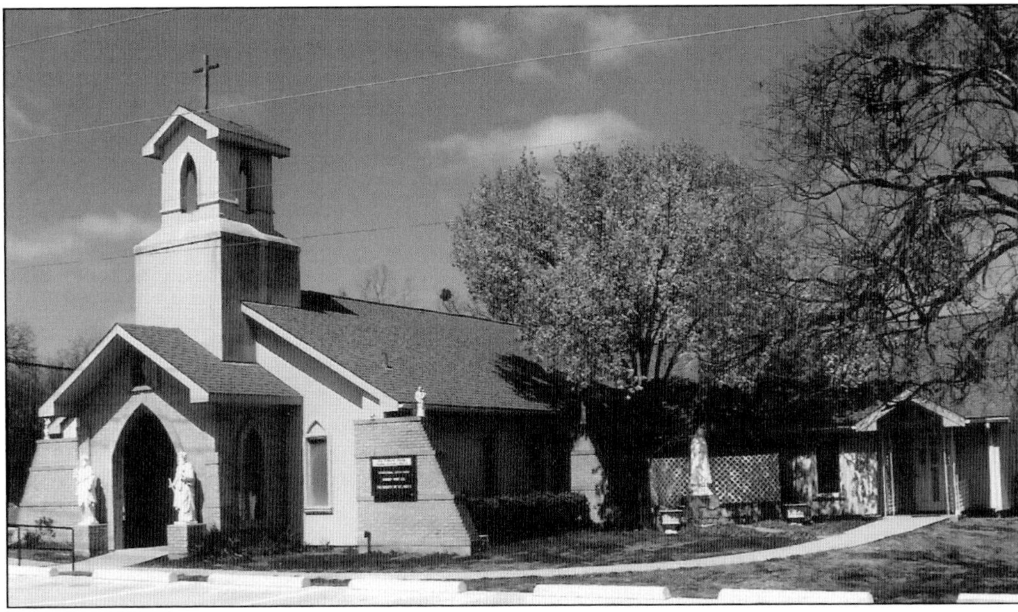

LADY OF FATIMA ROMAN CATHOLIC CHURCH. Becoming an official chapel of the Society of Saint Pius X in 1975, masses in Latin were held in Denton until 1979 when the Sanger building was purchased and a major remodeling project was completed in 1987. The building was formerly the Assembly of God Church and is still located at the northeast corner of Peach and Third Streets. (Photograph by Cindy (Mays) Bounds.)

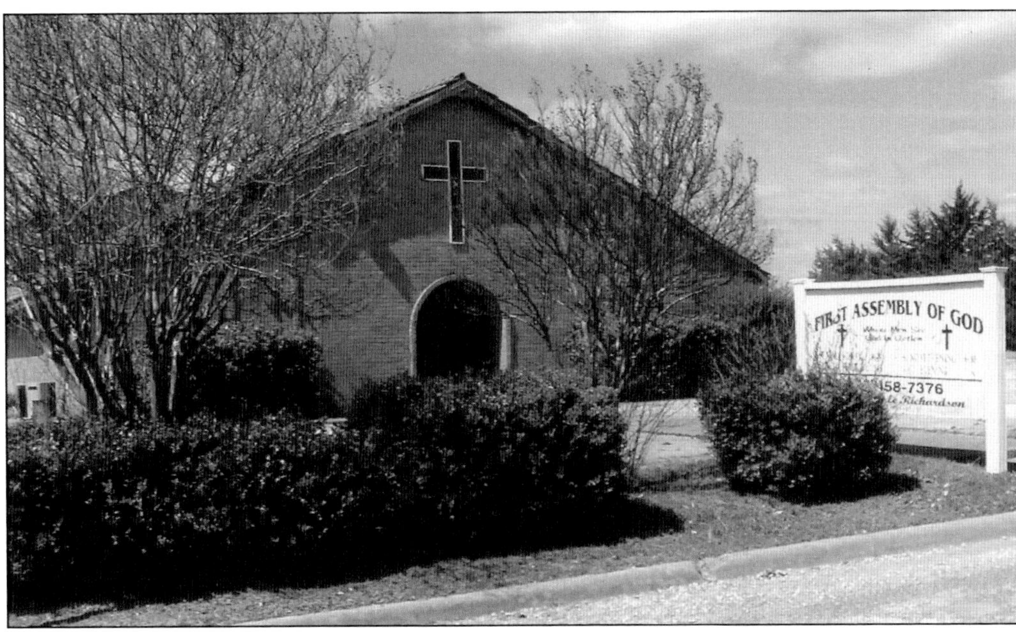

ASSEMBLY OF GOD CHURCH. The Assembly of God Church, established during a revival in 1938, was located on the northeast corner of Peach and Third Streets. The Rev. Burle Richardson began ministering at the church in 1975. The church relocated to a building on Freese Drive in 1979, and the original church building is now a Catholic church. (Photograph by Cindy (Mays) Bounds.)

Five

The Working

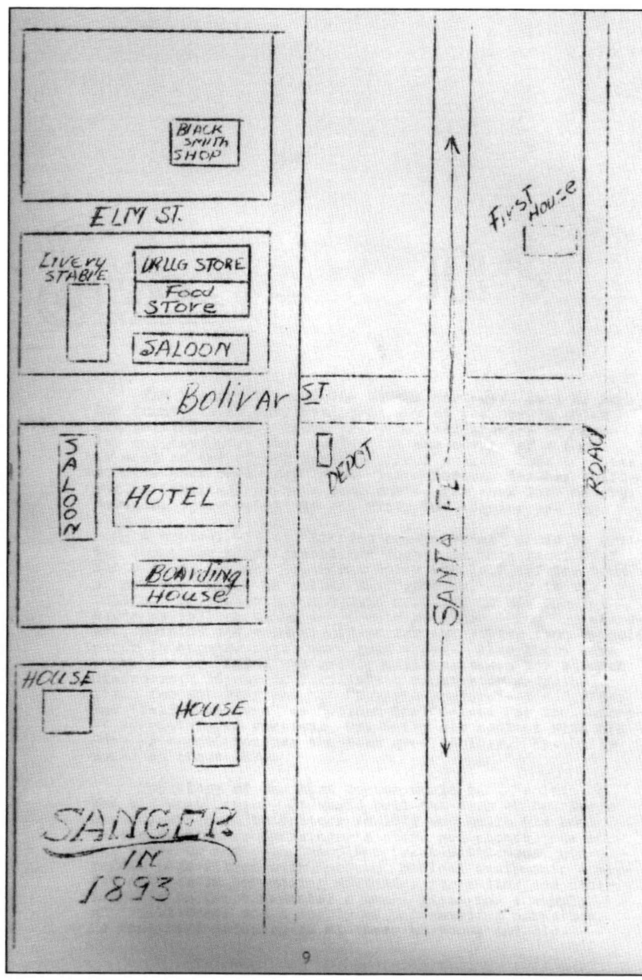

Sanger Map, 1893. The high school civics class of 1952–1953 was taught by Ina Grace Holt. They compiled *Story of Sanger, 1886–1953*, which contained this map that was prepared with the help of Gus Enlow and Emmitt Kirkland, men who remembered the early days of Sanger. The booklet was presented to the ex-students' association for distribution to the public. (SAHS.)

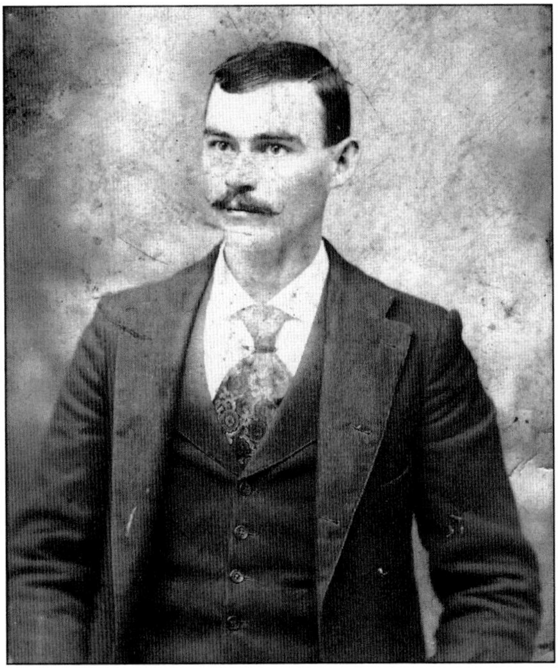

The Village Blacksmiths. James Flow "Jim" Campbell (1876–1915) was one of Sanger's earliest blacksmiths. His shop was on East Elm Street near the railroad. He learned his trade from his father's half-brother, James Flow of Denton. The blacksmith has been called "the most useful man in town" by Eunice (Sullivan) Gray in *Story of Sanger 1886–1986*. Other early blacksmiths included J.W. Milligan, J.O. and Cleo Strickland, and Jack and Cleve Campbell. (Courtesy of Nancy (Campbell) Smith.)

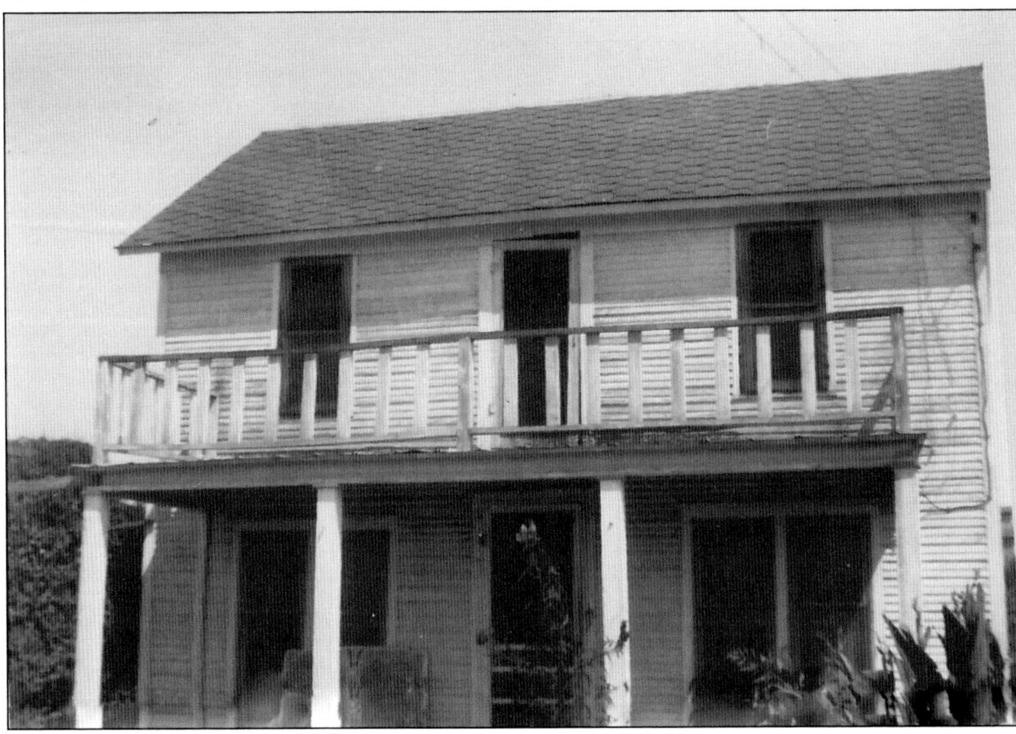

Burchard Hotel. Dora Lee (Rogers) Burchard operated her home as a hotel in 1900 when the local hotel next to the old depot site had no vacancies. The home had four upstairs bedrooms, and she served meals in the downstairs dining room. She and her husband, Harvey, eventually opened the Highway Cafe where the Sanger Public Library is currently located on Fifth Street. (Courtesy of Billy Ed Nance.)

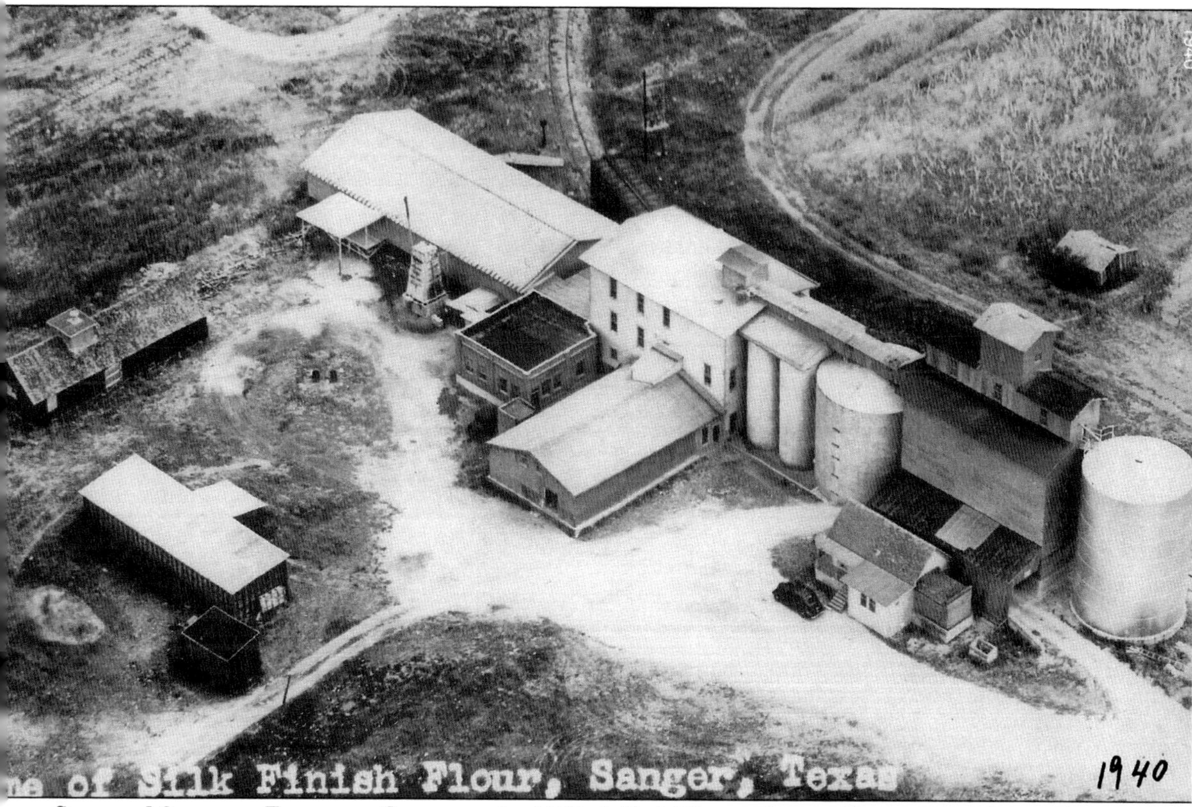

Sanger Mill and Elevator Company. In 1897, A.D. Miller, a flour miller, organized a stock company to establish and build the Sanger Mill and Elevator Company. A.J. "Squire" Nance was its first president (from 1897 to 1917), Phil F. Saltsman was chairman of the board, and J.T. Chambers was manager (from 1898 to 1925). Others involved in the early days of the mill include Jack Sullivan, E.L. Berry, and Frank Thatcher. It was known as the "Home of the Silk Finish Flour" while Willie Bush Chambers was manager (from 1925 to 1941). Sold in 1941 to Kimbell Milling Company of Fort Worth, the elevator, mill, public scale, and an upstairs residence continued in its location on the east side of Second Street between Plum and Pecan Streets for many years. Schertz Farms Feed Store now operates from this site, and old silos can be seen there still. (SAHS.)

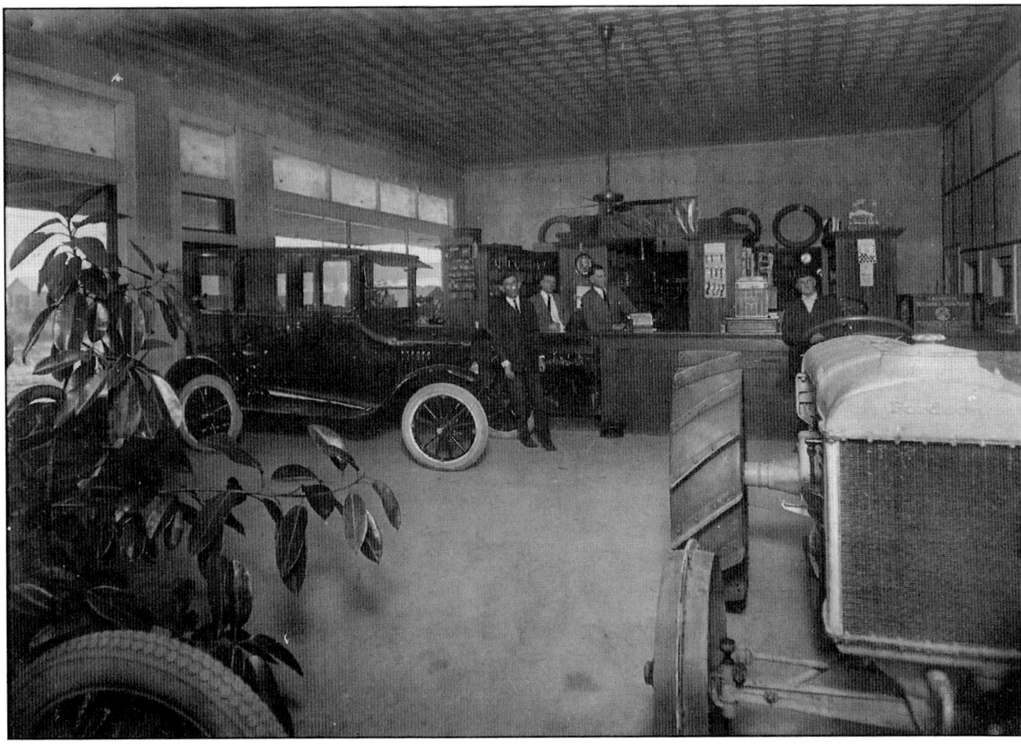

LeGear Motor Company. The showroom (above) of LeGear Motor Company, located at Highway 77 and Bolivar Street, began selling Ford products in 1925. E.L. "Lish" LeGear came to Texas at the age of one, and moved to Sanger at age eleven. The brick building (below) is still standing at the southeast corner of Fifth and Bolivar Streets. LeGear became the John Deere distributor with his son-in-law Henry Cooper as his partner, and the business was located at the northeast corner of Fifth and Cherry Streets but was eventually torn down. (Courtesy of Jerriann (Cooper) Shepard.)

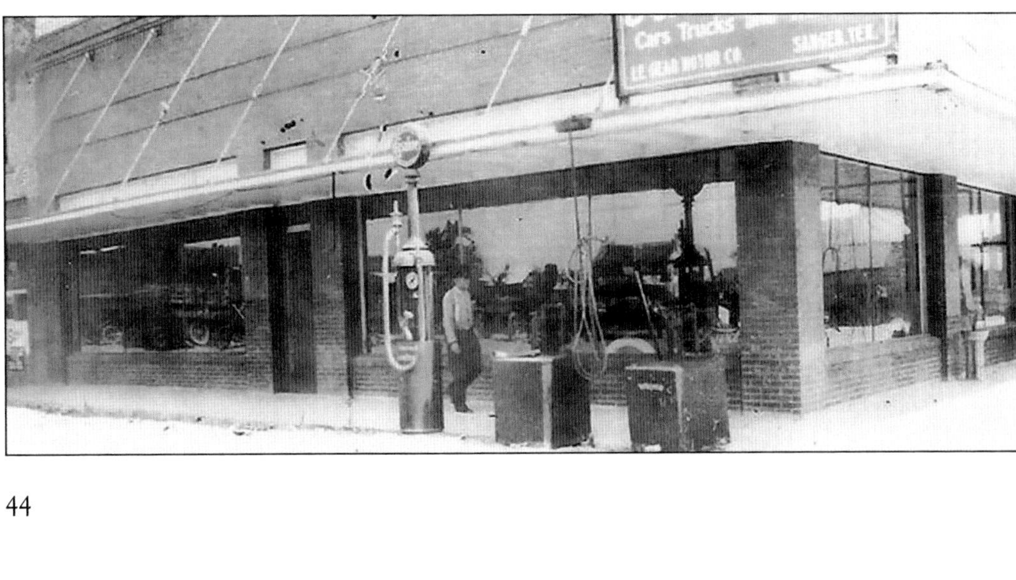

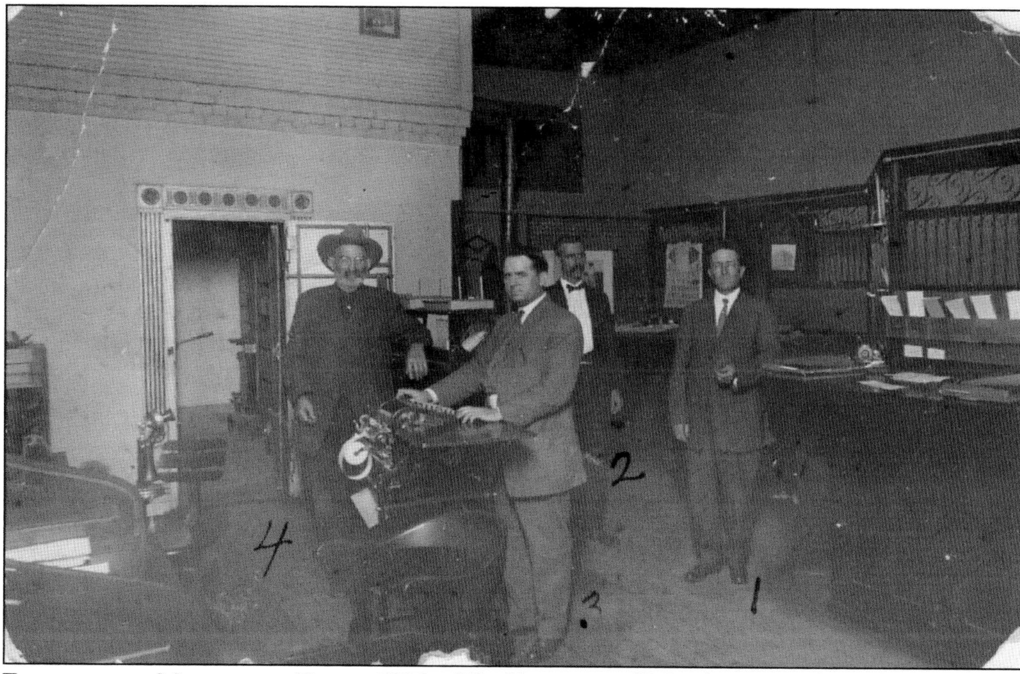

Farmers and Merchants Bank, 1890s. The Farmers and Merchants Bank was located in the two-story red brick Dunn Building on the east side of Fourth Street, facing the park. Pictured here, from left to right, are customer S.T. Sluder, assistant cashier W. Lee Sullivan, assistant cashier H.D. Greene, and cashier J.G. Wright. The vault stands open in the background, and the cashiers' cages can be seen to the right. (TWU.)

First National Bank, 1920. In 1899, E.L. Berry, B.L. Spencer, and J.W. Spencer bought Farmers Bank of Sanger and changed the name to Farmers and Merchants Bank. In 1905, it was chartered as First National Bank of Sanger and located on the northwest corner of Bolivar and Third Streets. The building is now used as the Sanger Law Enforcement Center. (SPL.)

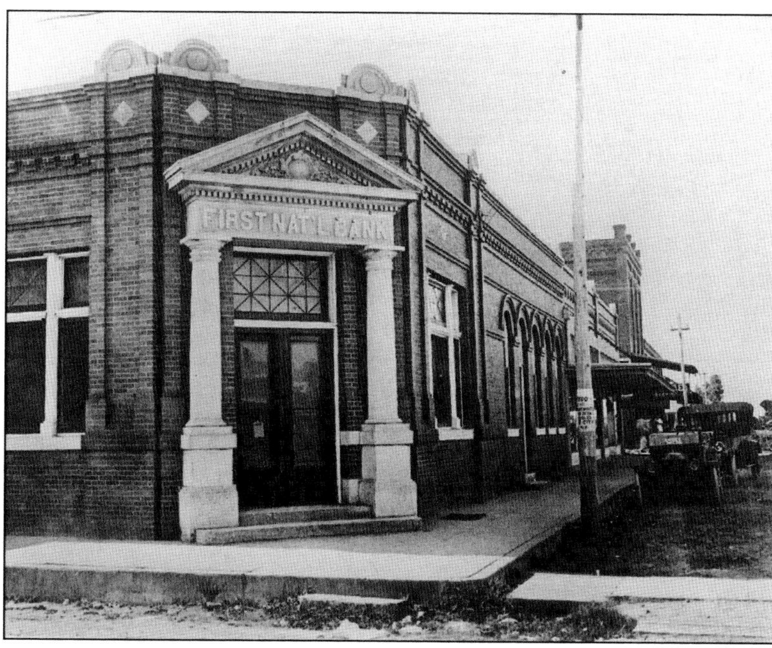

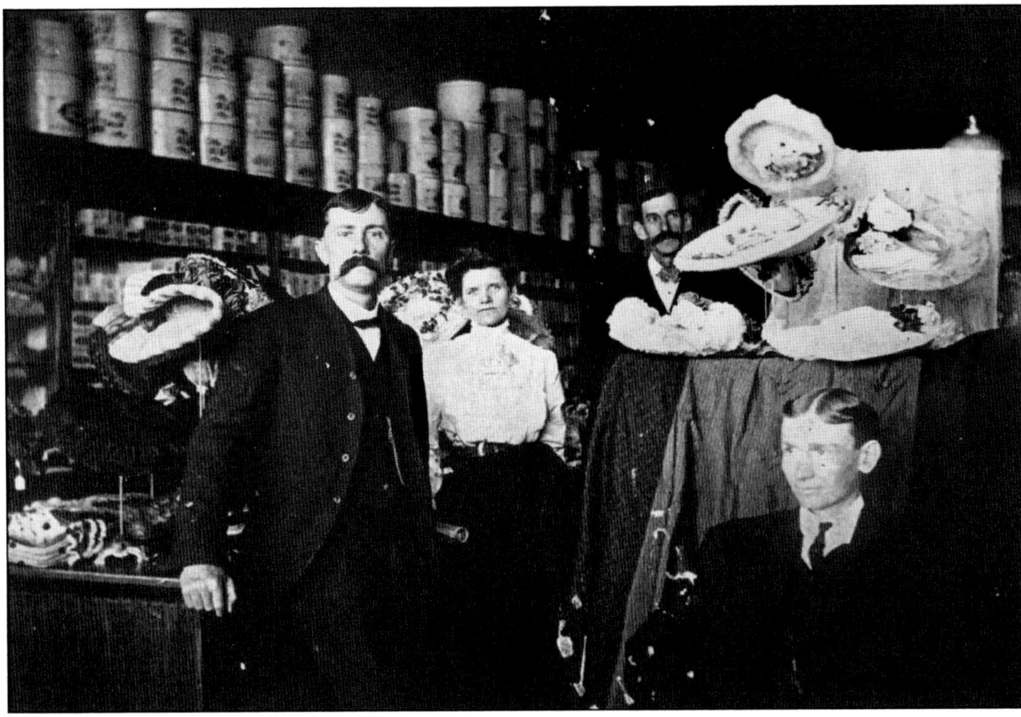

Collins and Andrews Dry Goods. In this picture, from left to right, Mr. Andrews, Mrs. Waide, Mr. Collins, and clerk Luther L. McNeil (seated) are in the dry goods store, which is reported to be the first business of its type in Sanger. The ladies' hats that are prominently displayed befit the mode of dress in that era, estimated to be in the early 1900s. (TWU.)

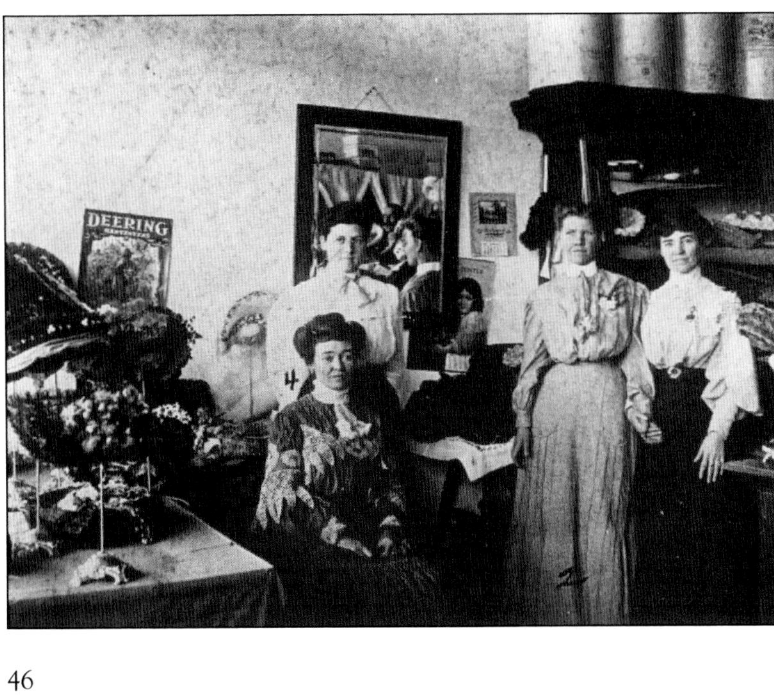

The Millinery Shop. Julia McMurtry (seated) and her sister, Nell Harter (far right), owned this shop in the early 1900s. Julia, Irene Berry, and Lina B. Koons, representing the Sanger Improvement Club, appeared before the city council in 1916 to request that the park be cleaned up and used for the purpose for which it had been donated. (SAHS.)

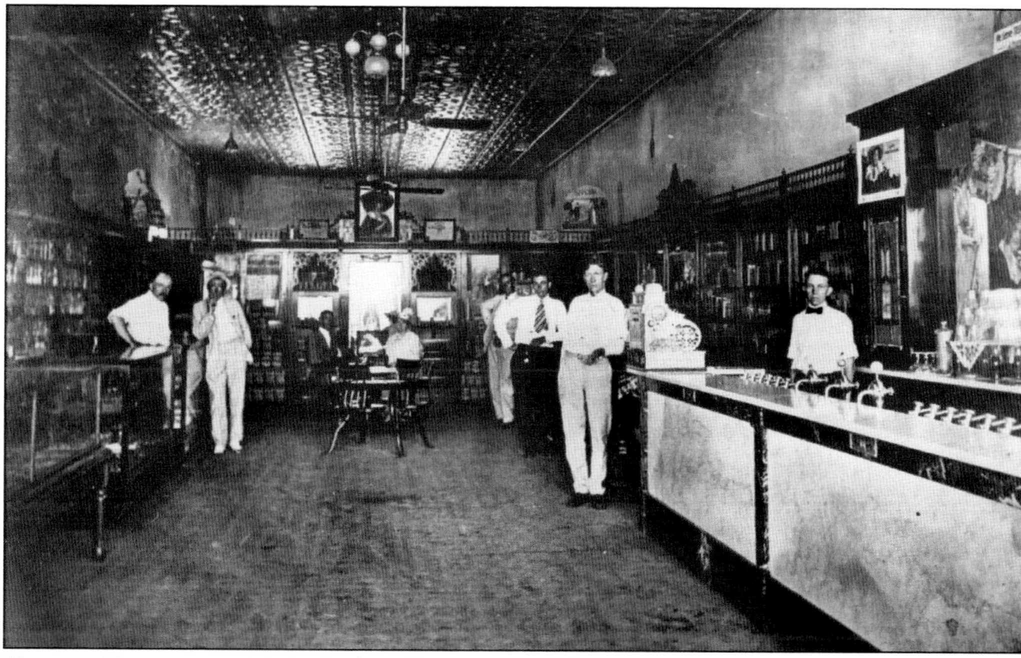

Gaskins Drugstore, 1912. Gaskins Drugstore was located on the north side of Bolivar Street. In the photograph above, W.H. Gaskins stands near the cash register with Duncan Davidson on his right. Dan Davis stands behind the jewelry counter opposite them. The tables in the back were furnished for customers to enjoy treats from the soda fountain prepared by the soda jerk. Note the tinned ceiling. (TWU.)

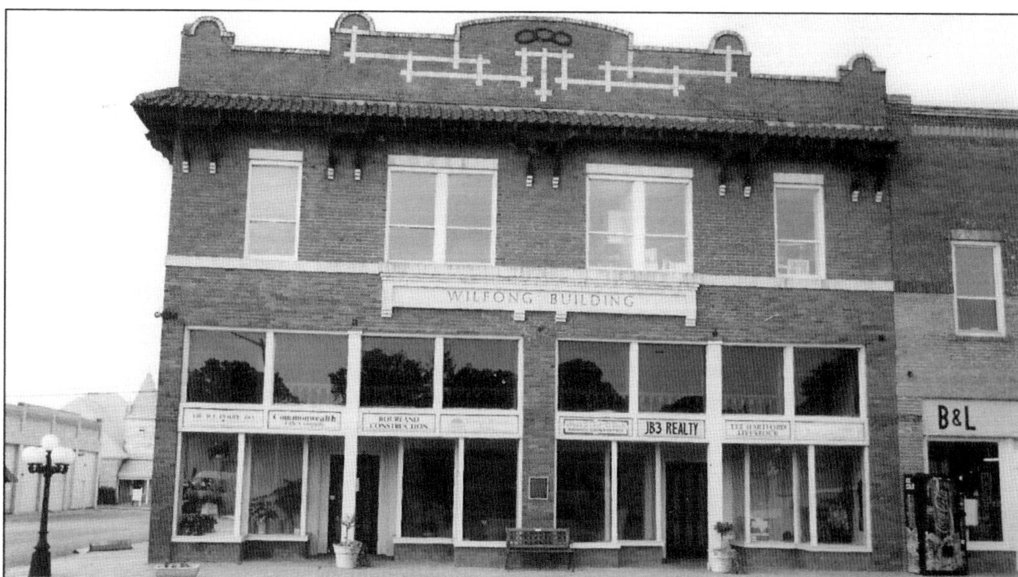

Wilfong Building. In 1917, J.M. Wilfong built a two-story brick building at the southwest corner of Bolivar and Fourth Streets to house his dry goods business. It included two front-entry doors. A side entry led to the second floor, which was used for various functions. Wilfong moved his business to Gainesville in the late 1930s, and Jess Smith Dry Goods was housed in this building for many years to come. (SAHS.)

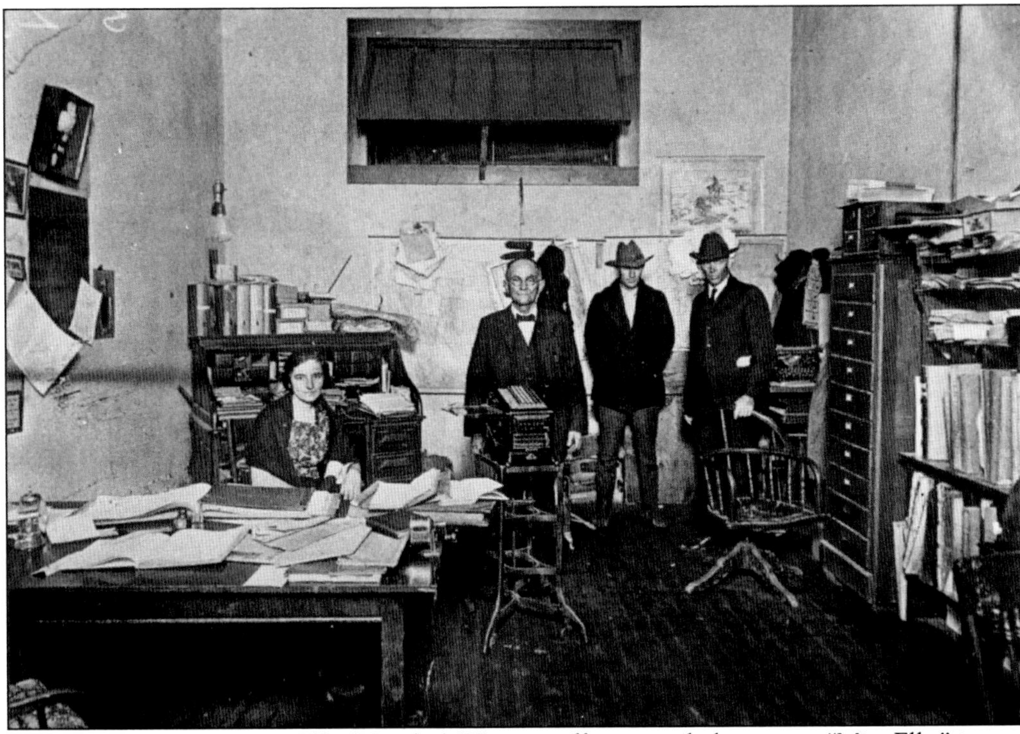

Insurance Office, 1923. Ella (Vaughn) Warren, affectionately known as "Miss Ella," is seen here in her insurance office located on North Third Street in the rear of the First National Bank building. With her are R.W. Walton, her partner; Curtis Warren, her husband; and J.L. Ratcliff, pastor of First Baptist Church. She was the first woman in Sanger to receive the Citizen of the Year award. (SPL.)

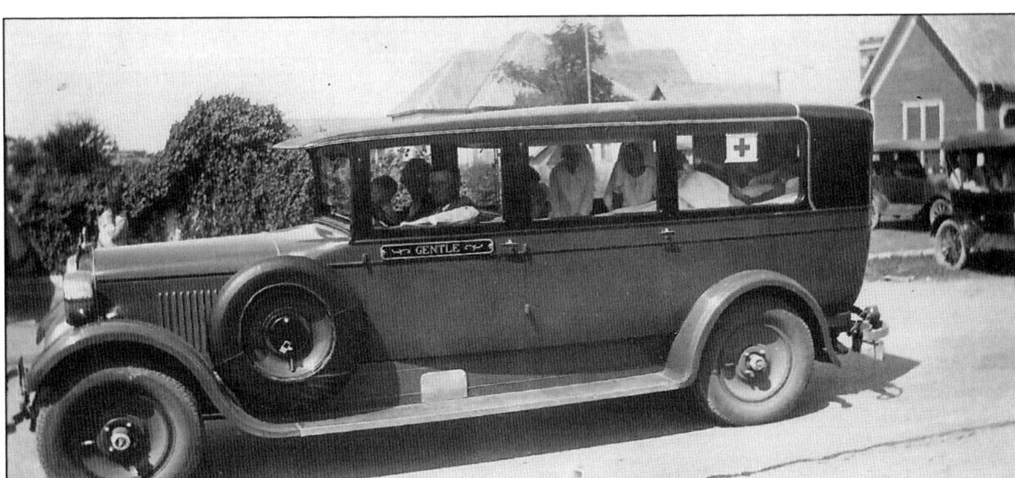

Gentle Ambulance, 1930. This automobile, which appears to be a 1928 Cadillac limousine, served as an ambulance. In this picture, a man, woman, and child are in the front seat and two nurses sit with a patient in the back. Notice the name "Gentle" on the driver's door and the Red Cross symbol on the back window. (SAHS.)

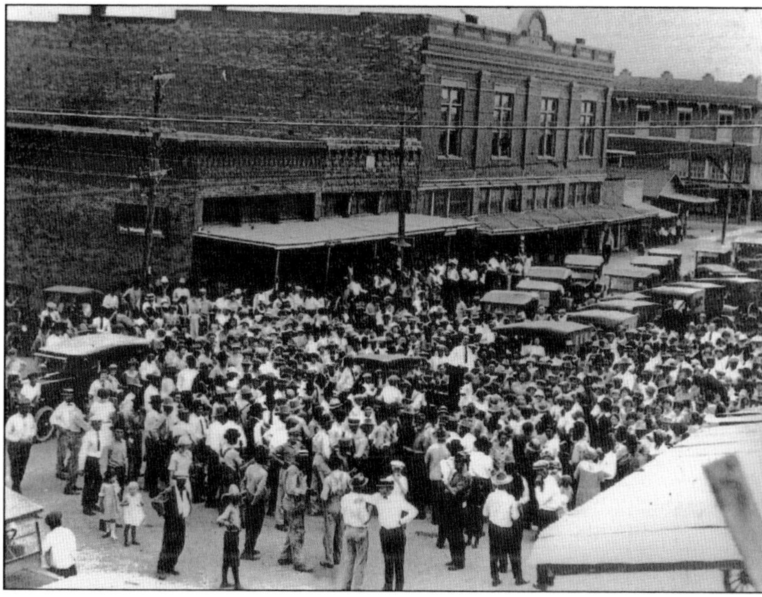

Saturday Drawing, 1920. The drawing on Saturday afternoon was a tradition in downtown Sanger for many years. Gordon W. "Speedy" Sullivan stands in a truck in the middle of the large crowd to announce the winning tickets for cash prizes donated by local merchants. The Opera House and the Wilfong Building can be seen in the background. (SPL.)

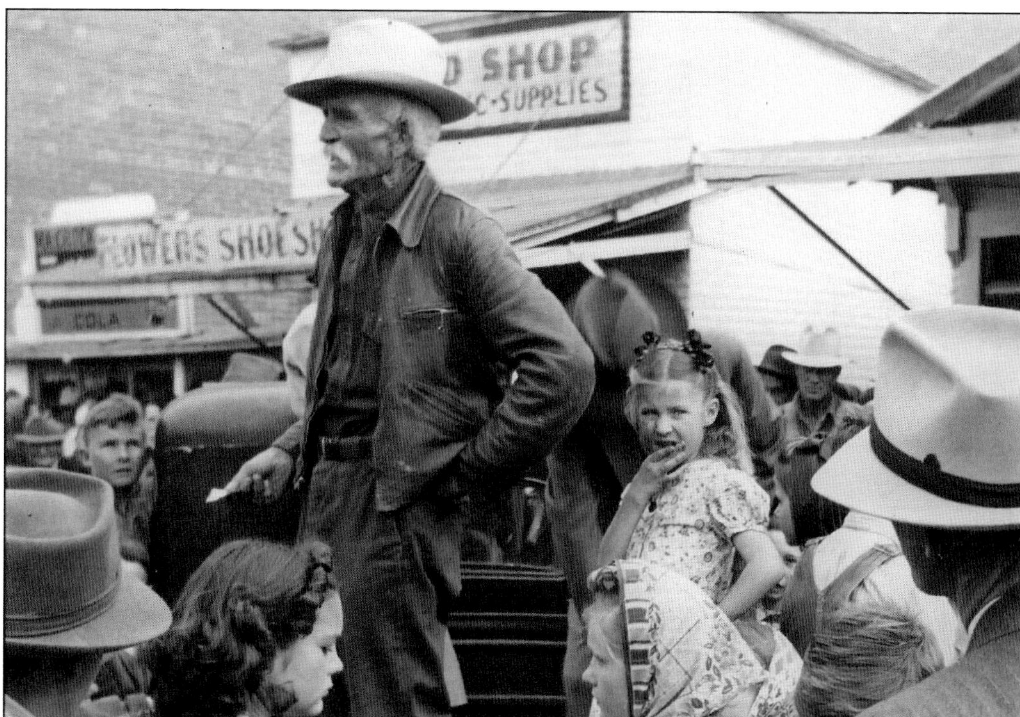

Another Saturday Drawing. The Saturday afternoon drawing was a big event that drew large crowds to town through the many years it was held. The man seen above is holding a winning ticket that was possibly drawn by the young girl behind him. Cash prizes furnished by local businesses were given to the lucky ones who had their names drawn. Notice the sign for the Flowers Shoe Shop. (SPL.)

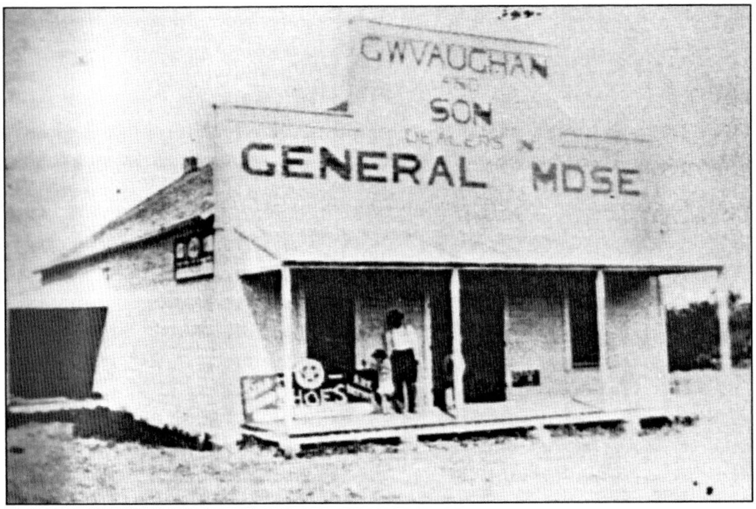

The Vaughantown Store. G.W. Vaughan Sr. and his son Aubrey operated this general store in Vaughantown, a community east of Sanger near Elm Creek of the Trinity River. The Vaughantown church building was moved to Gribble Springs in 1952. Lake Ray Roberts has covered this area since 1987. (Courtesy of Peggy (Vaughan) Pate.)

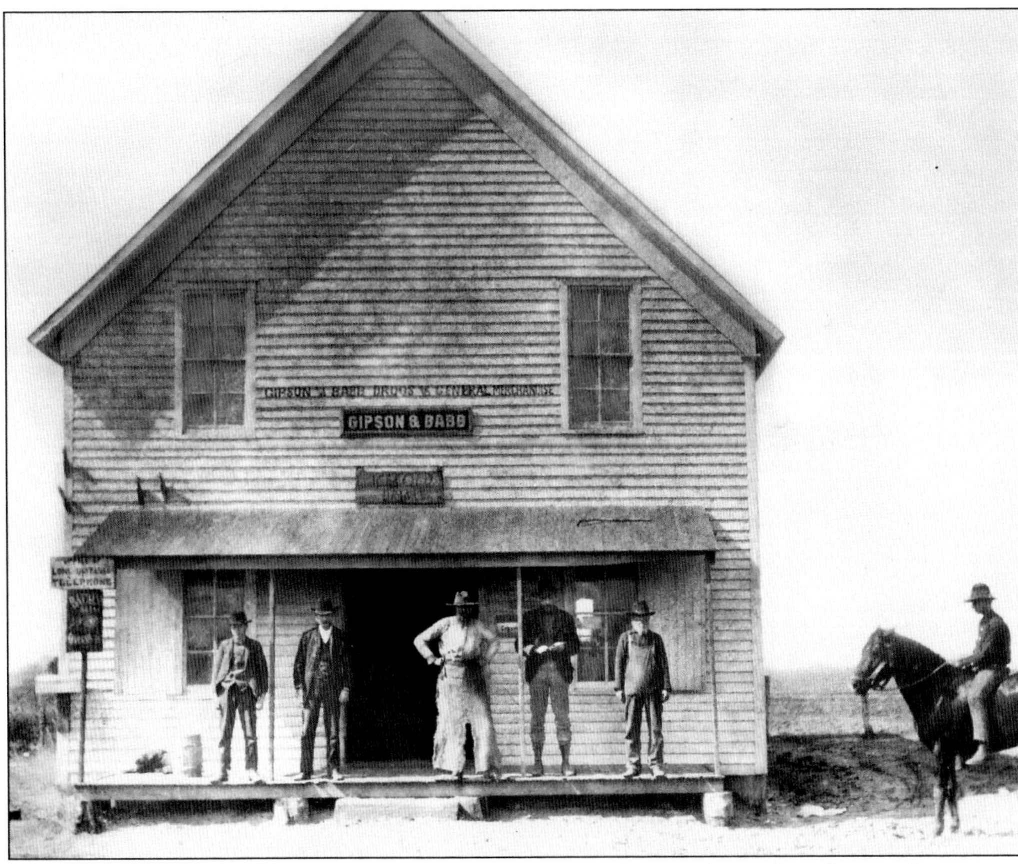

Gipson & Babb Store, 1915. This store sold drugs and general merchandise in the town of Bolivar, five miles west of Sanger. Pictured here are five men standing on the front porch and another man on horseback. Note the handmade sign for ice cold drinks above the porch roof, below the store's name. Another handmade sign for long distance telephone service is on the left. (SAHS.)

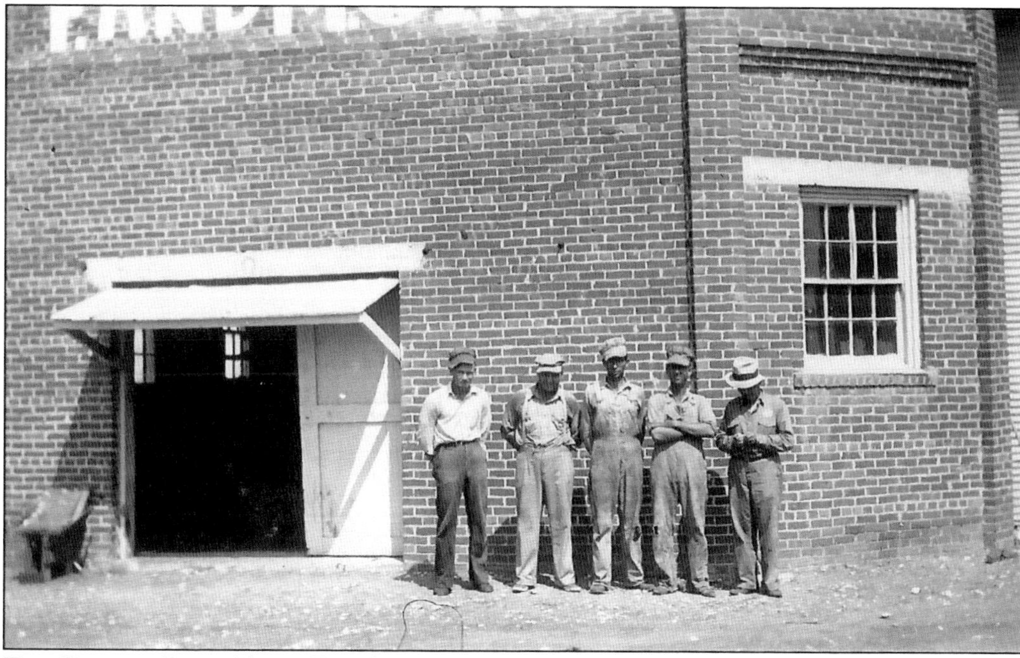

The Cotton Gins. Above, F and M Gin Company was one of several gin businesses serving farmers in and around Sanger. Two of these four employees pictured in the early 1940s were Tom Campbell and Homer Rogers (third and fourth from left). Butler Boydstun, who co-owned the gin company with his brother Joe, is on the far right. Joe Boydstun served as mayor of Sanger from 1923 to 1929. In earlier years, Sanger Gin Company was another gin business serving farmers around the Sanger community. The 1929 calendar shown below was gifted to customers. The name plate was attached by tabs, giving it a three-dimensional effect. (Above, courtesy of Nancy (Campbell) Smith; below, SPL.)

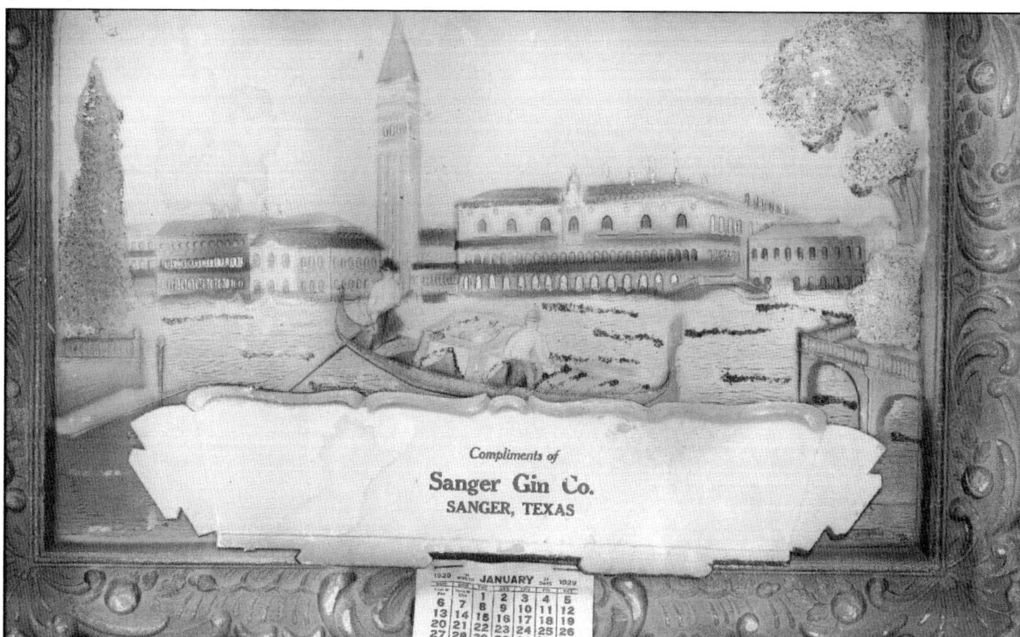

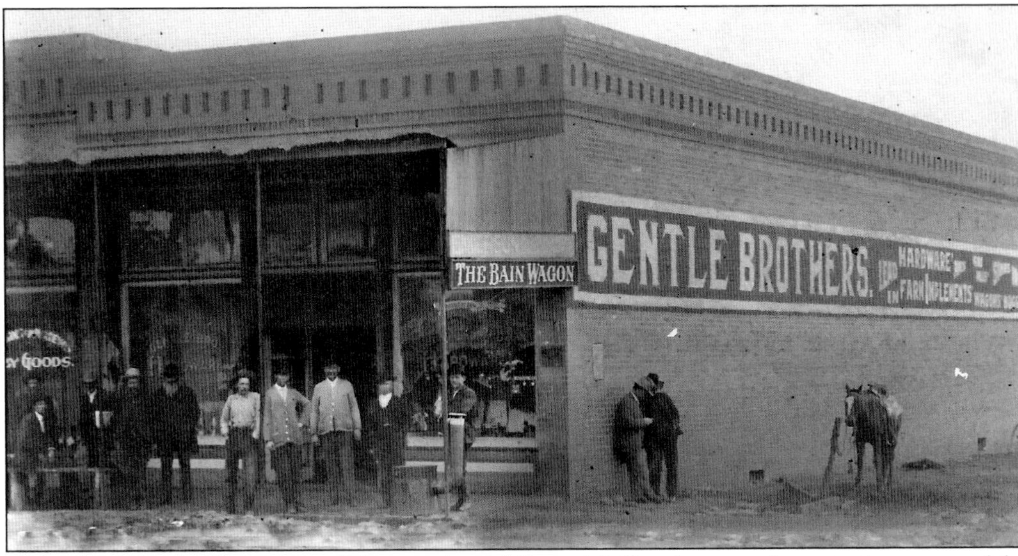

GENTLE BROTHERS HARDWARE. Thomas A. and Oscar M. Gentle, seen above in the center of the image wearing matching sweaters, opened a hardware store on the southeast corner of Bolivar and Third Streets in the late 1890s. Tom continued to operate the store in this location after Oscar opened another hardware store on the northeast corner of Bolivar and Fourth Streets around 1925. (Courtesy of Frances (Schertz) Gentle and Toni Gentle.)

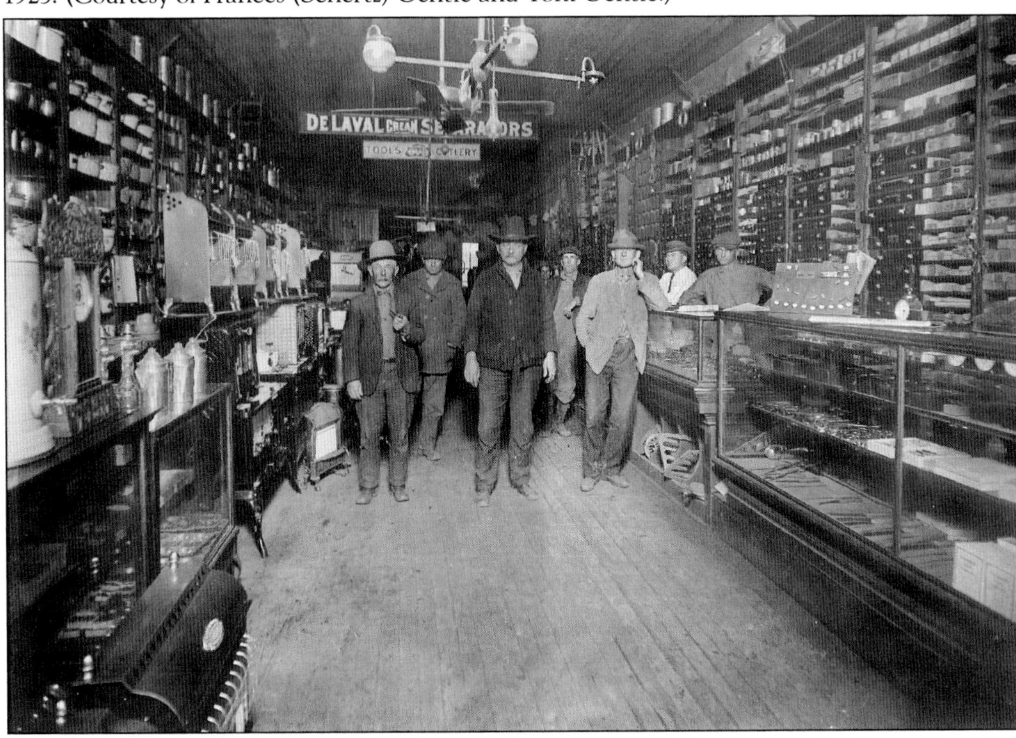

THOMAS GENTLE HARDWARE, 1927. Tom Gentle, third from left, is pictured in his well-stocked store with four customers, one of whom is Fred Amyx. His son Roy E. "Peggy" Gentle is behind the counter on the right; son Abb Gentle, also behind the counter, wears a white shirt. (Courtesy of Frances (Schertz) Gentle, Toni Gentle, and Janis (Bailey) Wetherbee.)

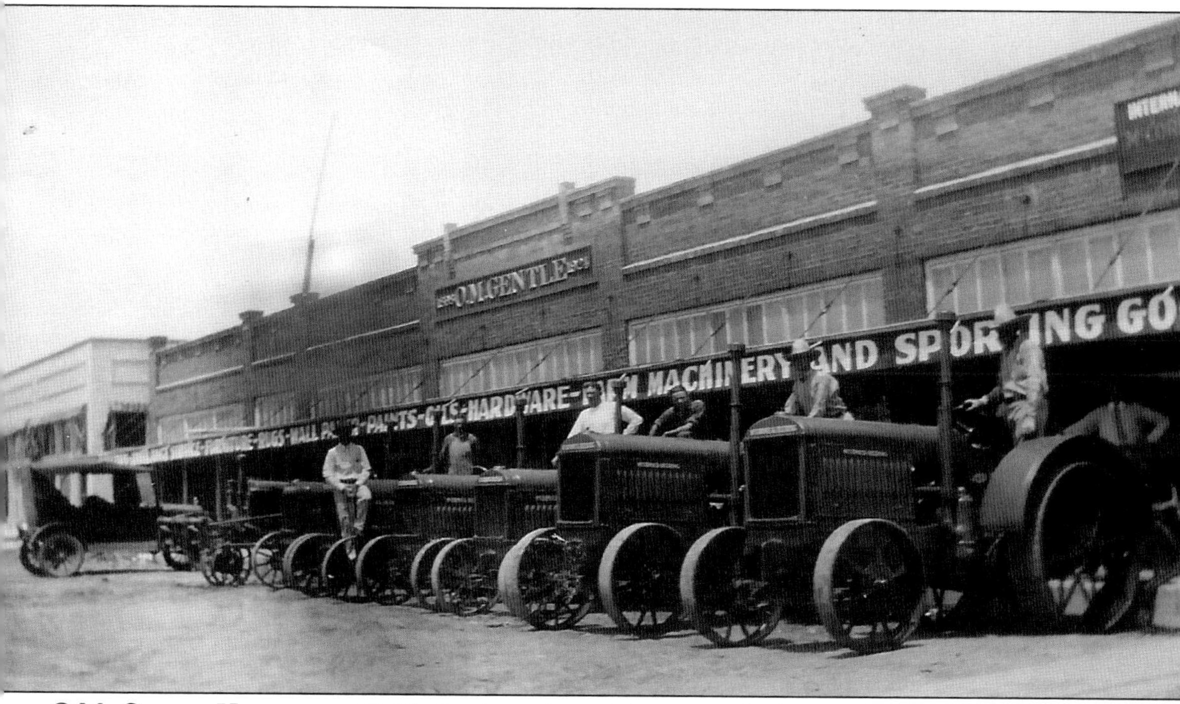

O.M. Gentle Hardware, 1928. Brothers Oscar Monroe and Thomas A. Gentle opened a hardware store in 1898. The store moved to this location on the corner of Bolivar and Fourth Streets about 1925. The store sold tractors, hardware, farm machinery, sporting goods, paint, oils, furniture, rugs, wallpaper, and a wide range of other merchandise. The building also housed the funeral home for a time. The business was sold in 1968 to Frank Smith. Smith's Country Store burned in 2000, leaving a corner lot that remains vacant in the middle of the downtown business district. Oscar's wife Bertie's maiden name was Harris. The Gentle home, located on the southwest corner of Seventh and Bolivar Streets, is now the home of Don and Dorcyle McClure. The Gentles' daughter Cathlene taught in the Sanger school for many years. They also had two sons: Oscar Monroe Jr., known as "Mon," and Lewis Gray, called "Red." (SAHS.)

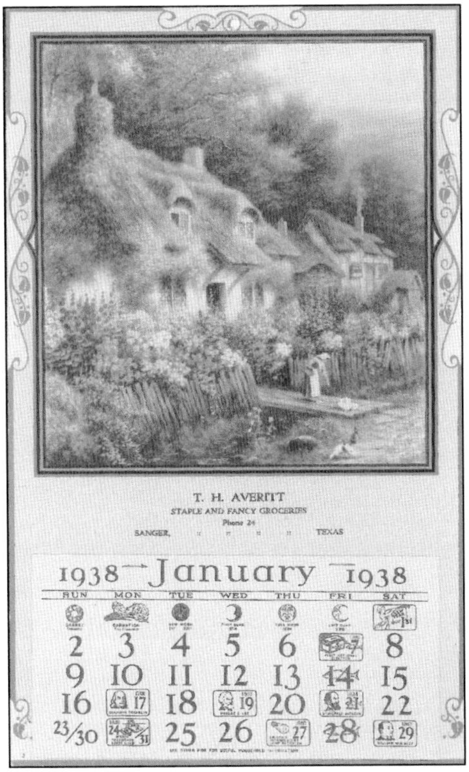

Advertisement Calendars. Although the practice still exists, in the early 1900s, calendars advertising local businesses were provided to the citizens of the community. At left is the January page from T.H. Averitt Groceries 1938 calendar. Short's Food Store offered a December 1939–1940 calendar with a photograph of a baby on the December page, as seen below. (Courtesy of Jim Bolz.)

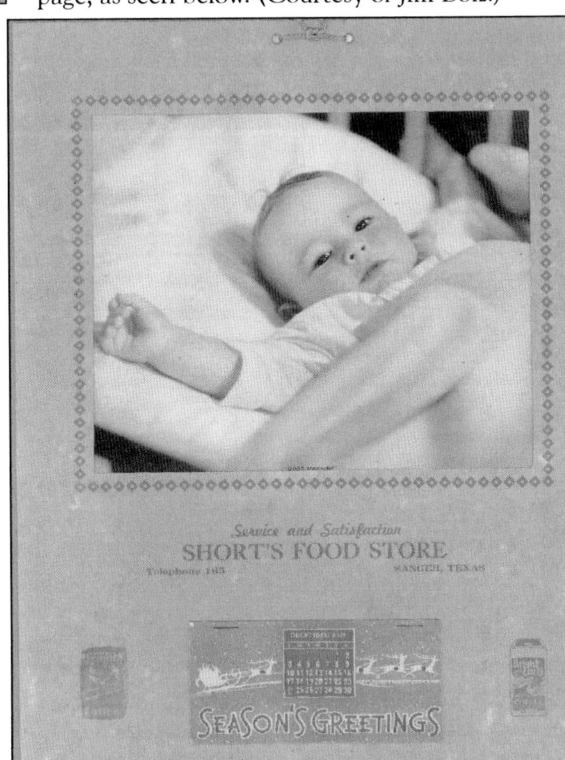

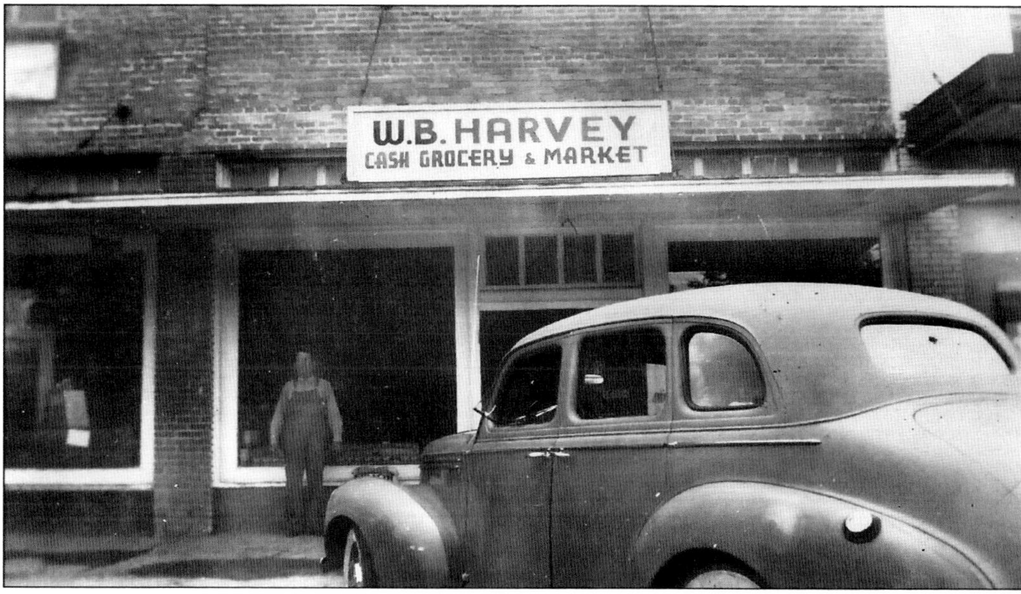

W.B. HARVEY CASH GROCERY AND MARKET. The grocery store owned by W.B. Harvey, father of Ben Harvey and grandfather to Linda Harvey Hewlett, was located on Bolivar Street across from the city park and next to the movie theater, which was later the location of the Cardinal Grocery (also known as Horst Brothers Grocers) between Fourth and Fifth Streets. This building still stands today. (Courtesy of Linda (Harvey) Hewlett.)

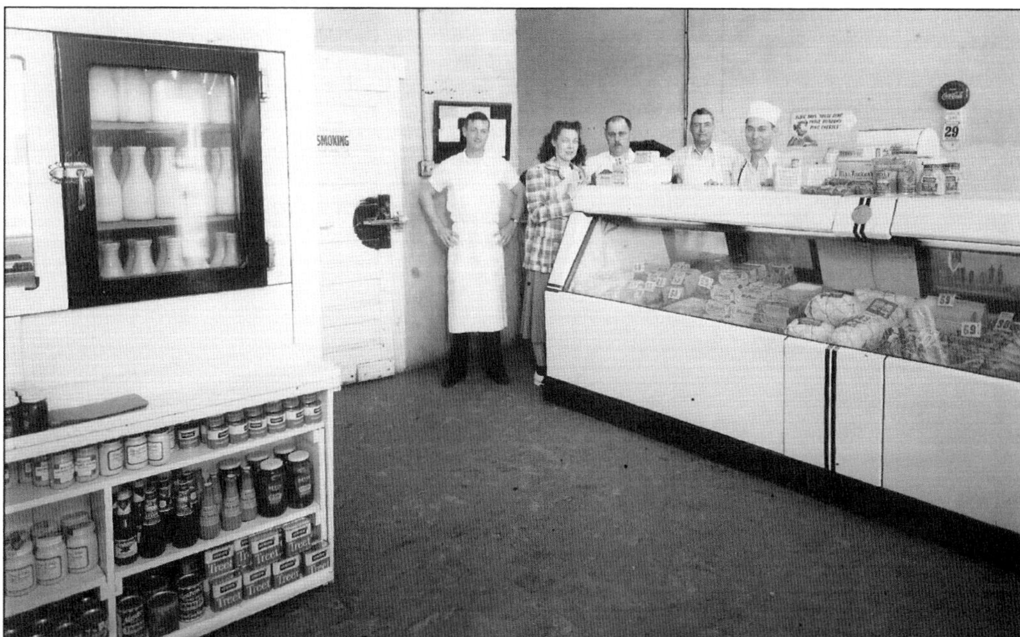

HORST BROTHERS GROCERY AND MEAT MARKET. The Horst brothers operated their store on east Bolivar Street before moving it further west, across from the park. Pictured are Dick Ready, Verdie (Horst) Ezell, Edwin Horst, Art Seely, and Lawrence Horst. Later, Seely owned and operated a frozen food locker at this location, which he sold to Ready. The door to the freezer can be seen. (Courtesy of Helen (Seely) Bounds.)

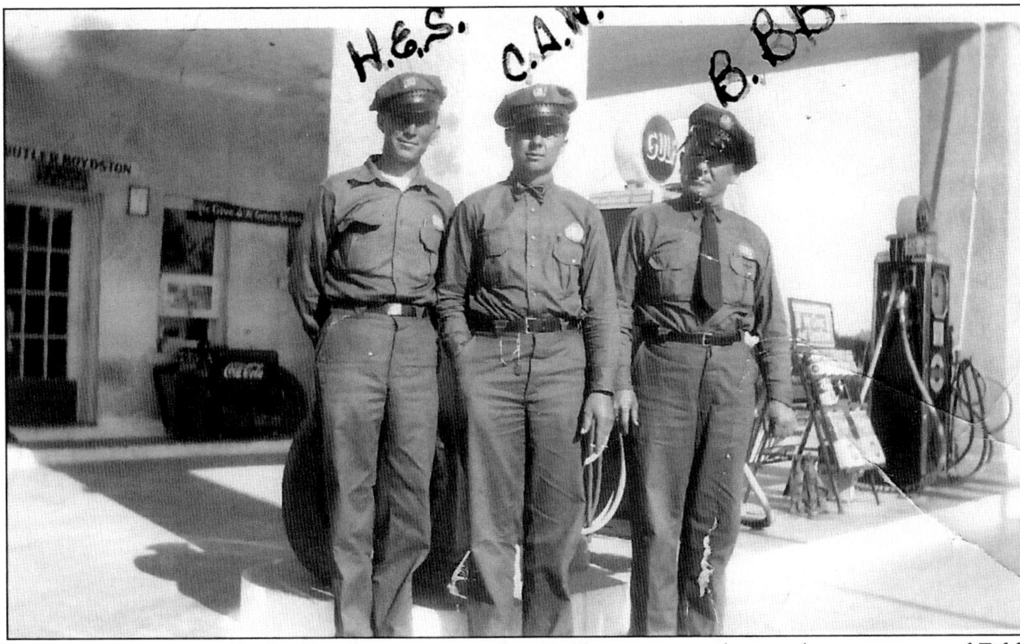

The Gulf Station. Butler Boydstun operated a Gulf station on the southwest corner of Fifth and Elm Streets. Boydstun (far right) is pictured here with two employees: Herman Sullivan, left, and Clarence Wright. Beneath the S&H Green Stamps sign, there is a Coca-Cola box where customers could help themselves to ice cold drinks while the uniformed attendants serviced their cars. (Courtesy of Elleece (Sullivan) Calvert.)

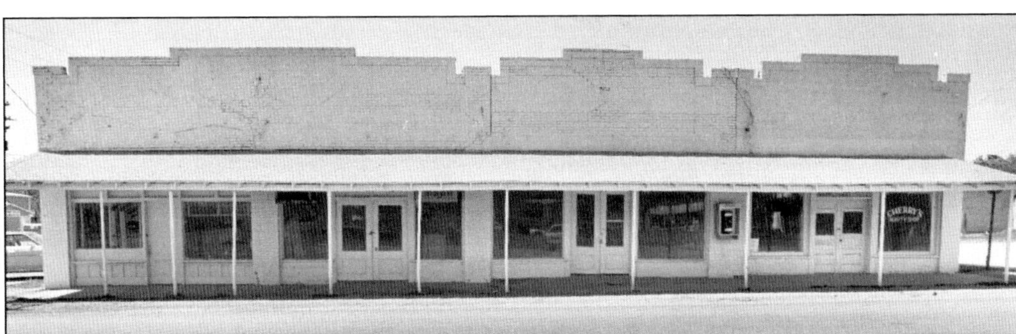

Future Site of Library. This building, located on the west side of Highway 77 (northwest corner of Fifth and Bolivar Streets) and across from the city park, was home to many local businesses for many years. A laundry, Cherry's Beauty Shop, Windle's Barbershop, and Fellers' Cafe were all located in this center. The building was later torn down, and the Sanger Public Library was built where it stood. (DCM.)

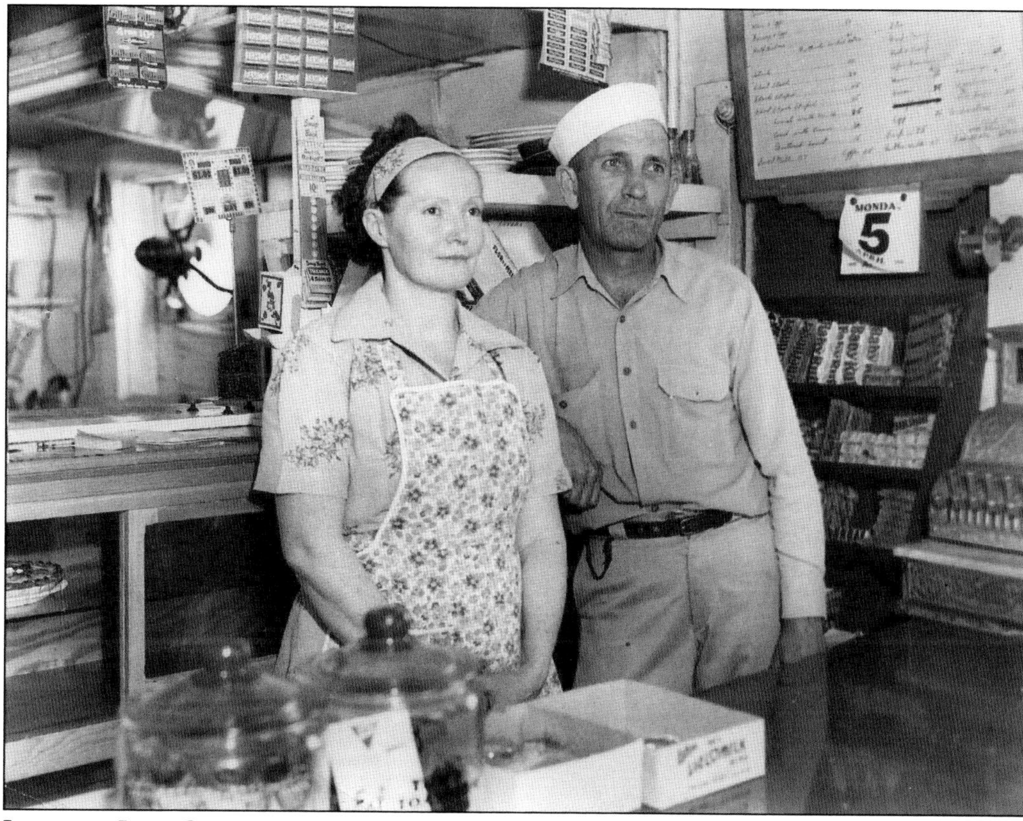

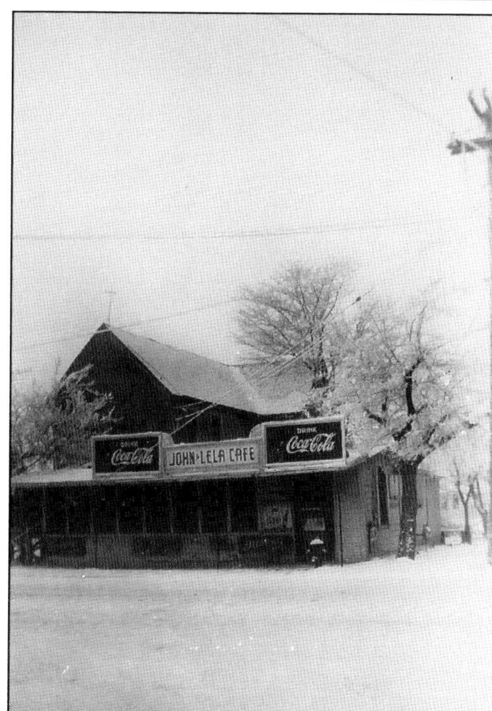

John and Lela Gary and Their Cafe. A winter storm enveloped the city with sleet and snow on January 26, 1949, and the cafe owned by John and Lela Gary is encrusted with ice in the image at right. The top of the home seen directly behind the cafe is that of Dr. Ervin Howard, John Gary's great grandfather. The cafe was at the southwest corner of Bolivar and Fifth Streets. Lela Gary was a sister to Dennis Windle, the local barber. The Garys' cafe was a popular eatery that included a counter with barstools and booths to serve the public. (Above, courtesy of Robert Windle; right; SAHS.)

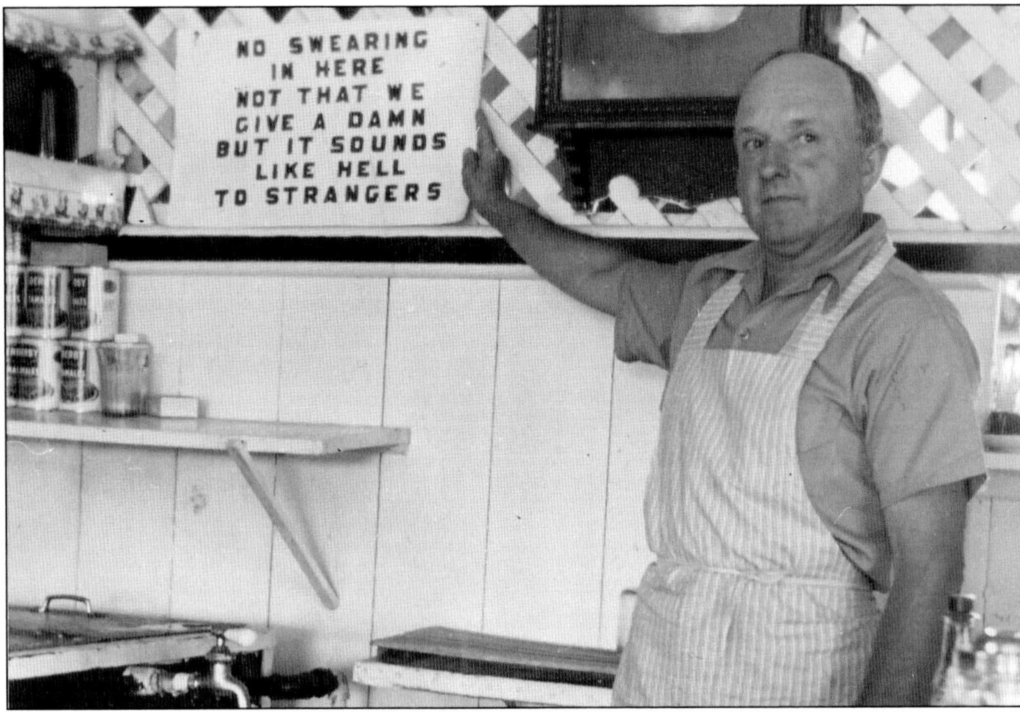

KEMP'S CAFE. Ray and Ida Kemp's cafe posted their rules of operation with a twist of humor, as shown here. The business was located on the south side of Bolivar between Third and Fourth Streets. (SAHS.)

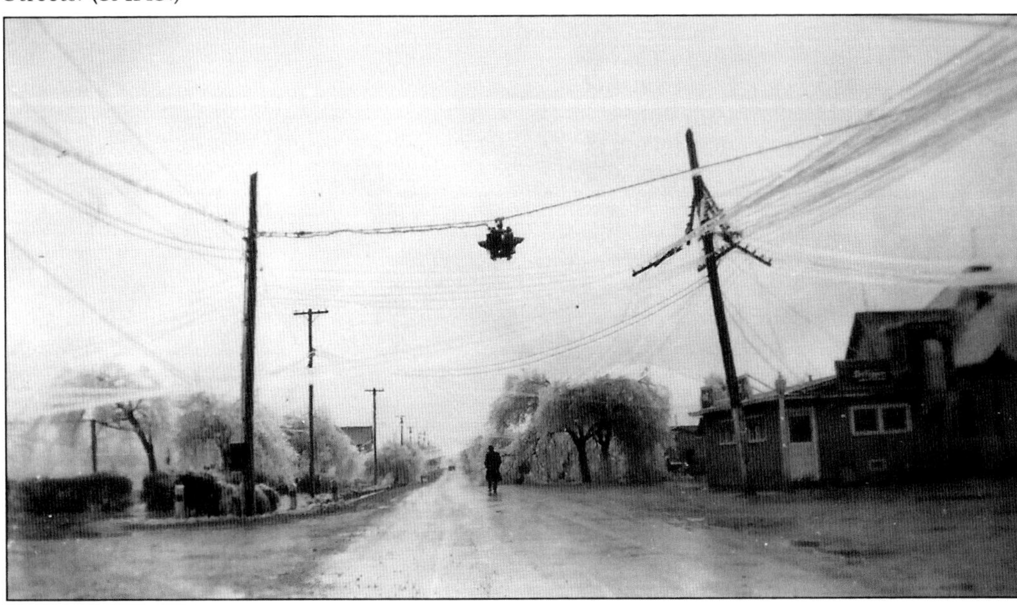

FELLERS' CAFE. Dave and Erma Fellers owned and operated this small diner at the northeast corner of Fifth and Elm Streets that included two booths, a counter with barstools, and the essential jukebox. The Fellers' cafe relocated to the current library site on Fifth Street and later to Bolivar Street between Third and Fourth Streets. Dave was an amazing one-armed man who performed cooking duties for many years. (SAHS.)

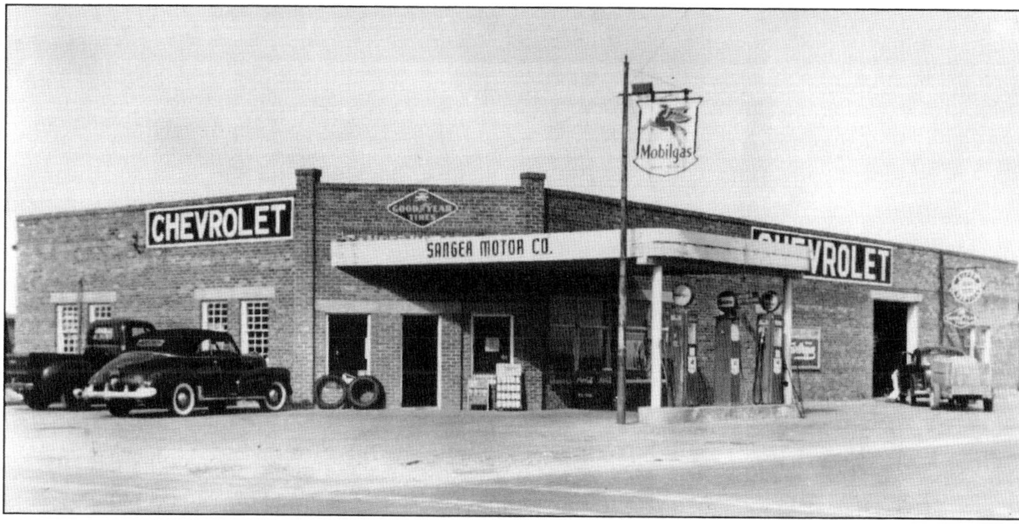

Sanger Motor Company. The Chevrolet dealership, established in 1928 by E.E. "Bud" Pate, was constructed by Ed Long at the northwest corner of Farm-to-Market Road 455 and Highway 77. The building's foundation, reinforced with old car parts and scrap iron, is still standing today. The business was later owned by Pate's son Willie Keith Pate and his wife, Peggy, until they sold it in 1981. (Courtesy of Peggy (Vaughan) Pate.)

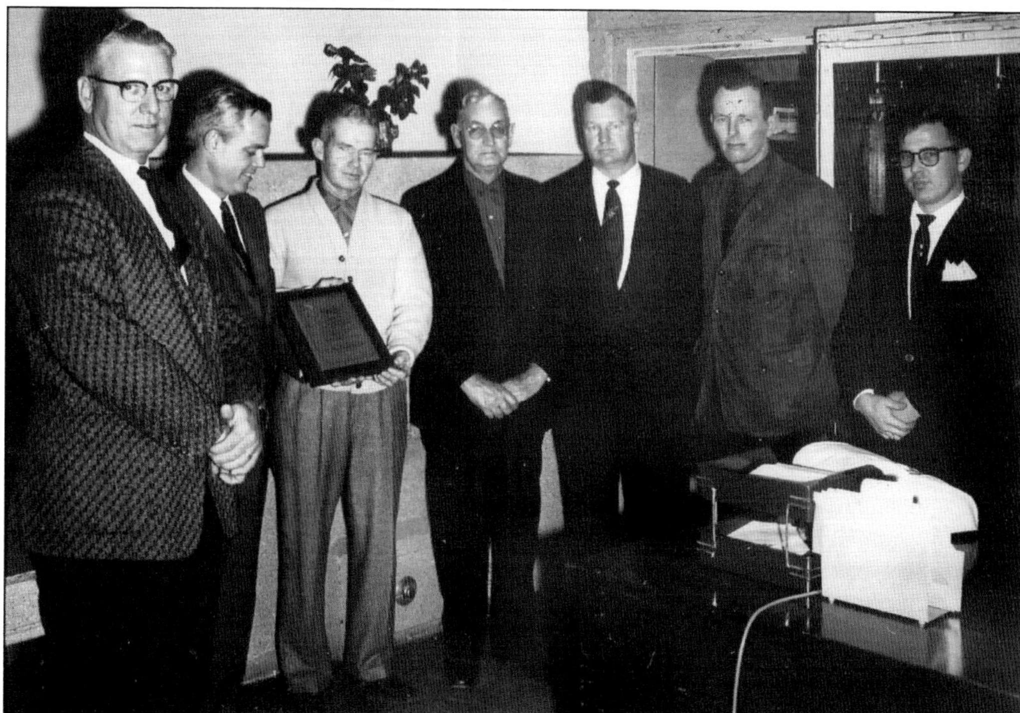

First National Bank Board, Sanger, Texas, 1960. Originally known as Farmers Bank of Sanger, First National Bank was chartered in 1905. Directors in 1960 were, from left to right, president Harold Easley, unidentified director of First National Bank of Fort Worth, Fred Johnson, Bud Pate, vice president Bobby Ready, Tommy Muir, and teller Billy Ezell. The bank was later acquired by GNB Financial in 1990. (Courtesy of Thomas Muir.)

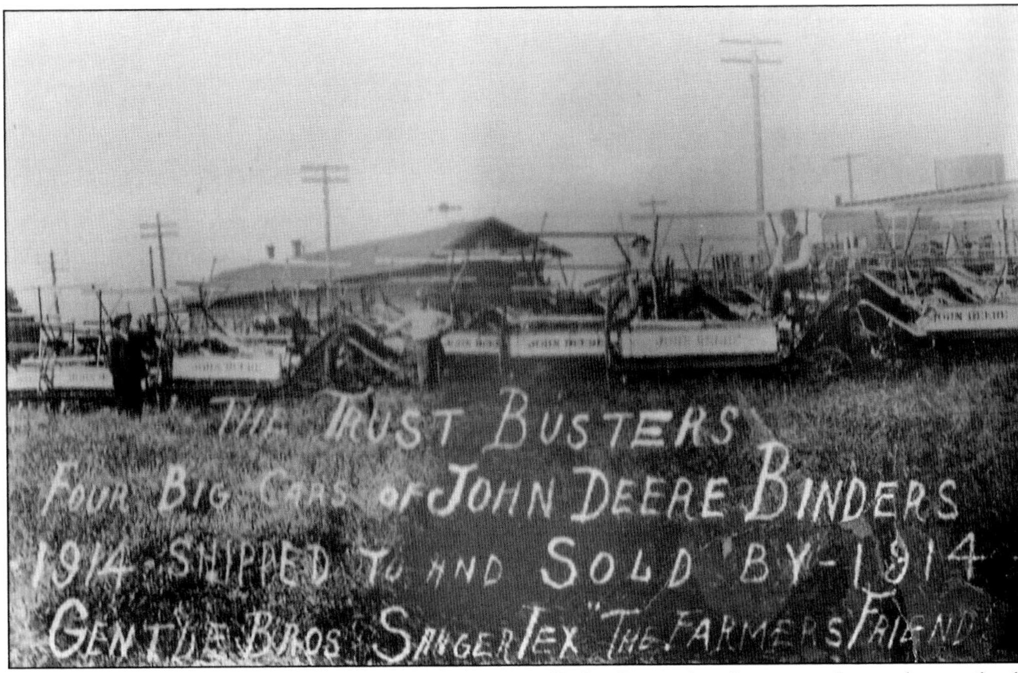

THE TRUST BUSTERS, 1914. Four big railroad cars of John Deere binders were shipped to and sold by Gentle Brothers—the "Farmers' Friend." These machines were unloaded, stored, and assembled in the building on the northeast corner of Fourth and Cherry Streets where Babe's Chicken Dinner House now feeds many happy customers. (Courtesy of Janis (Bailey) Wetherbee.)

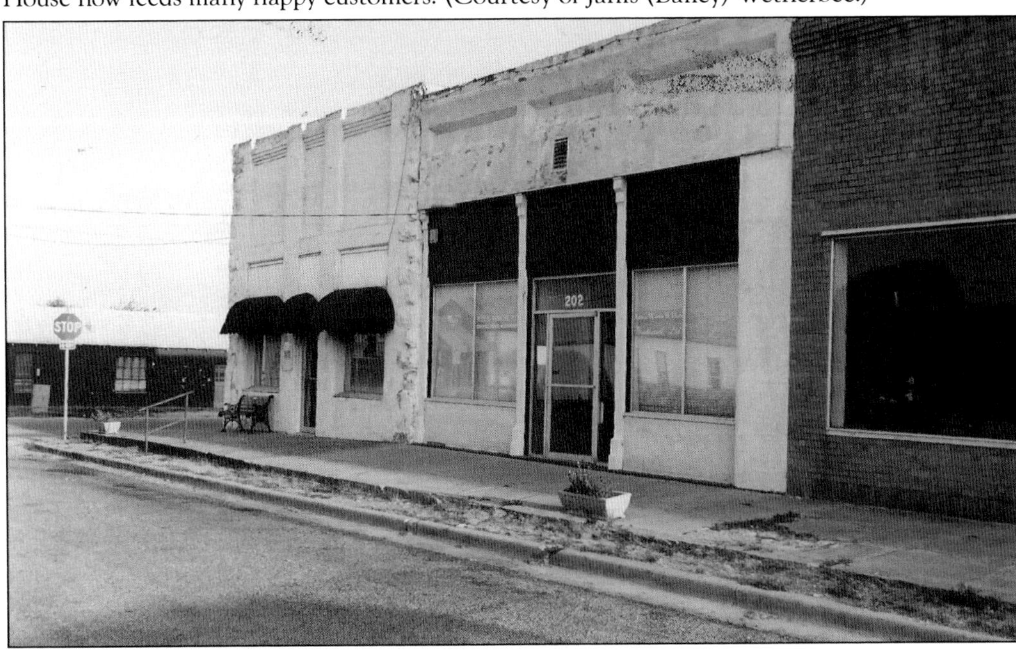

SANGER COURIER OFFICE. Just west of what was known as the Rock Building was the longtime office of the *Sanger Courier*, Sanger's newspaper since 1899. Many remember H.B. and Myrtle Toon, the owners for 43 years. Currently, the *Sanger Courier* is published by Lemons Newspapers Inc. with offices on Interstate 35 at the home that was built by E.L. Berry. (SAHS.)

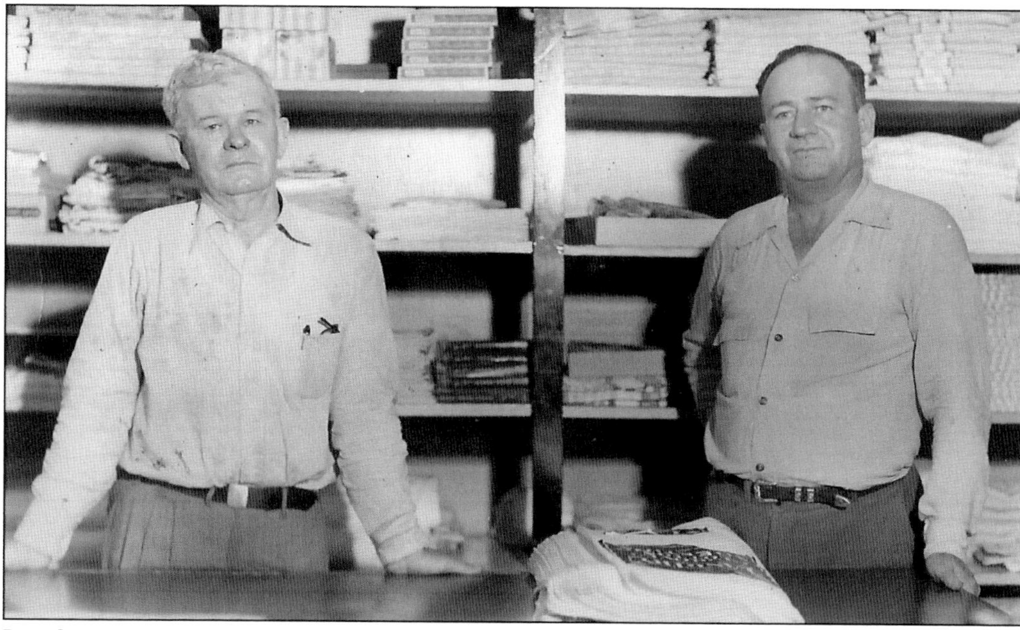

Jess Smith Dry Goods. Jess Smith (right) and his wife, Dottie Mae McBride, owned the dry goods store located at the southwest corner of Bolivar and Fourth Streets in the Wilfong Building, constructed in 1917. Dick Haynie (left) was a longtime employee. Sanger patrons depended upon this store for a variety of goods for their homes, as well as clothing from head to toe. The building still stands today. (Courtesy of Bill Mundy.)

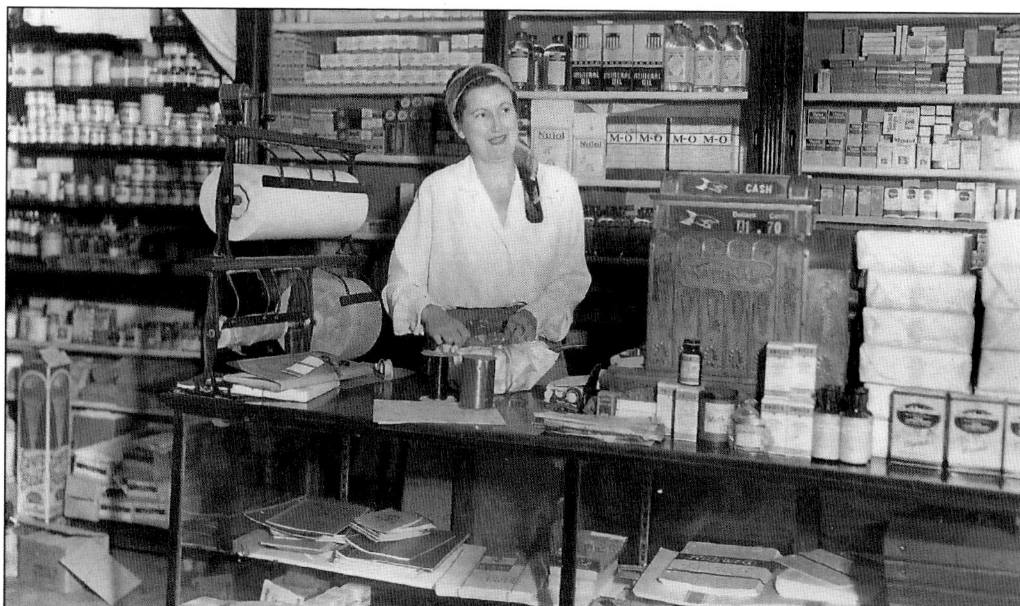

Palace Drugstore. Buck Bailey owned and operated the drugstore on Bolivar Street across from the city park. Bailey's wife is shown behind the counter with pharmacy supplies, a cash register, and a roll of paper to wrap purchased items. Dr. John Sullivan's medical office was located in the rear of the drugstore for many years. (Courtesy of Bill Mundy.)

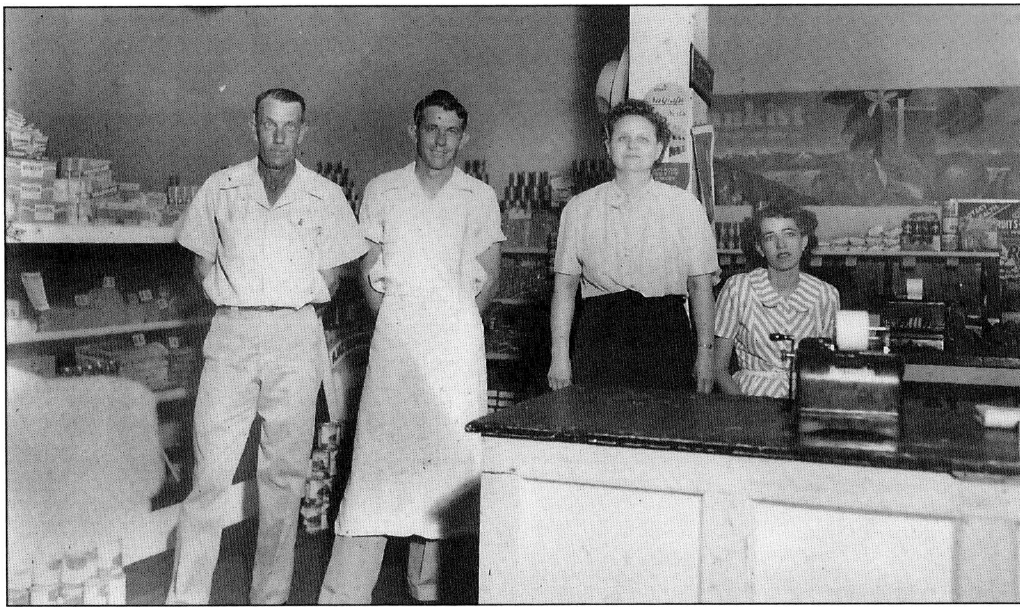

Kings' Grocery. Bob King, Harold B. King, Minnie King, and Billie Dean (Sullivan) King are shown in the grocery store located on Bolivar Street between Third and Fourth Streets. Over the years, Sanger had many grocery stores and each offered home delivery service to their patrons. Customers telephoned the store with their order, and delivery would arrive shortly thereafter, a service later to be forgotten. (Courtesy of Bill Mundy.)

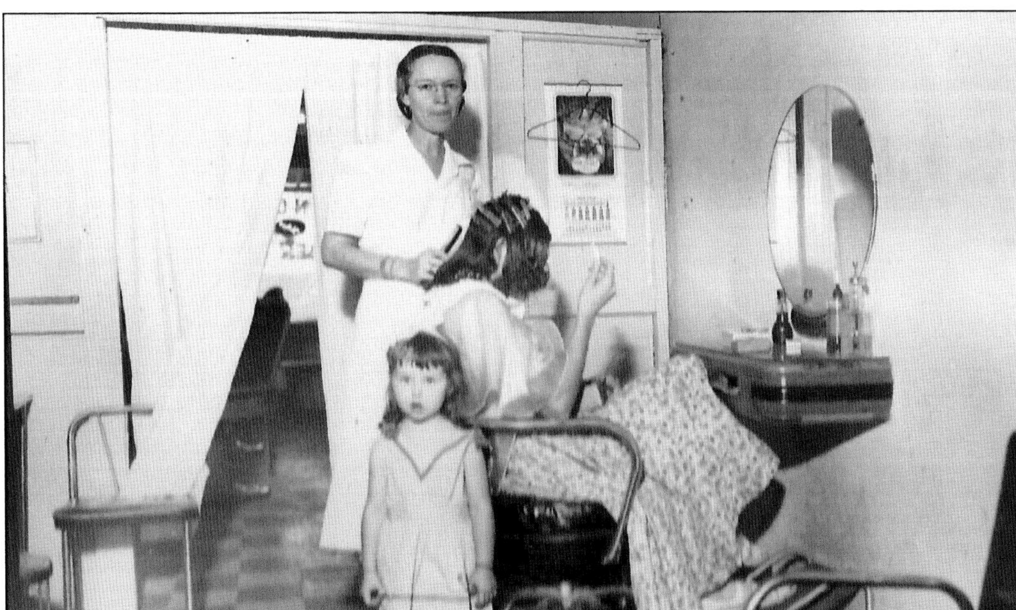

Cherry's Beauty Shop. Alma Cherry operated her beauty shop for the women of Sanger for many years. She had a one-chair operation in the rear of Windle's Barbershop located on Fifth Street. Theda, Alma's sister, is shown with her young daughter, Cherry Jones, having her hair attended to. (Courtesy of Bill Mundy.)

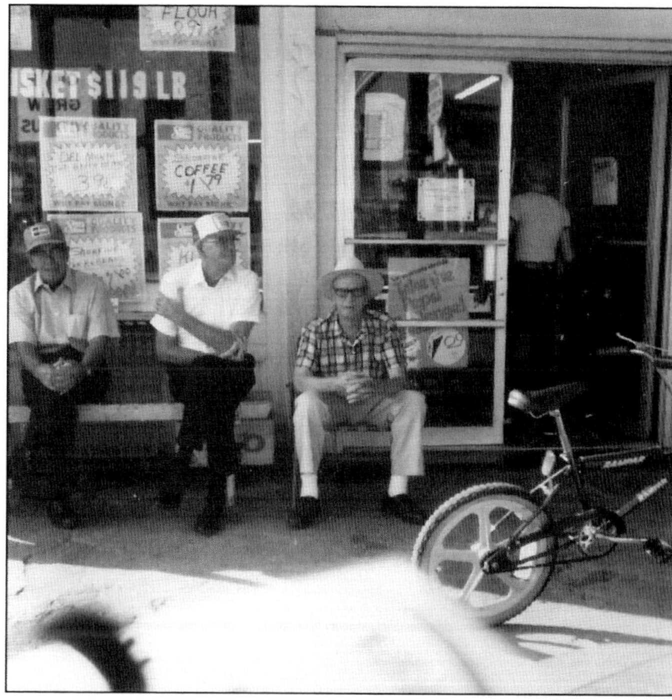

Sit and Spit Bench. From left to right, Will Shafer, Ed Nance, and Art Seely occupy one of several benches in the business area of downtown Sanger on what was known as the "Sit and Spit Bench," or the "Spit and Whittle Bench." Men of the community would gather here to discuss everyday life, problems, and mysteries of the universe. (Courtesy of Helen (Seely) Bounds.)

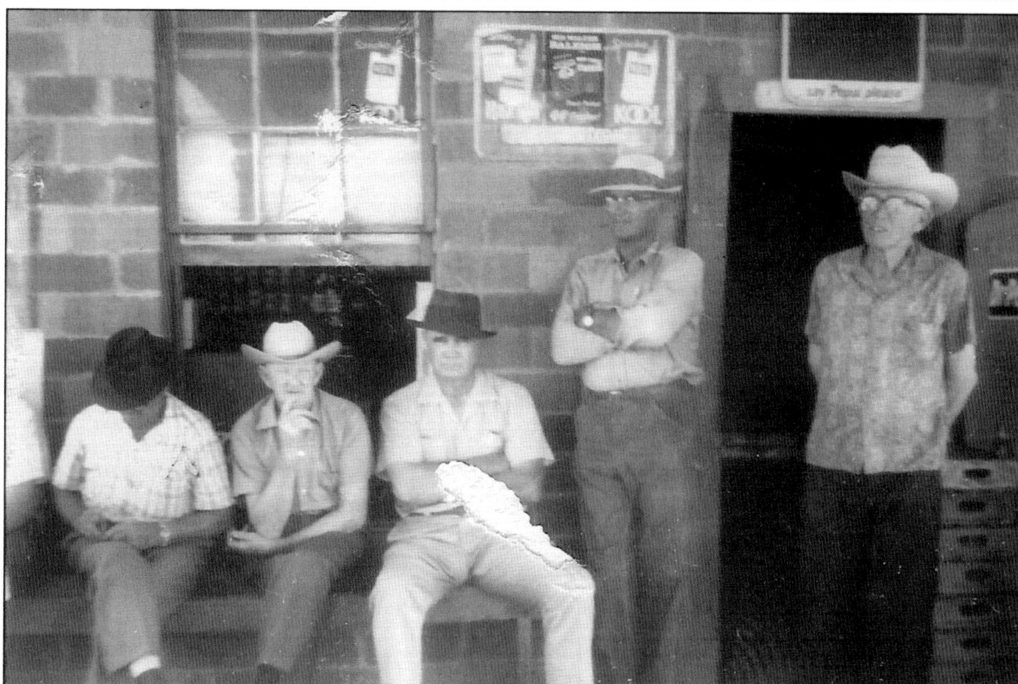

Bolivar Spit and Whittle Bench. Just as Sanger stores furnished benches for local men to relax on, there was also one at the Bolivar Oil Company, five miles west of Sanger, on the northeast corner of Farm-to-Market Road 455 and Farm-to-Market Road 2450. Those identified here include Bailey Garrison, B.R. Bentley (second and third from left), and Elmer Harvey (far right). (Courtesy of Linda (Harvey) Hewlett.)

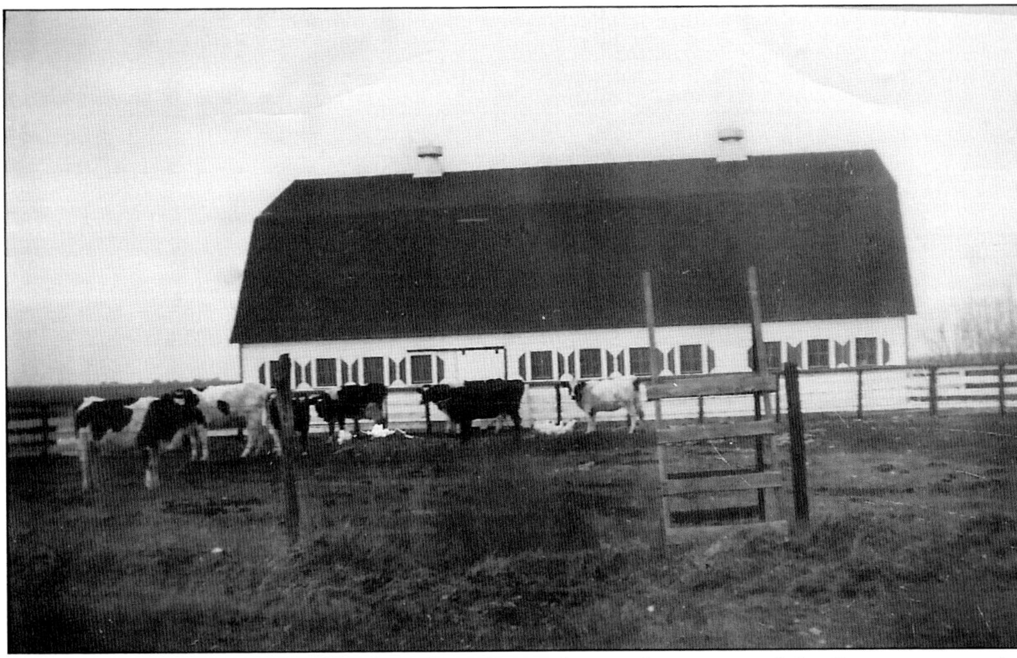

Major Moore's Barn. Agriculture has always been a large industry around the Sanger community. A familiar sight to those traveling west on Farm-to-Market Road 455 was this imposing structure on the north side of the road just after leaving Sanger. Moore was a farmer and cattleman. His wife, Jewell, was a member of the Bentley family from Bolivar. (Courtesy of Linda (Harvey) Hewlett.)

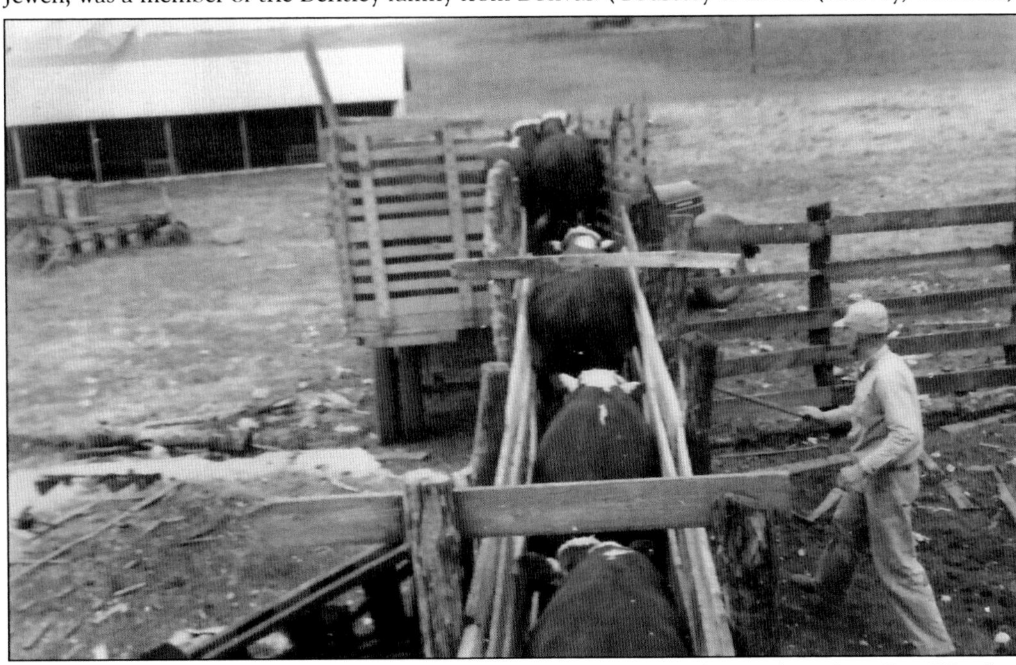

Getting Ready for Market. Farmers often took their cattle to the stockyards in Fort Worth to be sold. Many farms had loading chutes into which the animals could be herded single file into a trailer or truck for transporting to the cattle pens there. This scene is on the Glenn Waide farm northwest of Bolivar. (Courtesy of Judy (Knowles) Selph.)

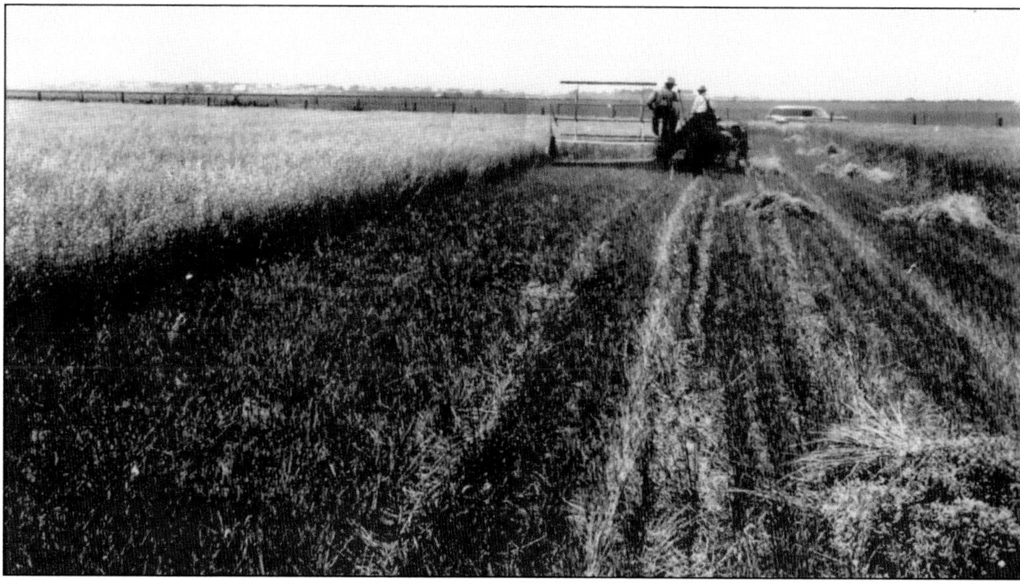

Binding the Grain. Binders pulled by teams or tractors were used to cut the grain and wrap portions of it with binder twine into bundles, as seen on the far right of this picture. This scene is on the Aaron Yeatts farm, north of Sanger. In later years, combines would take the place of binders and threshers. (Courtesy of Yvonne (Yeatts) Cain.)

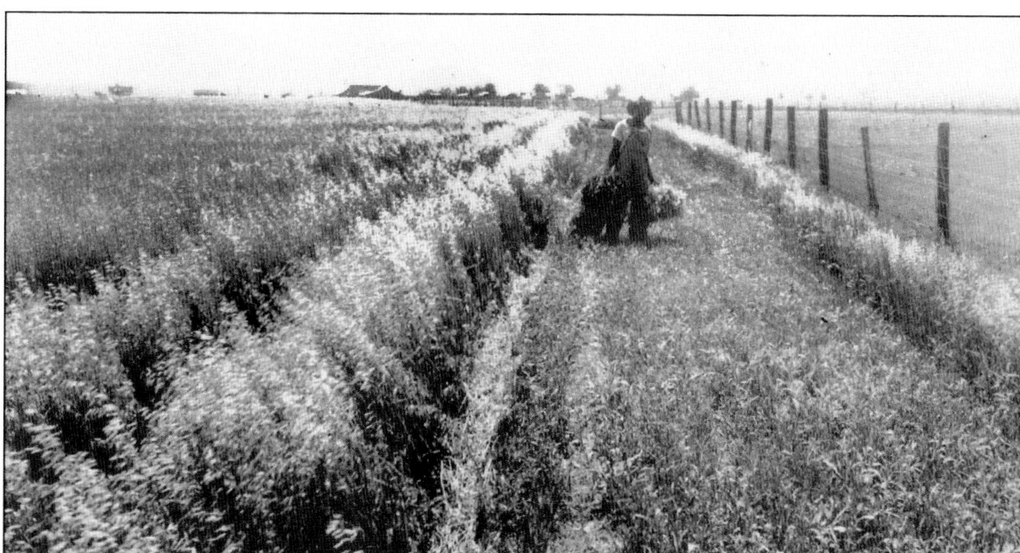

Shocking the Grain. Farm workers picked up the individual bundles and stacked them into shocks that looked like teepees in the field. There, they were picked up on wagons to be taken to the threshing machine for separating the grain head from the stalks. This work was usually dusty and itchy as the chaff went down workers' collars. (Courtesy of Yvonne (Yeatts) Cain.)

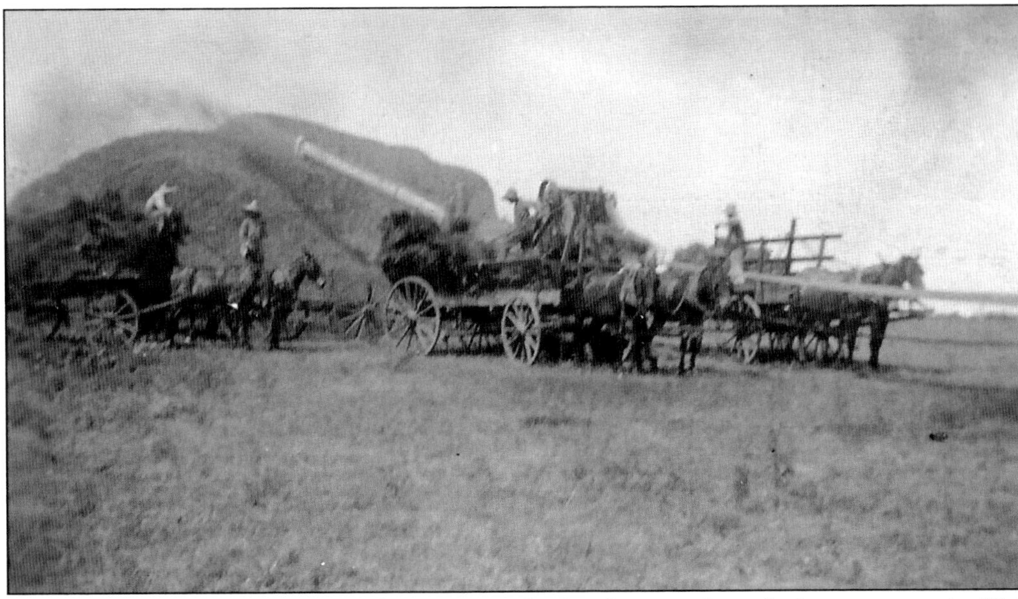

THRESHING THE GRAIN. John W. Schertz operated a threshing machine for harvesting grain. This picture shows horse-drawn wagons that were used to gather the shocks of grain from the field and deliver them to the thresher. There, men used pitchforks to throw the individual bundles into the machine. Notice the haystack formed in the background as the grain is separated from the straw. (Courtesy of Wanda (Schertz) Hollingsworth.)

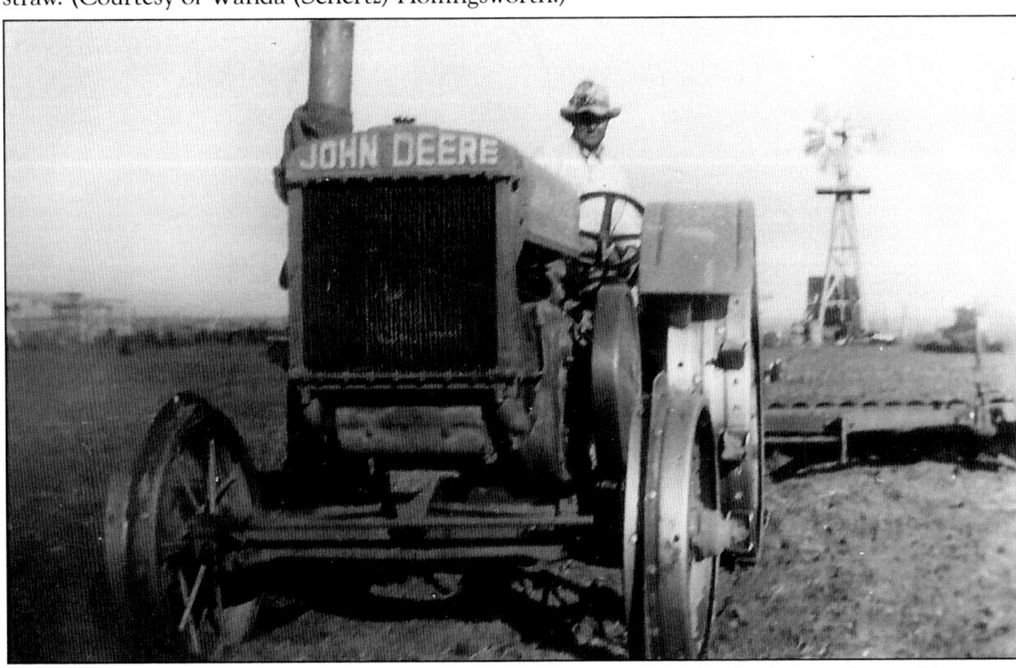

THE FARMER'S HELPER. Tractors were of great help to farmers who had formerly used horses or mules to pull their equipment. John Deere was a popular brand sold locally. Early rear tractor wheels had metal lugs to gain traction prior to rubber tires being used. Signs on roads often warned, "No lugs on highway." Windmills dotted the countryside, as seen in the background. (Courtesy of Linda (Harvey) Hewlett.)

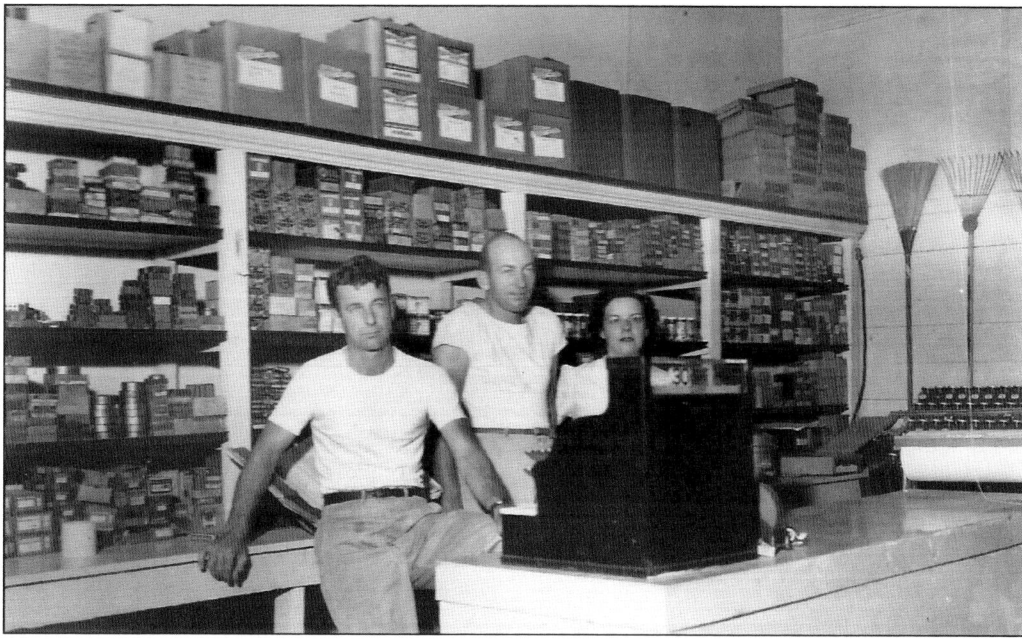

AUTOMOBILE SUPPLY STORE. Sanger's variety of businesses included an automobile parts and supply business for the community. Shown in front of the display of parts and supplies are, from left to right, James Ready, Romie Seely, and Norma (Omstead) Seely. The business was located on Bolivar Street in the downtown area. (Courtesy of Bill Mundy.)

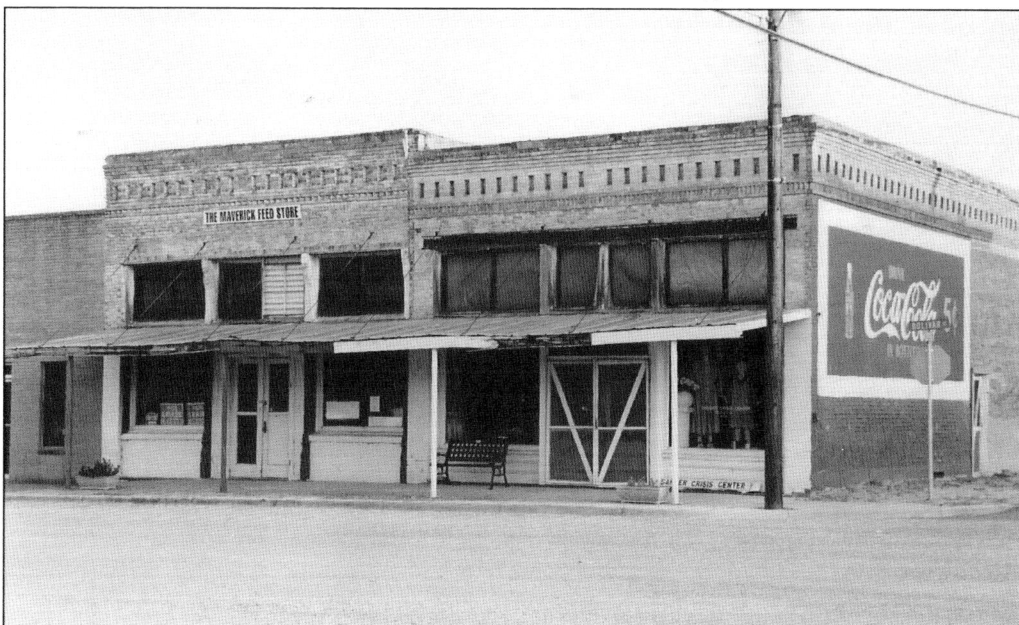

COCA-COLA SIGN. This building on the southeast corner of Bolivar and Third Streets, which once housed Gentle Brothers Hardware, has endured a variety of uses. At one time, it was home to Sanger Bargain Depot and Sanger Crisis Center, a local thrift store, food pantry, and a counseling service for the benefit of needy Sanger residents. The original Coca-Cola sign was repainted a few years ago. (SAHS.)

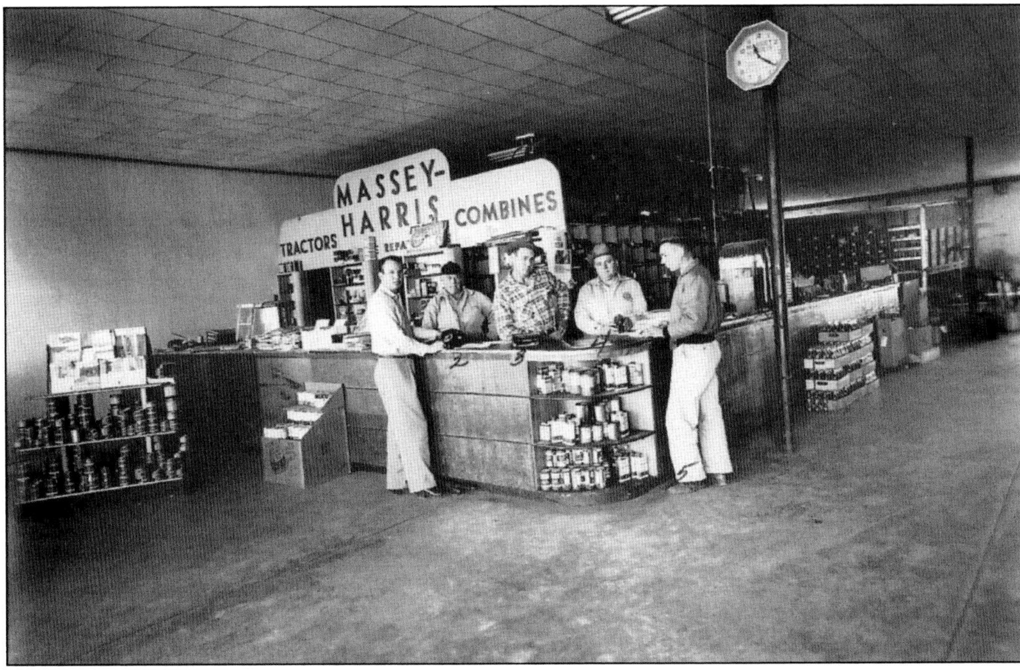

SCHERTZ IMPLEMENT SHOP. An unknown customer visits with John W. Schertz and three of his sons—Walter ("Buck"), Johnnie, and Bennie—in the shop where they sold and serviced Massey Harris tractors and combines. It was located on the south side of Bolivar Street where Hollingsworth Manufacturing now does business. (Courtesy of Frances (Schertz) Gentle and Toni Gentle.)

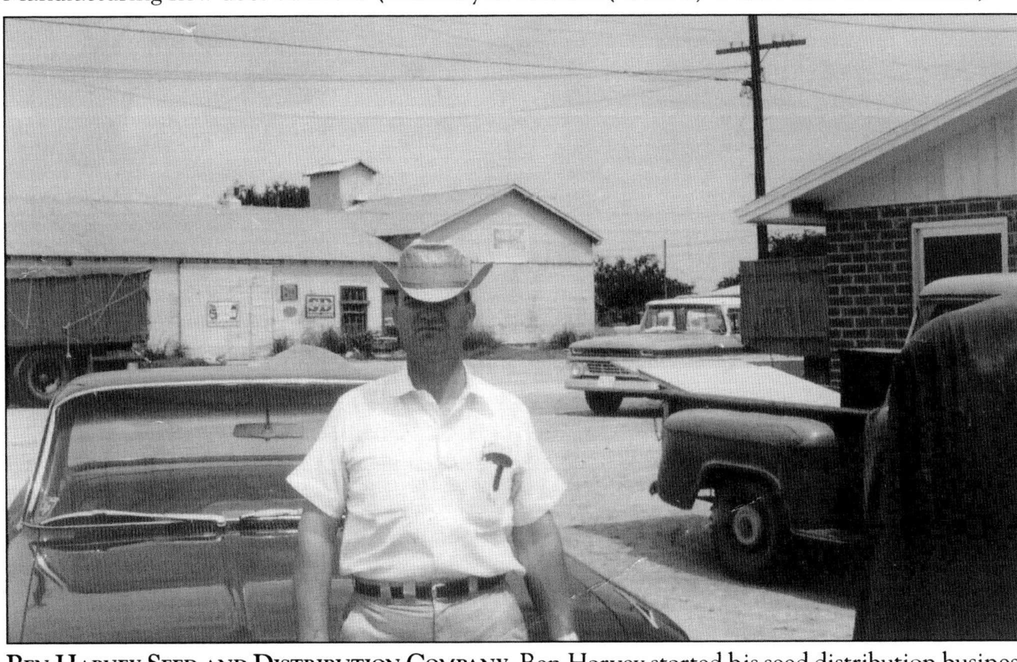

BEN HARVEY SEED AND DISTRIBUTION COMPANY. Ben Harvey started his seed distribution business on a small scale in the early 1950s in the Bolivar community. In 1954, Harvey opened his new operation on Farm-to-Market Road 455 in Sanger with several storage facilities and office buildings. His company was in business until 1967. (Courtesy of Linda (Harvey) Hewlett.)

Six

The Governing

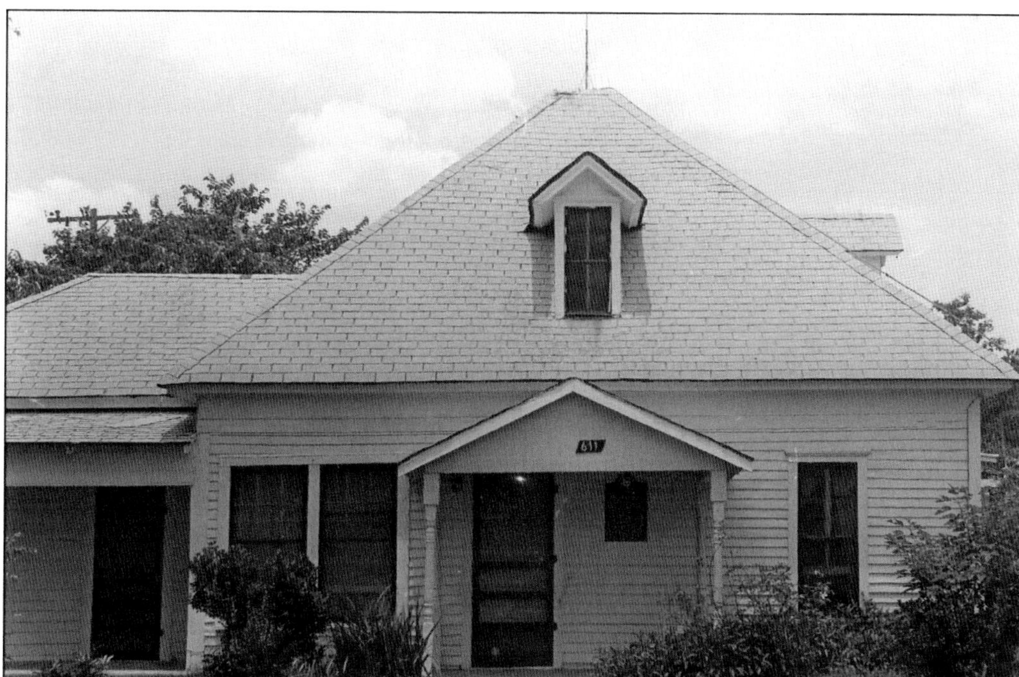

Partlow Home, Texas Historical Marker, 1976. Located at the northeast corner of Plum and Seventh Streets, the William E. Partlow home was one of the earliest built soon after the Civil War. Partlow surrendered with Gen. Robert E. Lee at Appomattox and was elected the first mayor of Sanger in 1892. This historic Sanger home was later demolished. (SAHS.)

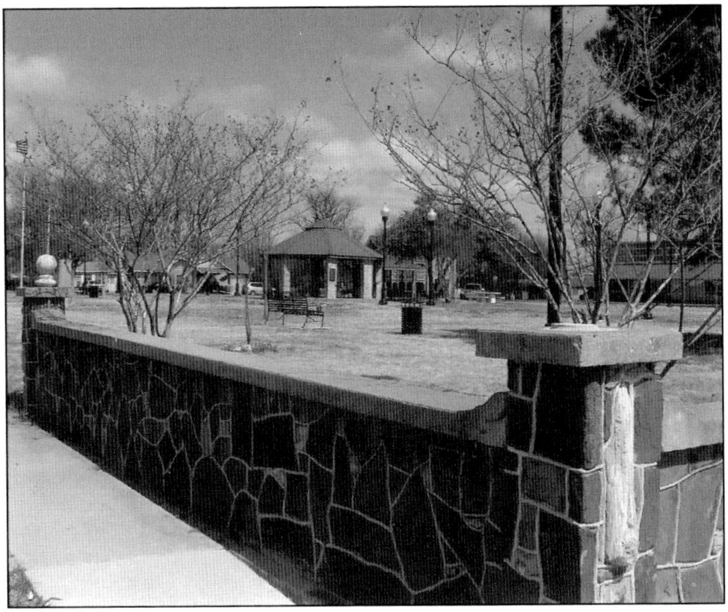

The Town Square. Elizabeth (Bullock) Huling donated land for a city park bounded by Bolivar, Elm, Fourth, and Fifth Streets. A well, dug by citizens, became a meeting place for residents who came for water and to socialize with others. It fell into disrepair until ladies from the Sanger Improvement Club organized to have it cleaned up. A rock fishpond was built in the center, and rock walls defined each corner. (Photograph by Cindy (Mays) Bounds.)

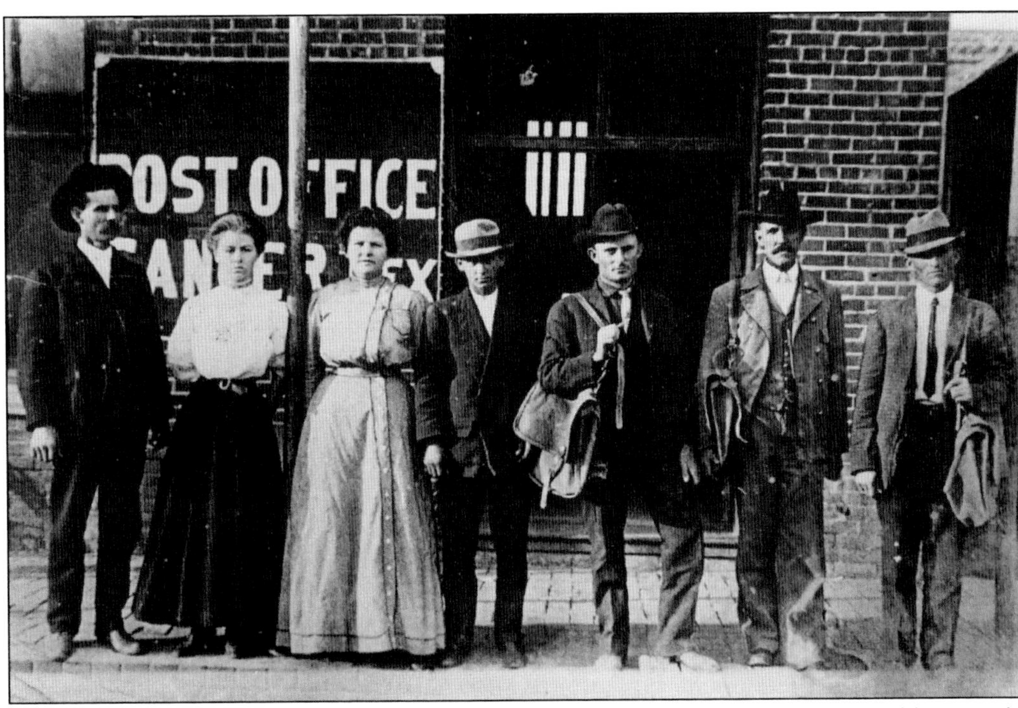

Sanger Post Office. This post office was located at the east end of the Dunn building on the north side of Bolivar Street and later became the location of O.M. Gentle's Hardware. Pictured from left to right are postmaster Howell D. Greene, Effie Greene, Sarah Greene, and Tyler Greene, and rural mail carriers Cleburne Warren, John Vaughan, and Curtis Warren. (SAHS.)

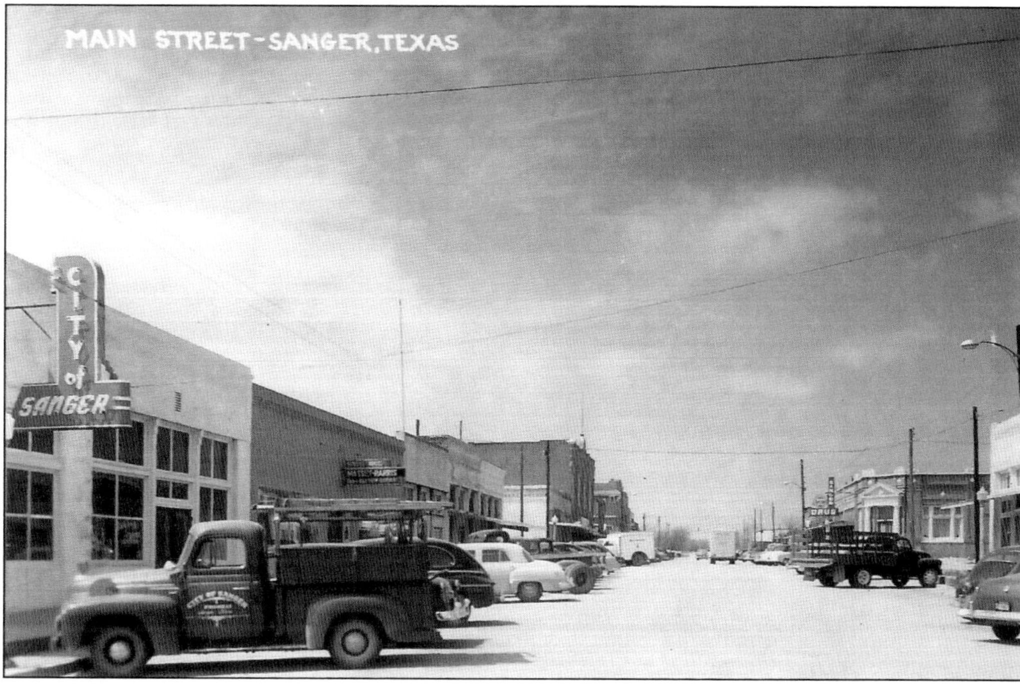

SANGER CITY HALL AND MAIN STREET. Pictured in the 1940s, city hall was located at the southwest corner of Bolivar and Second Streets. A new city hall was dedicated in 1959 across the street on the northwest corner. The city paid cash for its construction, and the post office occupied half of the building. A portion of this building housed the fire department. (Courtesy of Jim Bolz.)

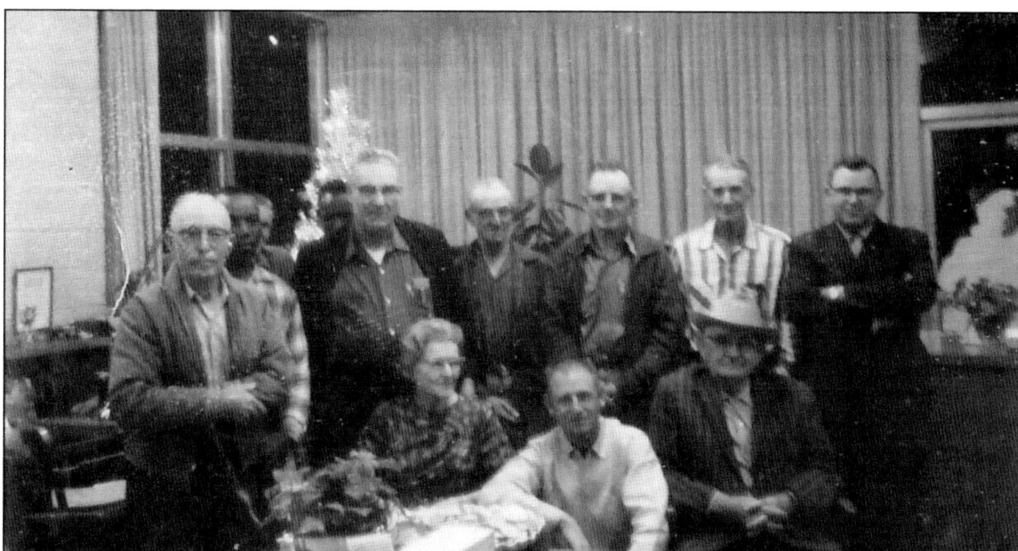

CITY EMPLOYEE HOLIDAY GATHERING, 1963. Pictured here are employees of the City of Sanger in 1963 as they gather for a Christmas party at city hall. They are, from left to right, (seated) Winnie Seal, Fred Denison Jr., and W.D. Lewis; (standing) Carl A. Batis, Charles Haskins, Dwight Howard, Paul Henderson, Bill Carter, Oscar Morris, Fred Denison, Ross Anderson, and Gene Hughes. (SPL.)

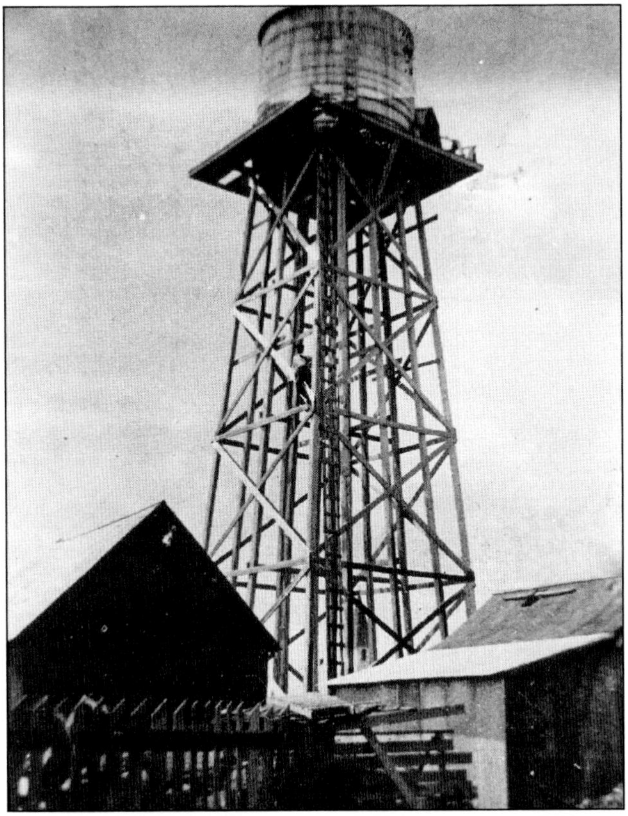

WATER TOWER. Frank Thatcher and Charlie Henderson built the first waterworks operation. The first public water tower, owned by Henderson and Dan Davis, was built in 1906 to serve the citizens of the growing community. The old wooden tower fell in 1910 and was replaced with a 900-gallon wooden and steel tank on Fourth Street. (SAHS.)

MUNICIPAL LIGHT AND POWER. In 1914, Sanger established its first power plant at Locust and Second Streets, but it was later closed due to acetylene issues. The power plant was purchased by the city of Sanger in 1923 from C.P. Dodson at a cost of $14,000. Three diesel motors were added in the late 1930s, and the power facility, now owned by the city, was still furnishing power and water for the municipality into the 1960s. (SAHS.)

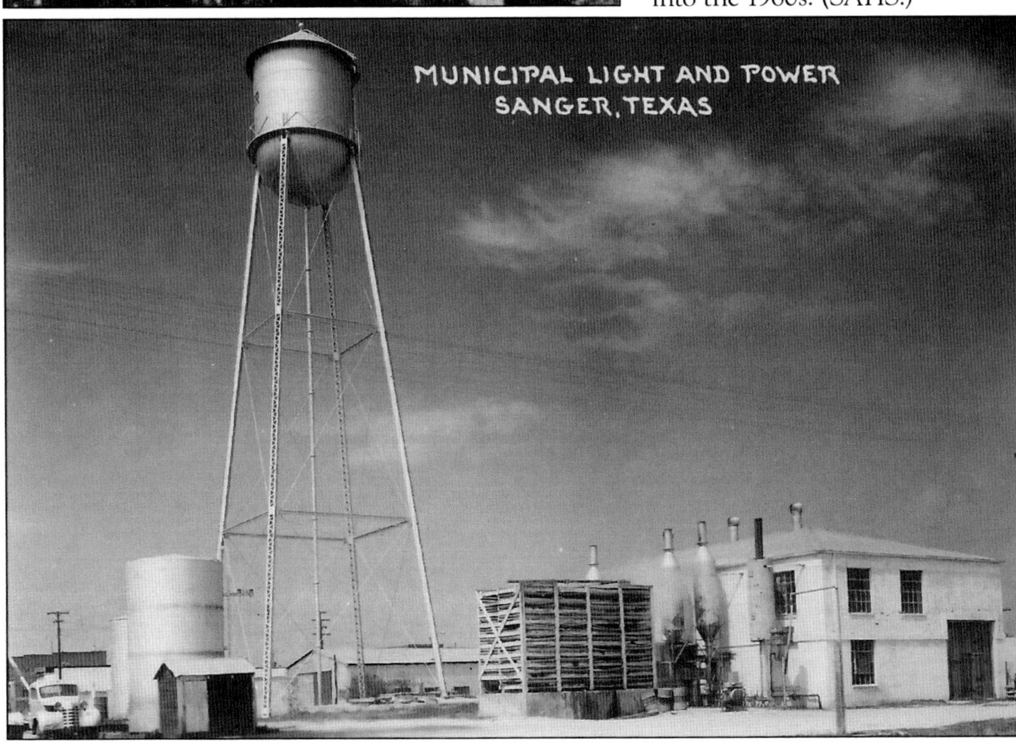

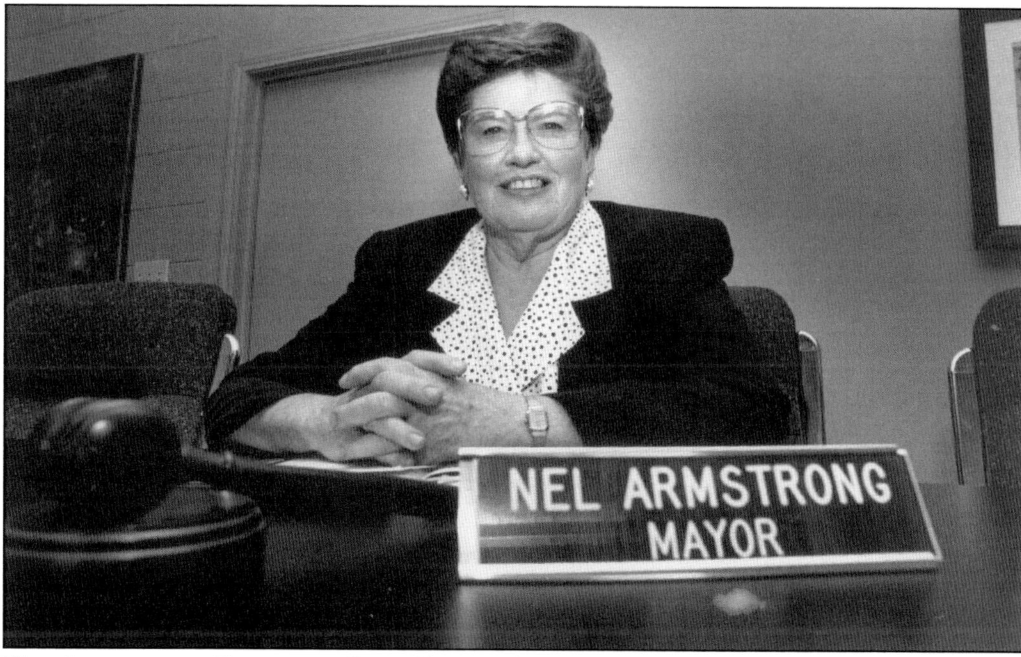

Nel Armstrong, First and Only Female Sanger Mayor. Sanger elected Nel (Haynie) Armstrong as its mayor in 1984. She graduated from Sanger High School before attending Baylor University. Armstrong was the first president of the Sanger Area Historical Society, was instrumental in obtaining a Texas Historical Landmark designation for the Presbyterian Church, and led the efforts to build a new structure for the public library. She is still an active community leader today. (SAHS.)

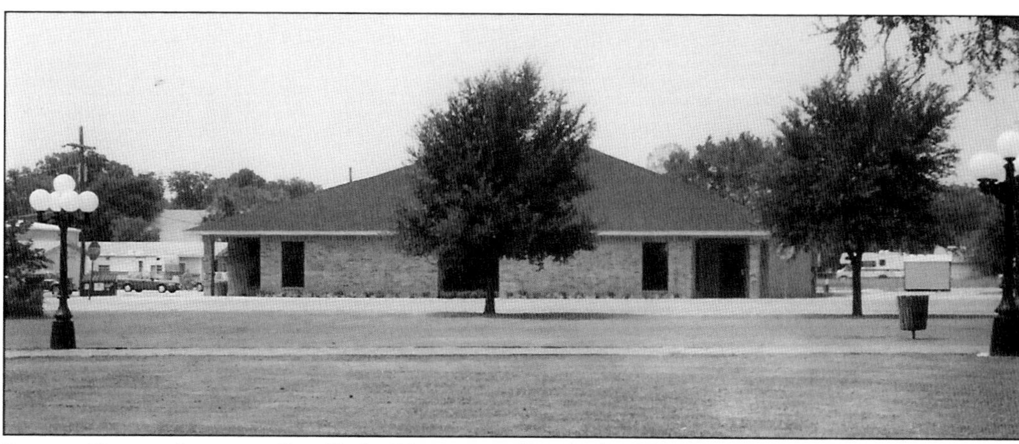

Sanger Public Library. Dr. Clyde Chapman offered a building on East Bolivar Street to house the library, which was founded in 1970. After outgrowing its original location, the library was moved to the historic Presbyterian church on the northwest corner of Seventh and Elm Streets. It remained there until a new building was constructed on the northwest corner of Fifth and Bolivar Streets in 1995. (Courtesy of Nancy (Campbell) Smith.)

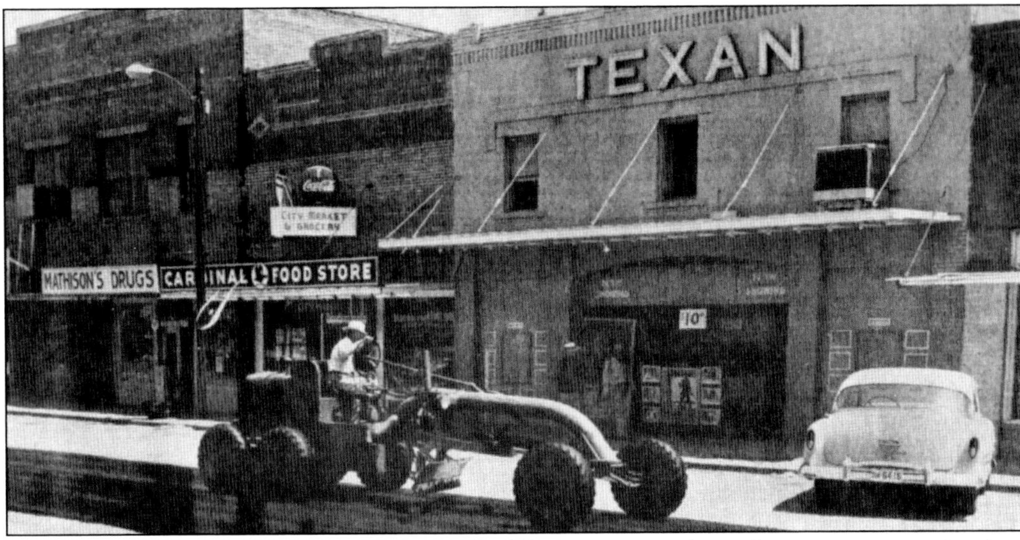

Carl A. Batis, City Road Maintenance. Carl Batis, a city employee for many years, maintained the streets and roads for Sanger. Here Batis operates the road grader, or maintainer, on Bolivar Street across from the park. Nearby is the Texan Theater owned by Gene Hughes and Cardinal Food Store (also known as City Market and Grocery) owned by the Horst Brothers, adjacent to Mathison's Drugstore, a popular establishment in the 1960s. (SAHS.)

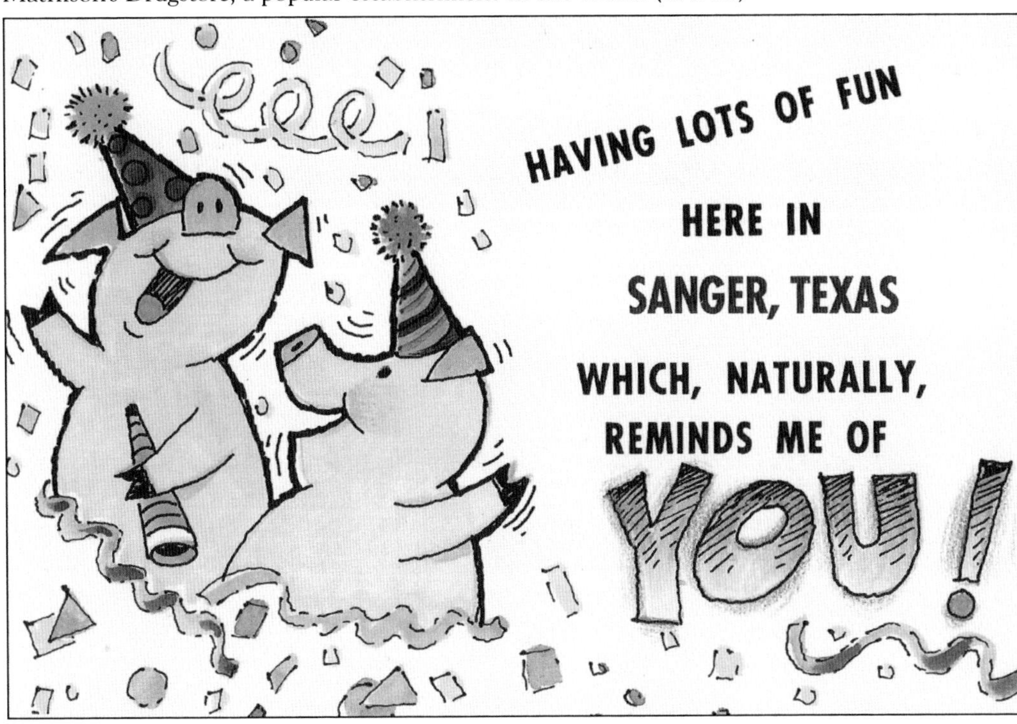

Postcards of Old. Postcards were available to residents and visitors of Sanger to either send to friends or place in their memory books of the beautiful little town. Sanger was known as the "town with the white trees," as all the trees, mostly hackberry trees along Highway 77, were whitewashed from the ground up to the branching of the tree. This feature definitely caught the eye of the traveler. (Courtesy of Helen (Seely) Bounds.)

Seven

The Organizing

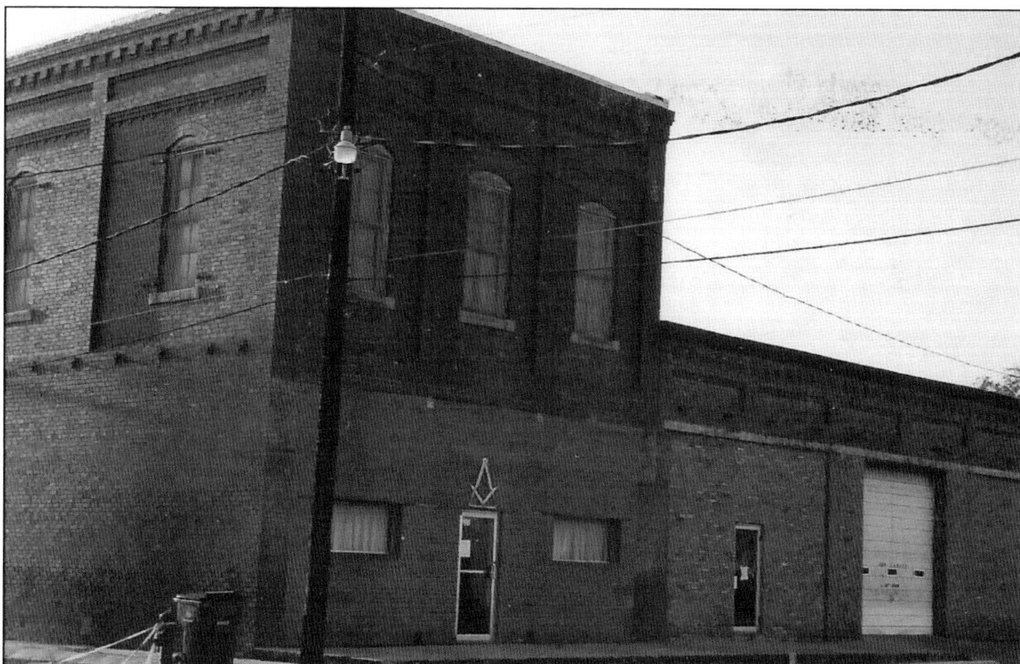

Bolivar Masonic Lodge Building. Lodge 418, chartered in 1875 in Bolivar, relocated to Sanger when Mason J.W. Milligan constructed a second floor to his building in Sanger for use as a Mason meeting hall in 1905. The lodge purchased the building in 1965, and the organization continues to meet in the location on the west side of Third Street between Bolivar and Elm Streets. (SAHS.)

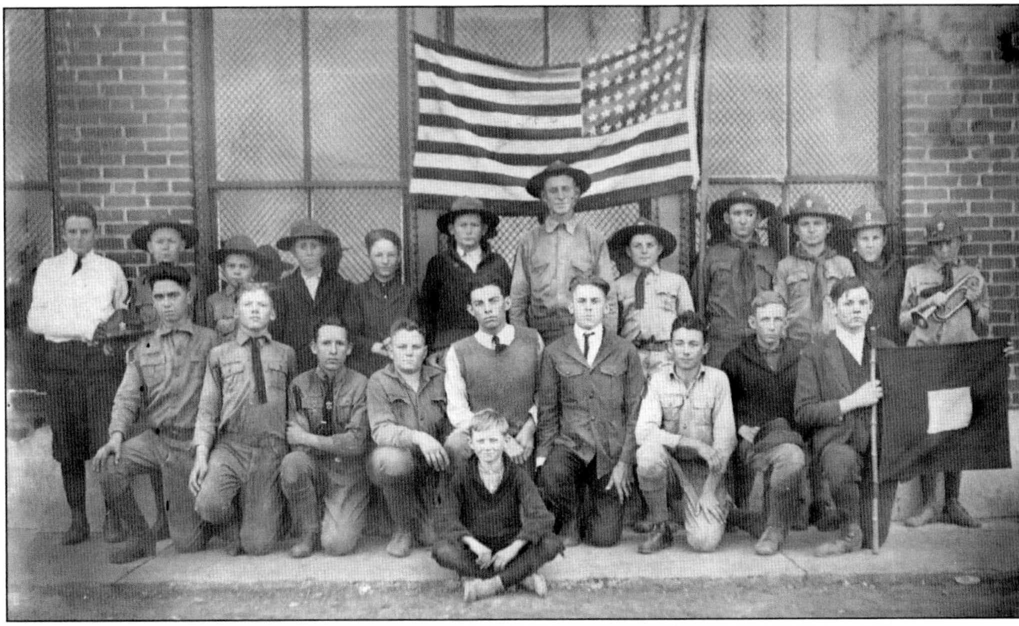

Boy Scouts of America, 1922. Early years provided scout activities for the young men of the community. Many were involved in the Sanger scouting organization in 1922, as seen in the image above. Dressed in their uniforms, the scouts display the American flag, as well as their troop flag. (TWU.)

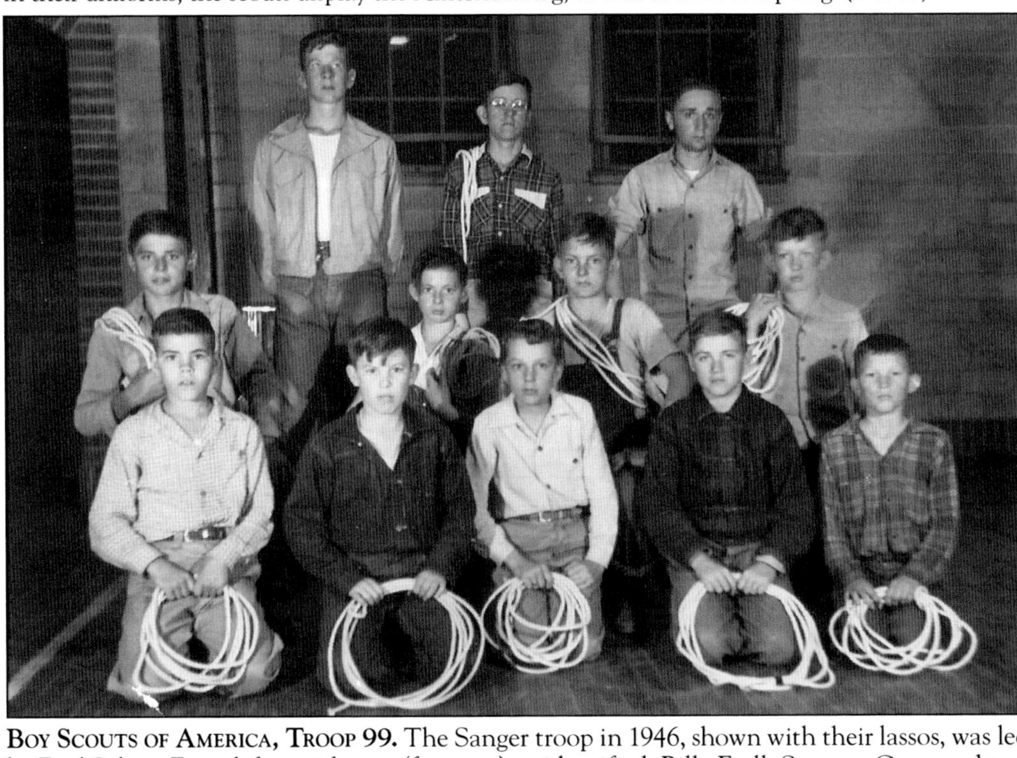

Boy Scouts of America, Troop 99. The Sanger troop in 1946, shown with their lassos, was led by Fred Scheu. From left to right are (first row) unidentified, Billy Ezell, Spencer Gary, and two unidentified; (second row) two unidentified, Paul Pace, and Robert Windle; (third row) Melvin Chapman, Murray Phillips, and Sammy Spratt. (Courtesy of Billy Ezell.)

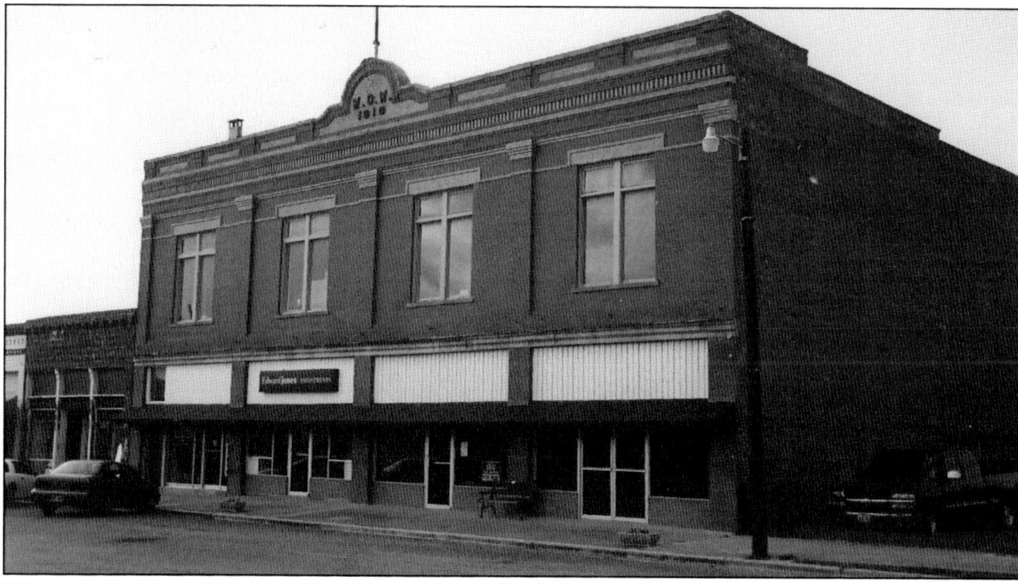

Woodmen of the World. The Opera House, built by the Woodmen of the World in 1910, was later used as a silent movie theater and a wrestling match venue. Unique headstones in the shape of a tree stump or a fallen tree can be found in cemeteries denoting members. The building seen above, located on the south side of Bolivar Street between Third and Fourth Streets, is still intact. (DCM.)

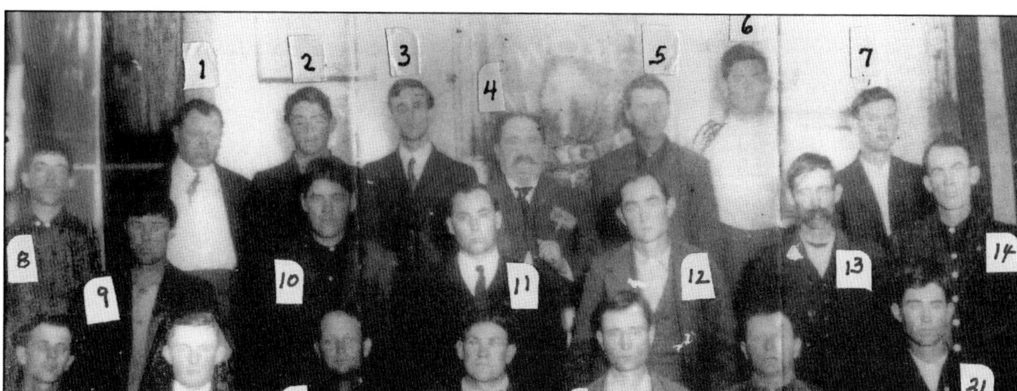

The Praetorians. The Praetorian group, Council 290, held their meeting with 19 members at the Woodmen of the World Opera House in May 1908. Deputy Lowe of Dallas conducted the meeting and was pleased with the turnout. Further information about this council and if there is any relation to the Woodmen of the World has been undetermined. (SAHS.)

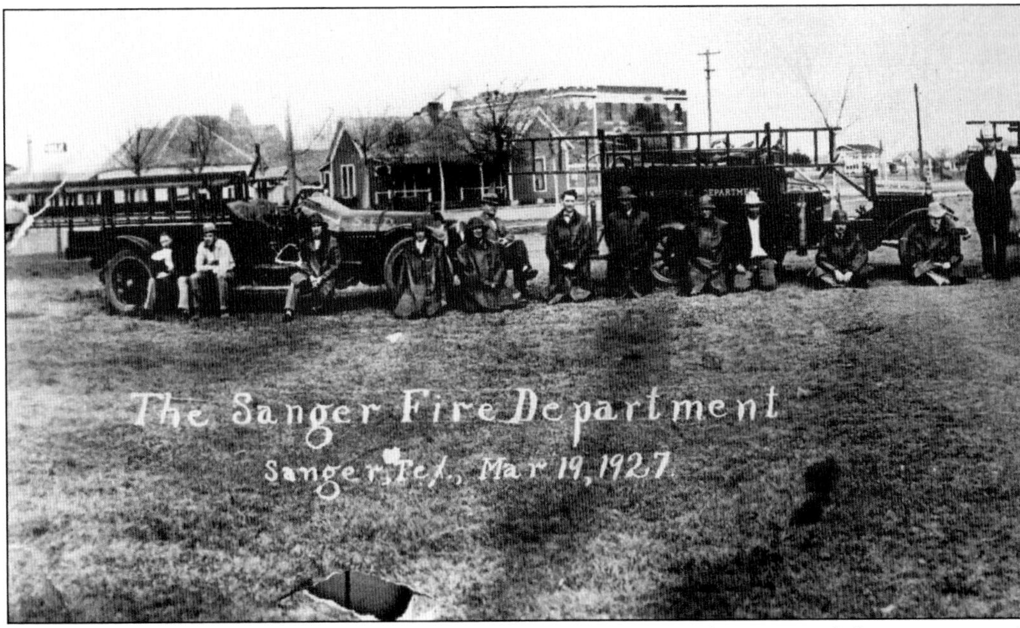

VOLUNTEER FIRE DEPARTMENT. Men of the Sanger community have served the citizens with many years of firefighting for the town. An early photograph of the department in 1927 (above) includes, from left to right, volunteers George A. Sullivan, Charles Milligan, W.D. Lewis, Glen Rieger, A.H. Haynie, A.L. Gentle, W.B. Chambers, John McClendon, R.E. Gentle, H.W. Ezell, John Hughes, Otis Jones, and Chief Bud Gentle. In the photograph below are, from left to right, Otis Jones, Chief Bud Gentle, A.G. Nance, Joe Hughes, Alton Gentle, S.C. Moore, L.B. Daniels, D.C. Gheen, G.W. Sullivan, Troy Stinson, Elmer Hulse, Jack McReynolds and John Richardson. Members not shown are Butler Boydstun, Chester Ausband, Jeff Cornett, and Jim Kline. The small girl on the fire truck is unidentified. (SPL.)

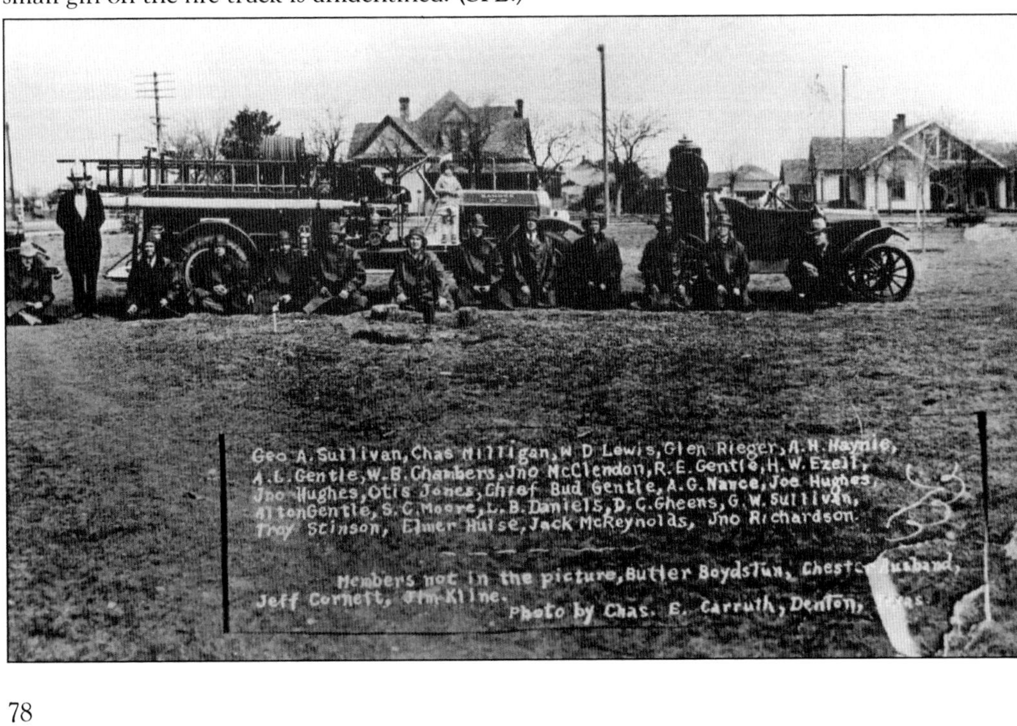

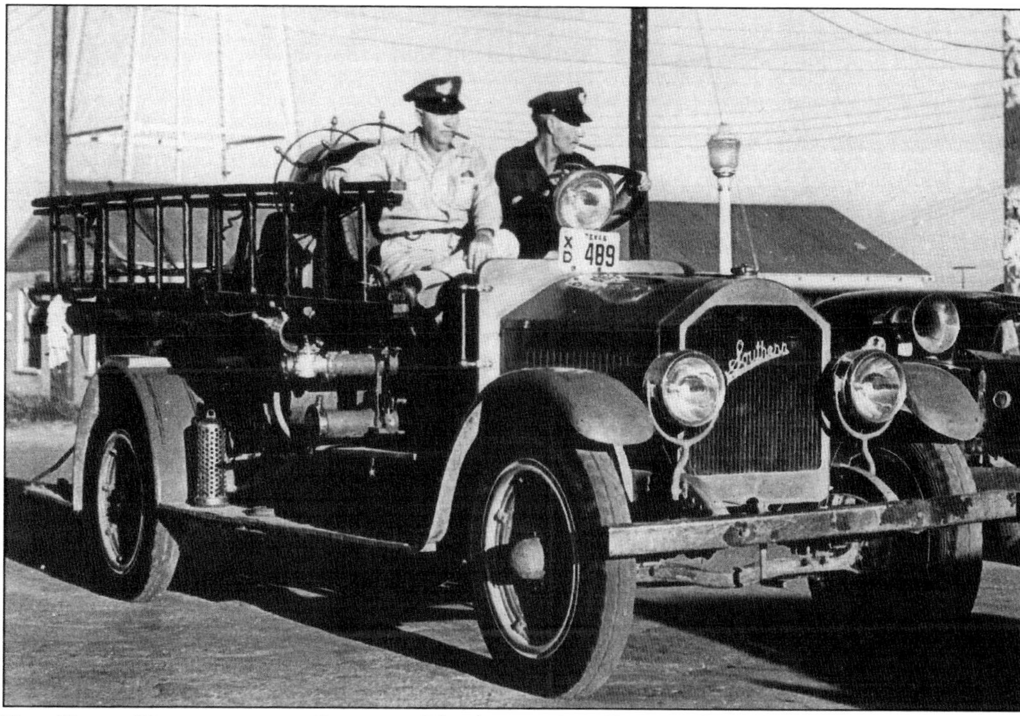

Fire Truck Departing the Station. The fire truck pulls away from the station at Second and Bolivar Streets as ? Parker (left) and Bob King smoke big stogies. Note the framework of the base of the water tower to the left and the street lamp to the right. The building behind the truck is still located at the site near the fire station to the right. (Courtesy of Oscar Shelton.)

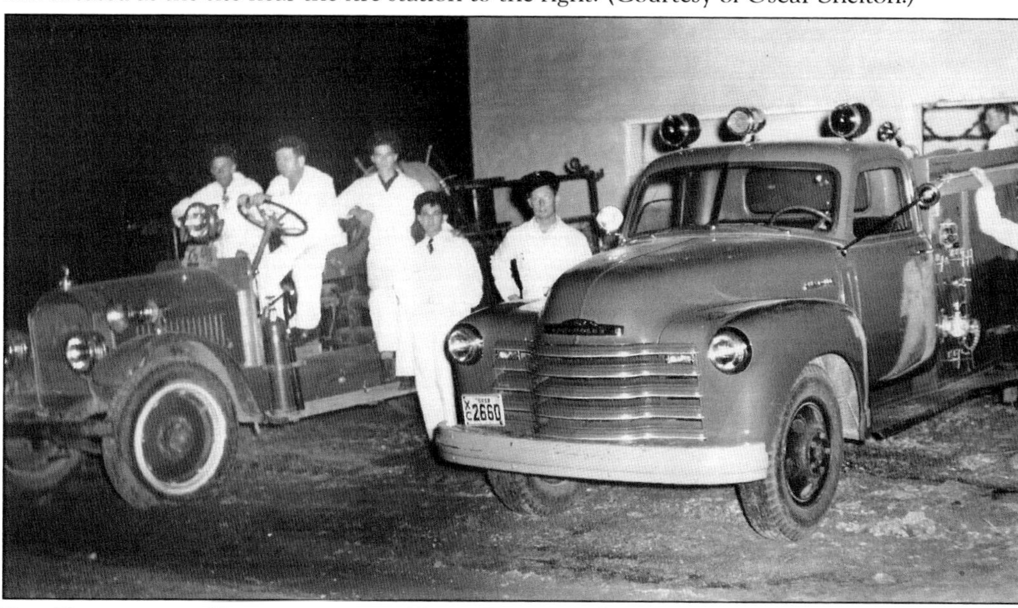

Fire Department Volunteers and Their Trucks. The men seen here in their white, zipped uniforms kept the fire trucks in top condition. During the 1950s, the fire station was located at the corner of Second and Bolivar Streets on the southwest corner. A pool hall and domino tables completed the station as a gathering place for the men. (Courtesy of Jerriann (Cooper) Shepard.)

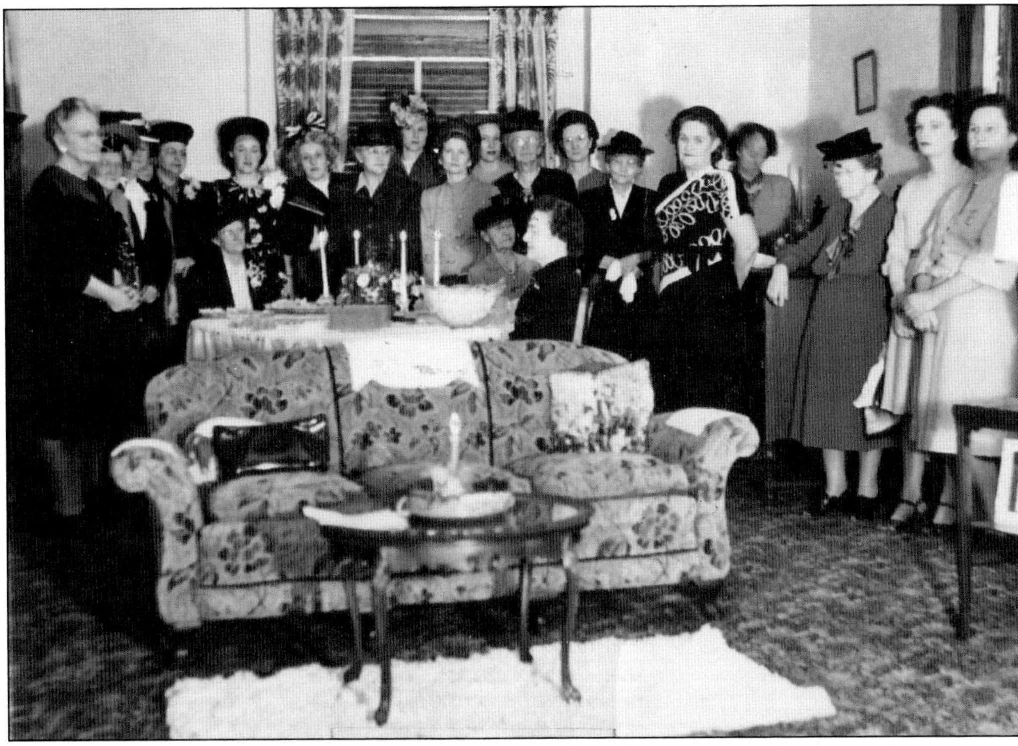

WEDNESDAY STUDY CLUB. The Civic Improvement Club, also known as the Sanger Improvement Club, organized in 1916, preceded the formation of the Wednesday Study Club for the ladies of Sanger in 1929. The club was organized for study and cultural growth with a prescribed course of study each year. Alma (Lain) Chambers wrote about the club's history from 1916 until 1948. Above, a typical occasion in the 1950s shows ladies dressed up for the meeting in the home of one of the members. Below, a float in the 1974 local parade was graced by several of the well-dressed members. As a part of the Texas Federation of Women's Clubs, it continues today. (Above, courtesy of Jerriann (Cooper) Shepard; below, TWU.)

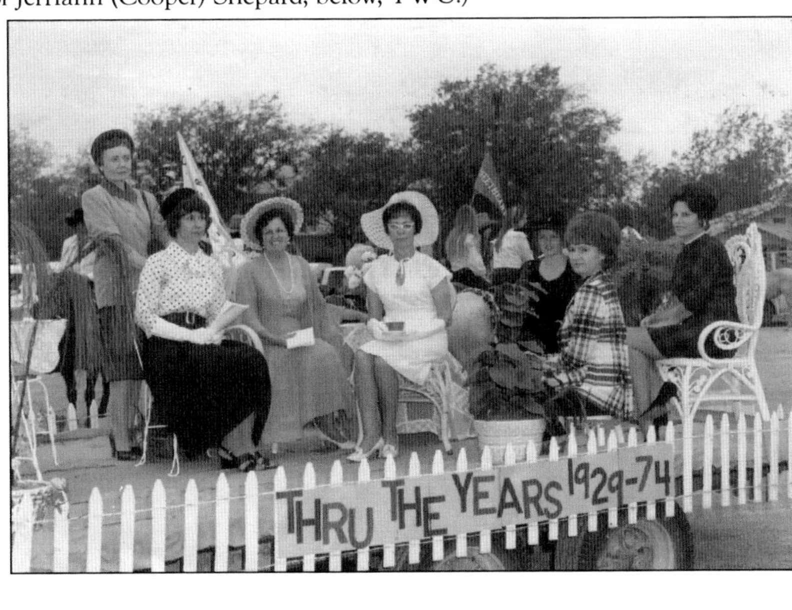

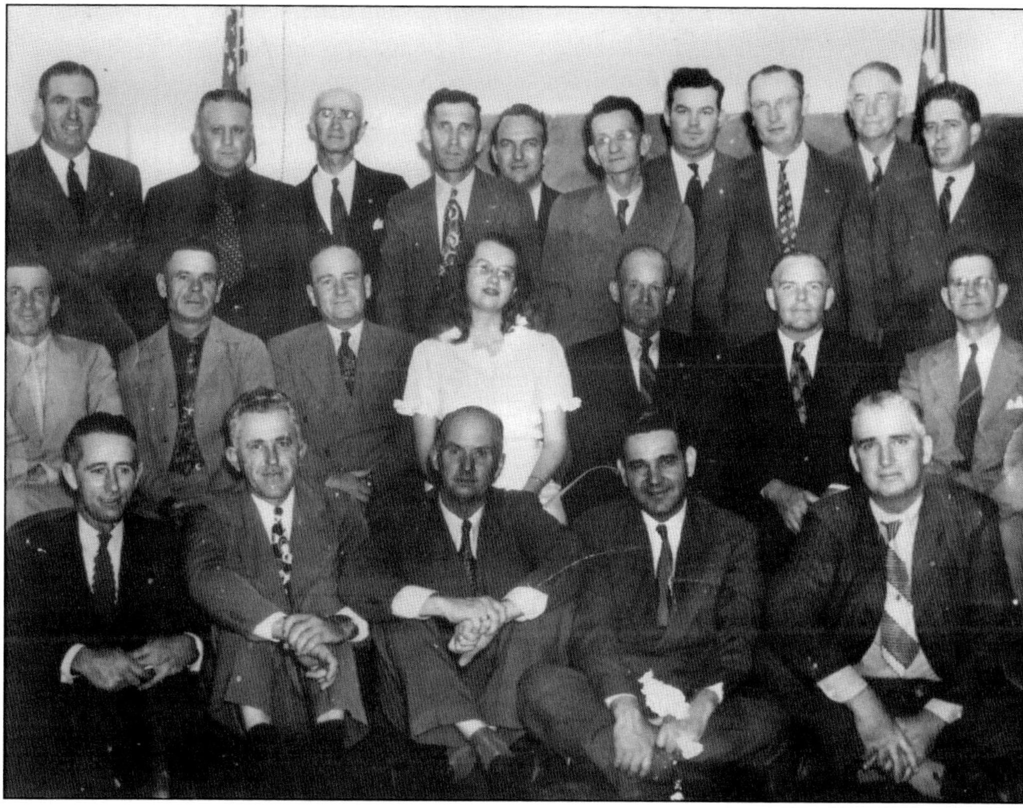

Lions Clubs International. Established as an international organization in the late 1900s, the Sanger Lions have long been dedicated to the mission of betterment of the community. Henry Cooper, E.M. Acker, Dr. Clyde Chapman, and Jess Smith were among the members seen above with their club sweetheart, Yvonne Harris. (Courtesy of Jerriann (Cooper) Shepard.)

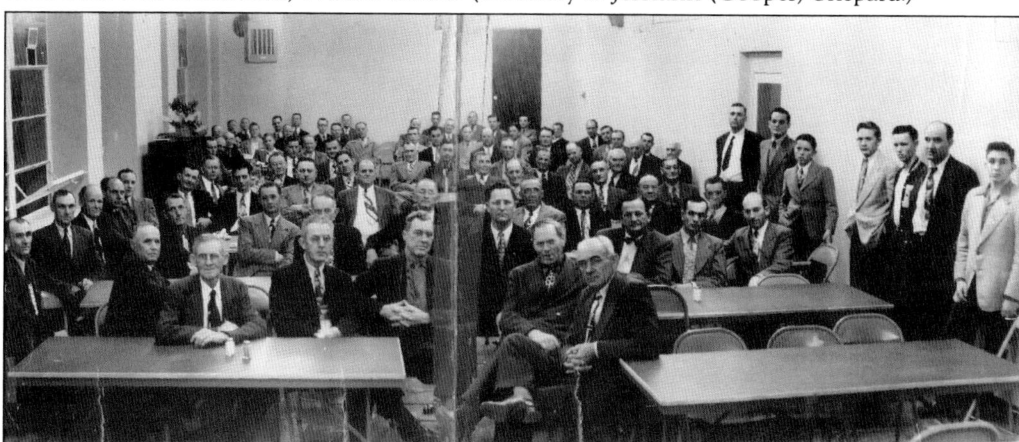

Community Leaders Gather. This gathering of community men and boys, believed to have been conducted in the new Sanger school building cafeteria between 1948 and 1950, included Willard Bounds, Art Seely, Virgil Ward, Bud Pate, Jess Smith, Bud Gentle, Jack McReynolds, Dr. J.S. Stubbs, Arthur "Romie" Seely, Bunk Lewis, Bob King, Ray McClendon, H.W. Ezell, Billy Ezell, Charlie Green, Fred Johnson, Bryan Clement, U.A. Burkholder, and Tom Muir. The reason for the meeting is unknown. (SAHS.)

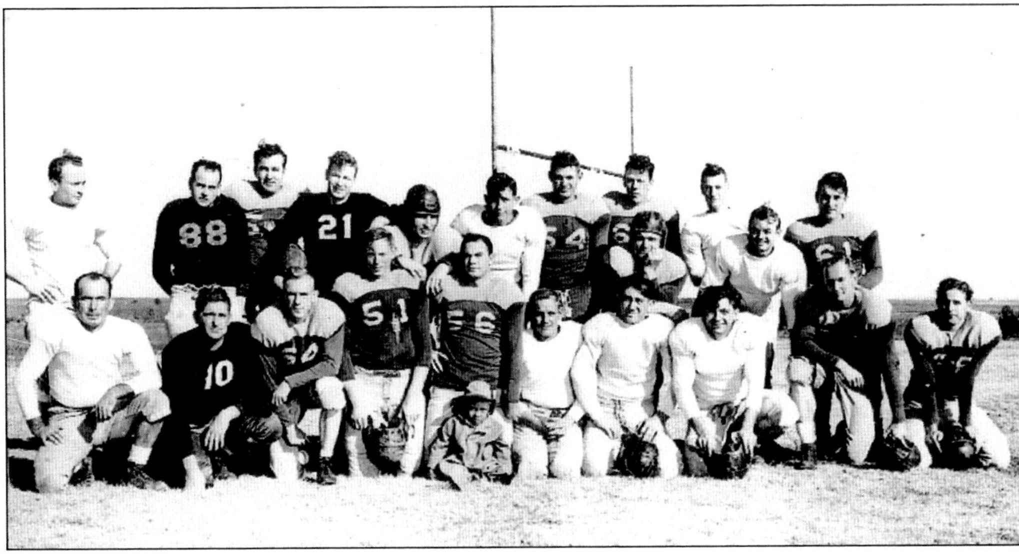

Sanger Outlaws, 1947. Many of the young men of Sanger returning from World War II began a football team, playing in uniforms loaned to them by the Sanger High School. They competed against Era, the only other team in the area that was not high school related. Kenneth Frady, number 56, was one of many who returned from the war and participated in Outlaws football games. (Courtesy of Kenneth Frady.)

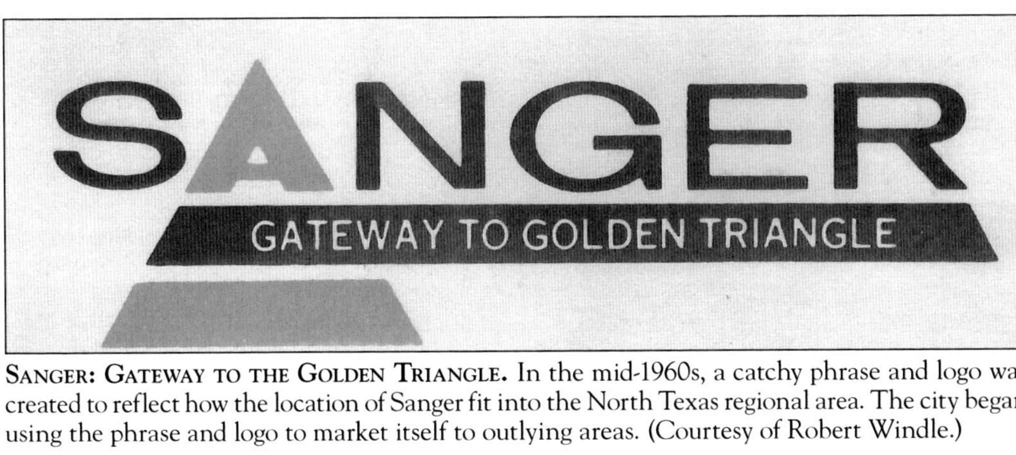

Sanger: Gateway to the Golden Triangle. In the mid-1960s, a catchy phrase and logo was created to reflect how the location of Sanger fit into the North Texas regional area. The city began using the phrase and logo to market itself to outlying areas. (Courtesy of Robert Windle.)

Eight

The Interesting

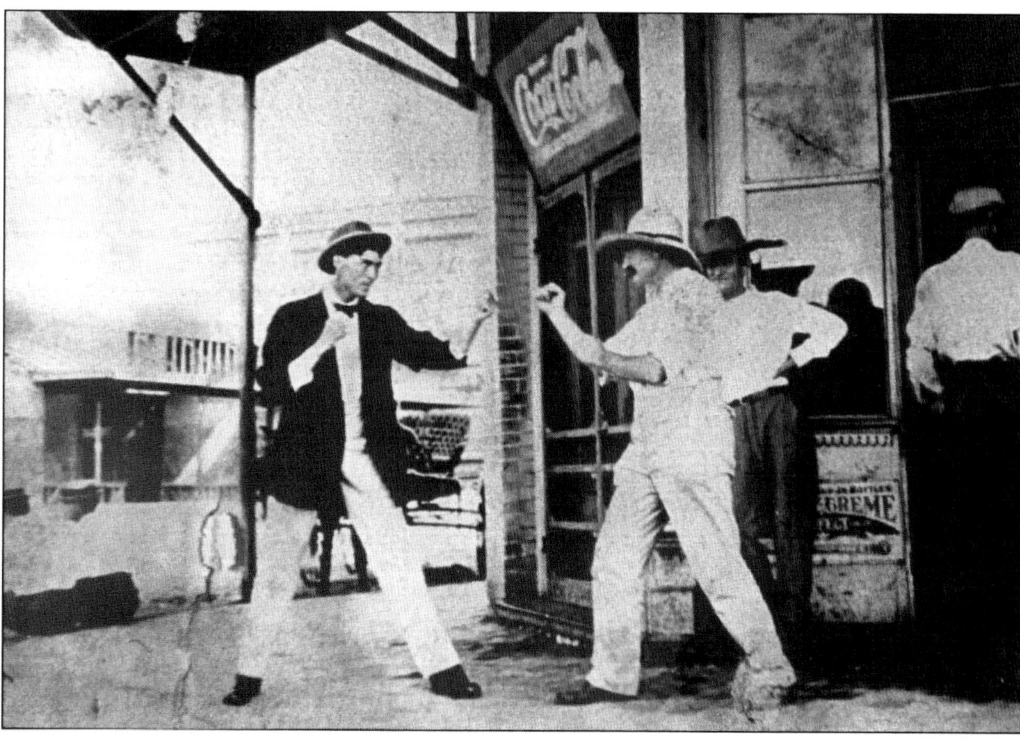

Mock Fight, 1915. An amused bystander watches Dan Davis and Dr. Townsend as they stage a "brawl" in front of a store in downtown Sanger. Notice the horseless carriage in the street behind Davis and the Coca-Cola sign above the entrance to the store. A bottled creme-type drink is advertised on the sign on the lower right. (TWU.)

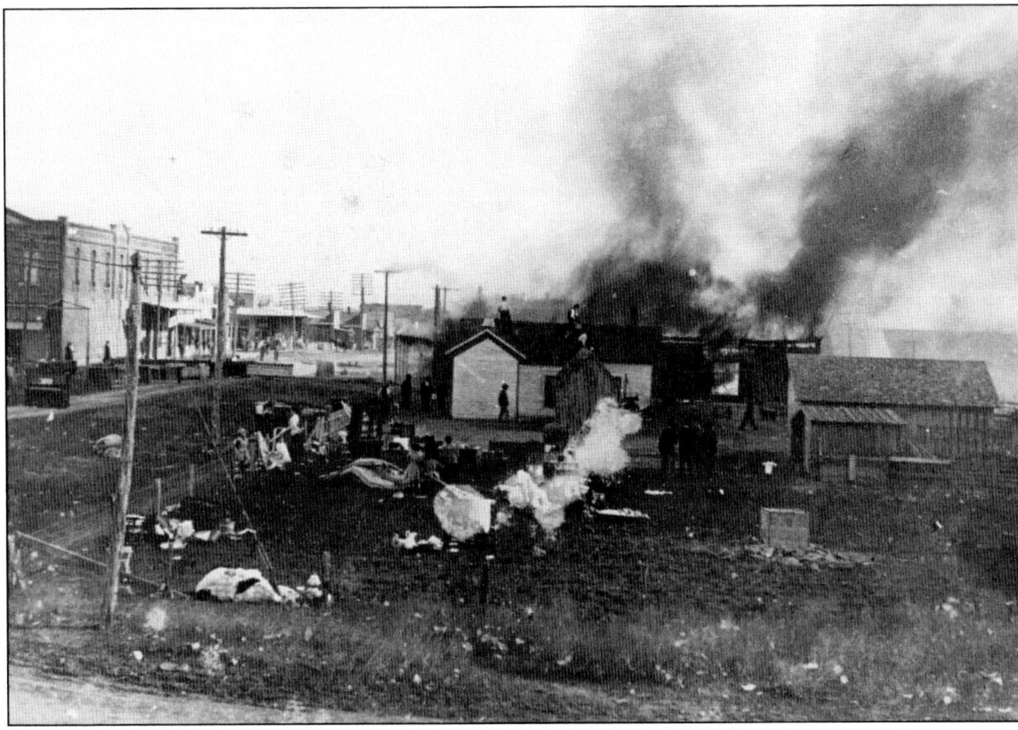

1909 Fire Destroys Building. A bucket brigade managed to save the home of N.P. Kirkland, but the fire destroyed the site of the future Sanger Variety Store, located across the street from the Dunn Dry Goods Store, which later became the O.M. Gentle Hardware business. The dry cleaner business was the suspected source of the fire. (TWU.)

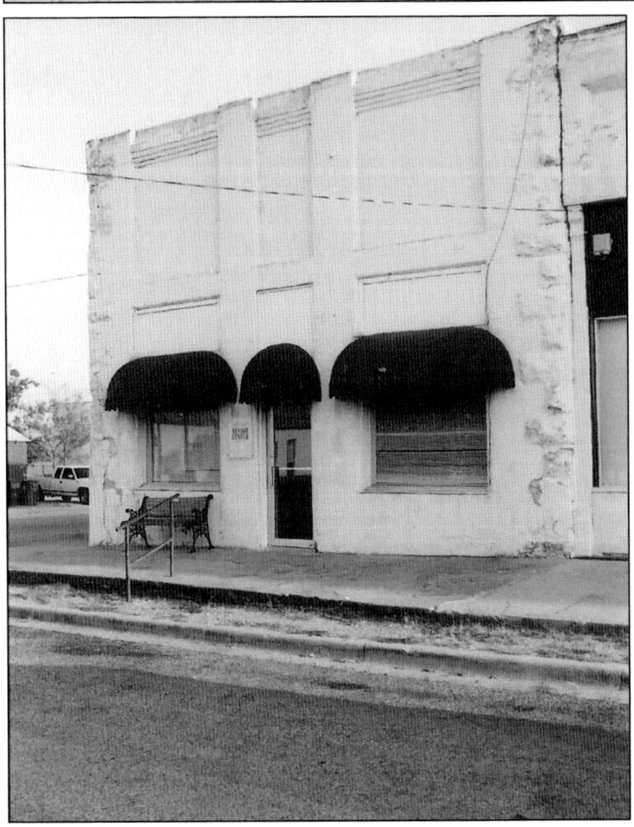

The Rock Building. The first permanent structure in Sanger was built in 1890 by W.J. Wheeler on the southwest corner of Bolivar and Second Streets. In 1985, it was donated to the city by Nelson Gambill Sullivan in memory of his parents and brother. It now serves as the Senior Citizens' Center and has a historical marker, awarded by Sanger Area Historical Society in 2002. (SAHS.)

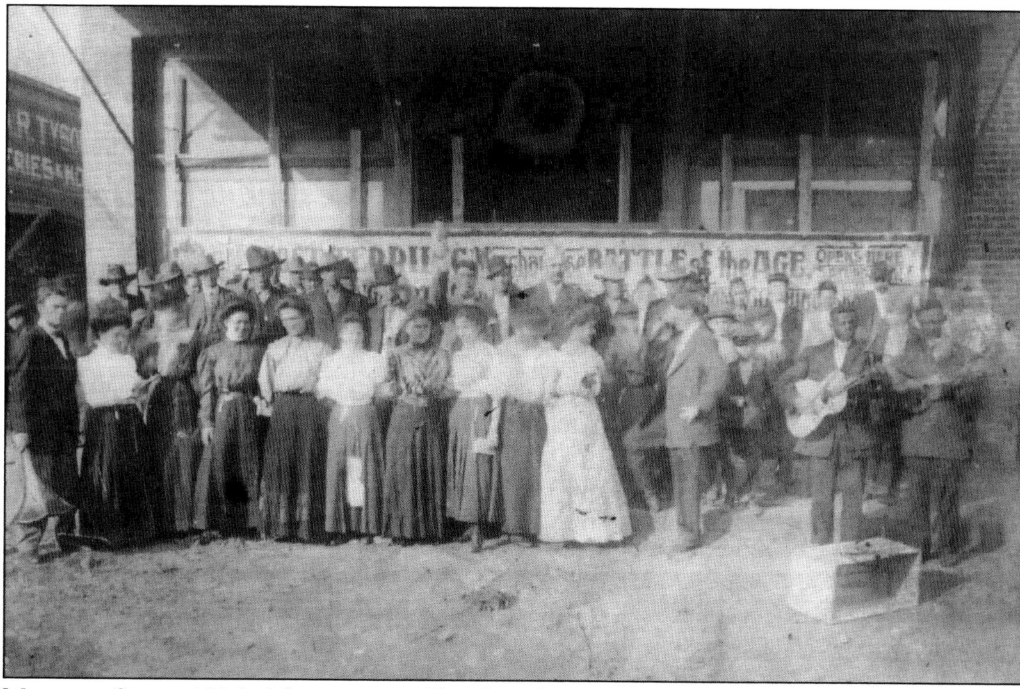

MEDICINE SHOW, 1896. A large group of local residents gather for a medicine show in downtown Sanger about 1896. Usually, medicine shows consisted of traveling horse-and-wagon teams that peddled "miracle cure" medications and other products between various acts of entertainment. The men in the front row on the right have musical instruments. A sign for Tyson Grocery can be seen in the upper left. (Courtesy of Sanger Chamber of Commerce.)

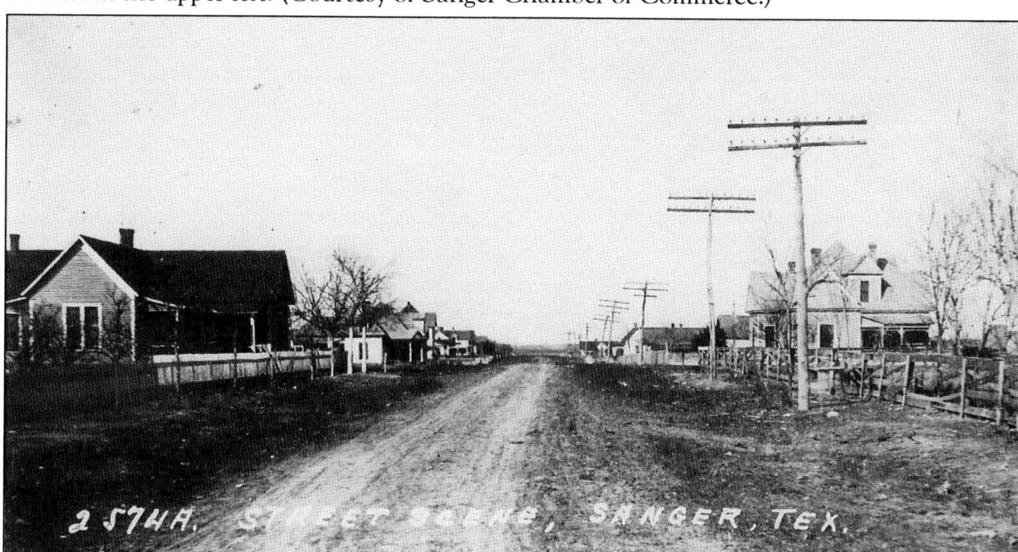

EARLY STREET SCENE. Looking north from Bolivar Street, many houses lined the Pike (now known as Fifth Street). Tall poles were in place to furnish utilities to the residents of a growing community. The pink house that still occupies the northeast corner of Elm and Fifth Streets can be recognized on the right beyond the plank ranch-style fence bordering the park, where there once was a flowing artesian well. (Courtesy of Jim Bolz.)

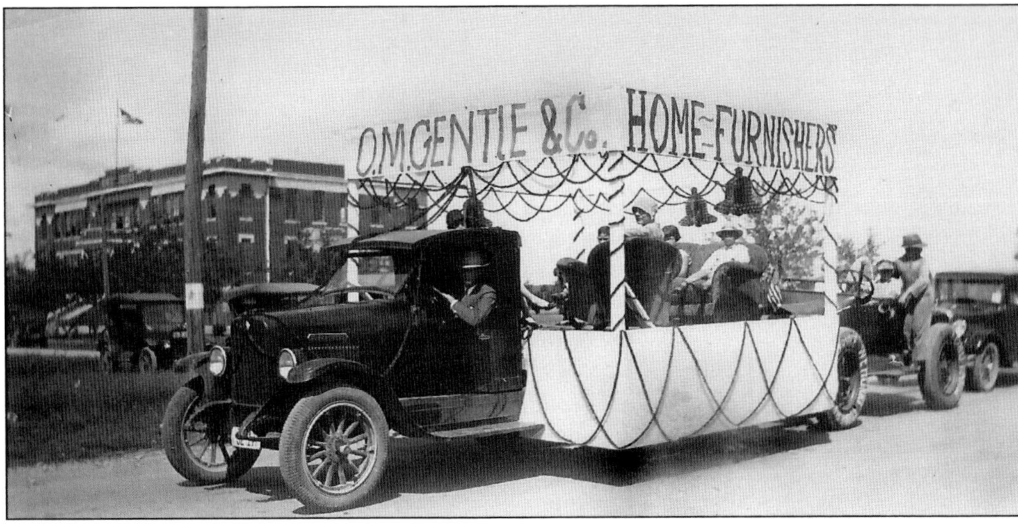

Early Sanger Parade. This float was sponsored by "O.M. Gentle & Co. Home Furnishers." The date this photograph was taken must have been after 1917, as the Sanger school building constructed in that year can be seen in the background with the American flag flying above it. A convertible automobile follows the float as a man stands on the running board beside the car's driver. (SAHS.)

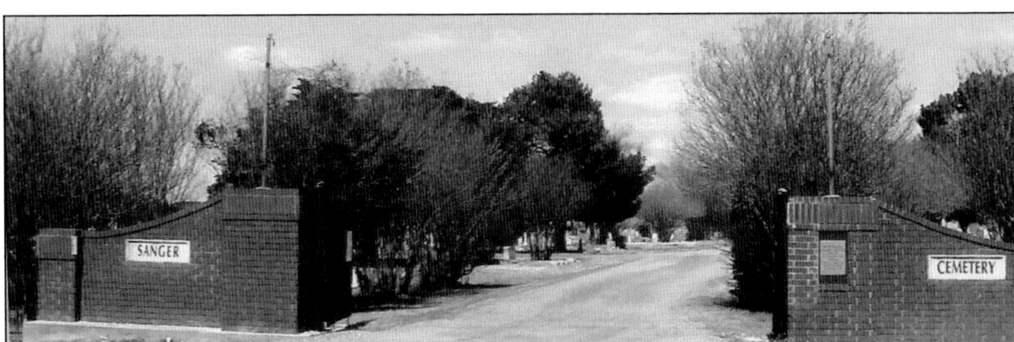

Sanger Cemetery. The cemetery land was donated by Elizabeth (Bullock) Huling, while the fence, brick walls, and entryway were donated by the McReynolds family. A strong association oversees this well-maintained cemetery. The Kirkland family, traveling through the area in 1885, lost their newborn infant Nancy Matilda Kirkland, who was the first to be buried in the cemetery. The cemetery is located on McReynolds Road just east of town. (Photograph by Cindy (Mays) Bounds.)

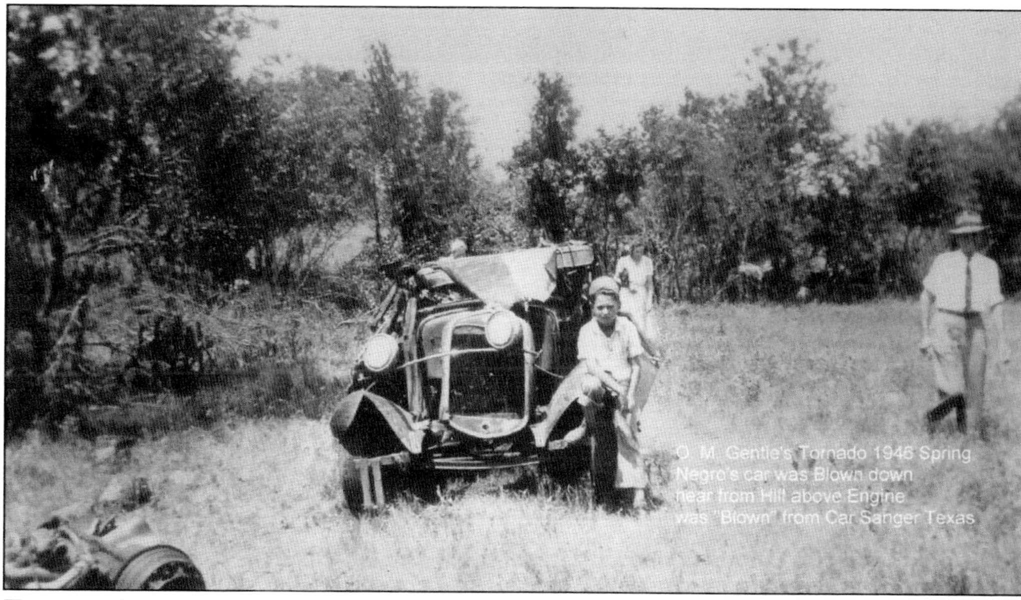

TORNADO STRIKES, MAY 18, 1946. Three miles east of Sanger, young Bill Mundy is sitting on the front of a car blown from the hill during a tornado passing through. The motor, torn from the car, is shown to the left. 10-year-old Charlene Joyce Hammons was killed and homes and barns were destroyed as a result of the storm. (Courtesy of Oscar Shelton and Bill Mundy.)

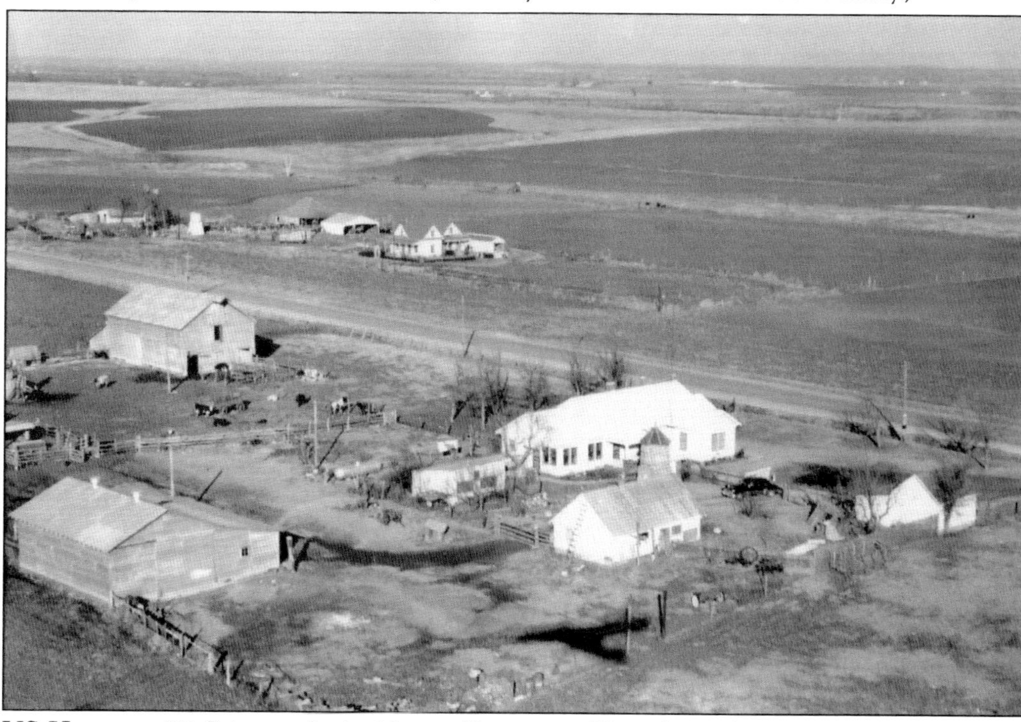

US HIGHWAY 77. Prior to the building of Interstate 35 in the early 1960s, Highway 77 went through the middle of Sanger. Travelers often remembered the town where the many trees lining the highway were whitewashed. This aerial view shows the area just north of town where farms dotted the landscape. (Courtesy of Yvonne (Yeatts) Cain.)

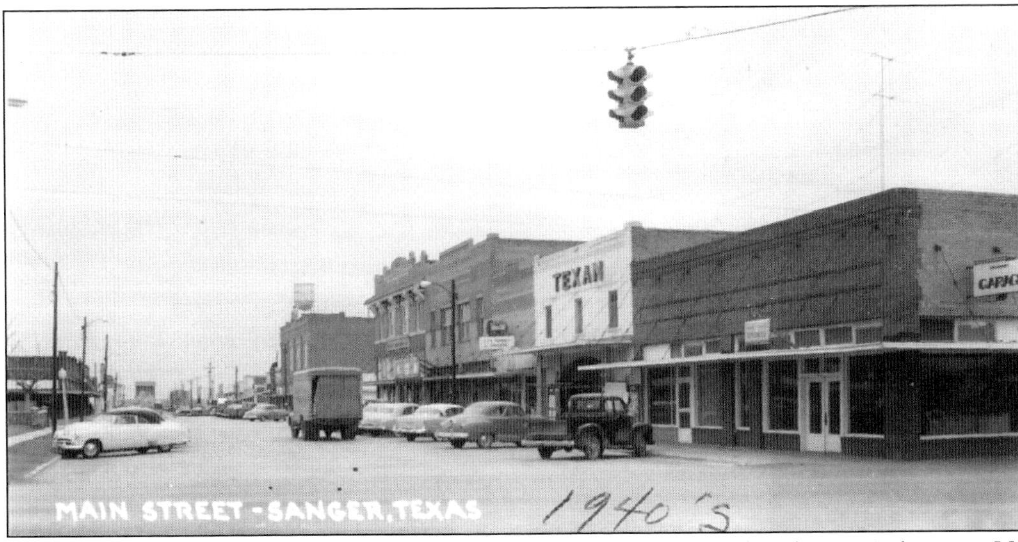

Downtown of the 1940s. The single traffic light was necessary in the 1940s because US Highway 77, the main thoroughfare, passed through the intersection of Fifth and Bolivar Streets. This image depicts a bustling Sanger with the Texan Theater, Brown's Garage, and vehicles of the decade. The railway depot is at the eastern end of Bolivar Street, where the town originally began. (Courtesy of Idaleene (Scheu) Fuqua.)

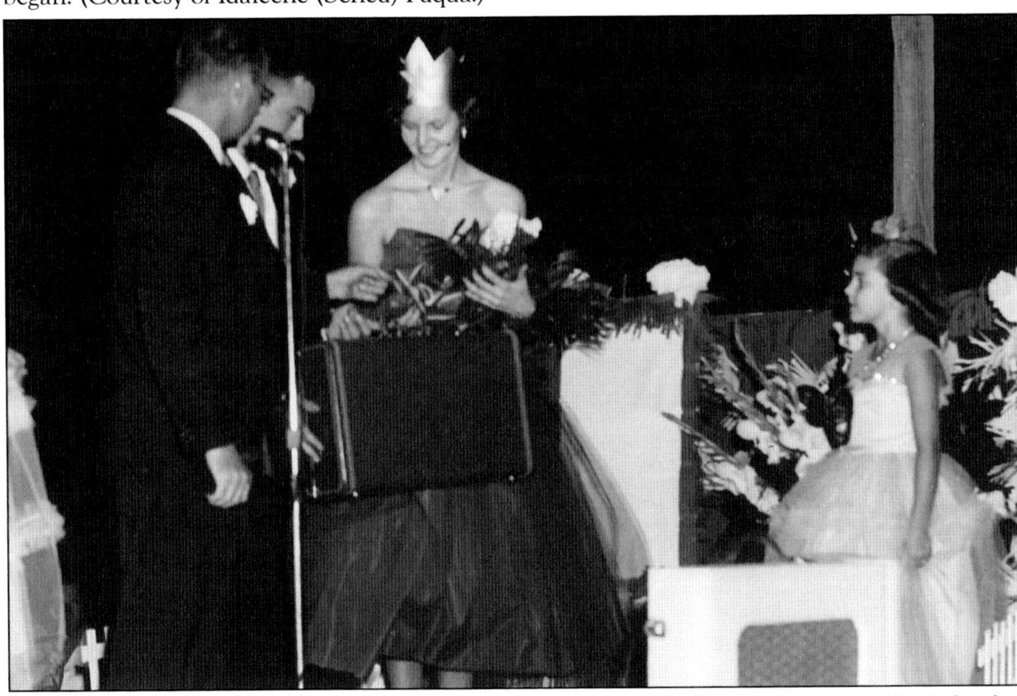

1956 Sanger Fair. The community fair in the city park was held in August 1956. The first queen coronation candidates were selected by a penny-per-vote system, with containers placed in businesses throughout the community. Candidates included Darrelene Ramsey, Nancy Campbell, JoAnn Dyer, Janice Spratt, and Valorie Brumbaugh. As seen above, Paula Harberson, sponsored by Sanger Fire Department, won the title to be crowned queen by Robert Cudd. Her young attendant was Tona Batis. (SAHS.)

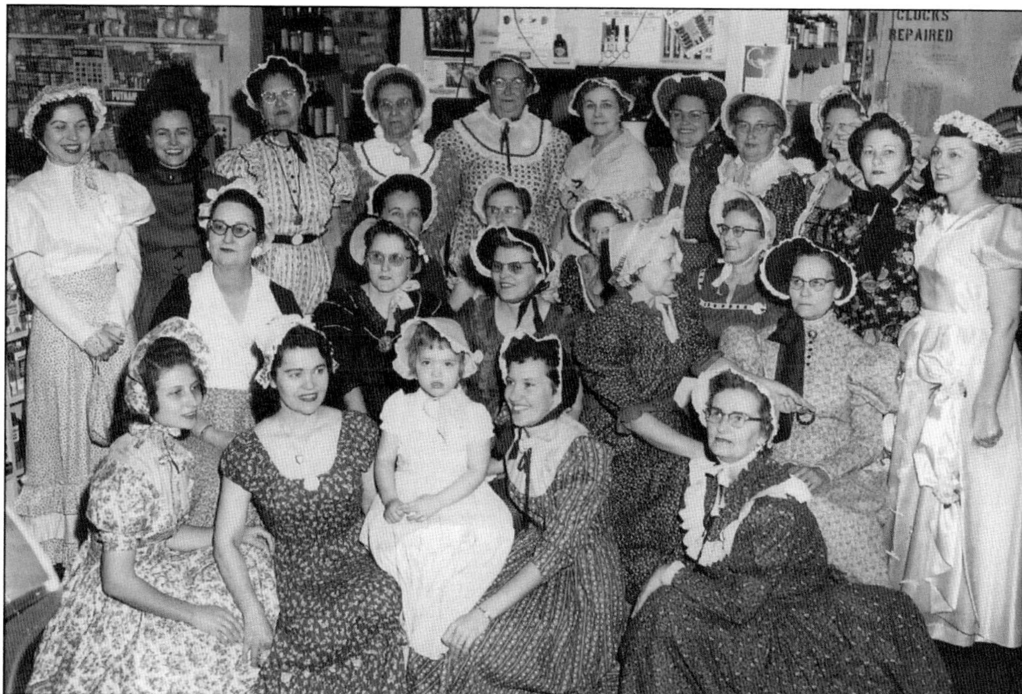

CENTENNIAL CELEBRATION, 1957. The City of Denton was established in 1857, becoming the county seat of Denton County. A countywide celebration was held a century later in which Sanger residents participated. Many Sanger citizens dressed in period costumes, with some of the gentlemen growing beards and sporting bowler hats while the ladies wore long dresses and bonnets. The 25 ladies pictured above are in the Palace Drugstore that later became Lillian's Drugstore. Below are, from left to right, Monroe Sims, Jack McReynolds, Leo Sebastian, J.D. Jones Jr., and an unidentified man. It seems that the unidentified man has been captured for causing trouble, as indicated by the chain around his leg and the coffee can he holds, hoping to collect enough money to pay his fine. (SAHS.)

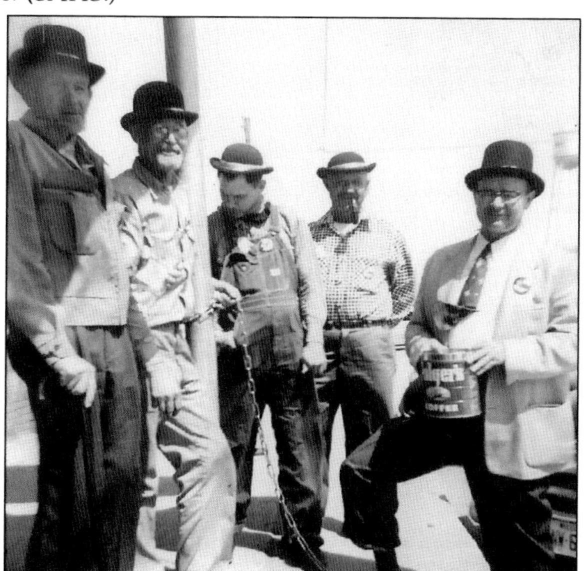

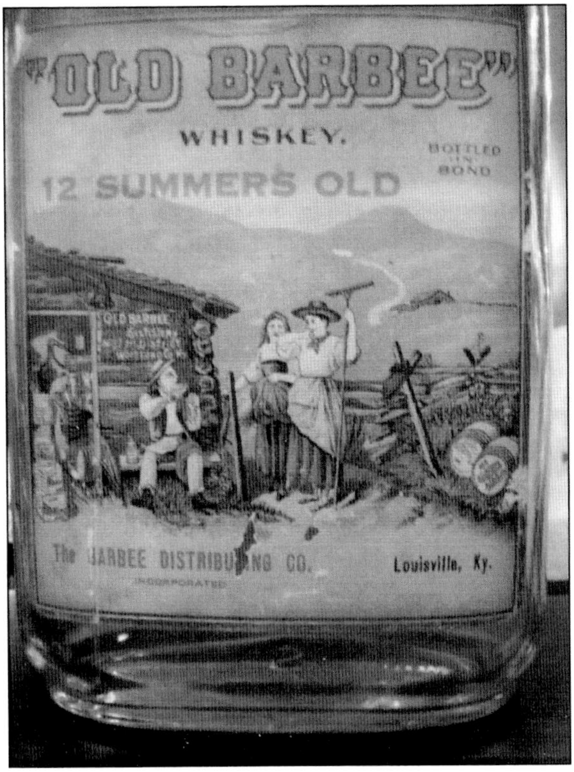

Prohibition Prescription. During the prohibition of 1919 to 1933, a colorful label indicates the brand of the "Old Barbee" whiskey bottle from the Barbee Distributing Company of Louisville, Kentucky. Attached to the back of the bottle is a prescription written by a physician to J.O. Nance for one pint of 100-proof whiskey, with directions to take six teaspoons every eight hours. Garrison Drug Store filled the prescription in 1925 in Denton, Texas. Note that the bottle label also indicates it was made prior to January 17, 1920, that it is in adherence to the prohibition laws, and is to be used for medicinal purposes only. (Courtesy of Billy Ed Nance and Oscar Shelton.)

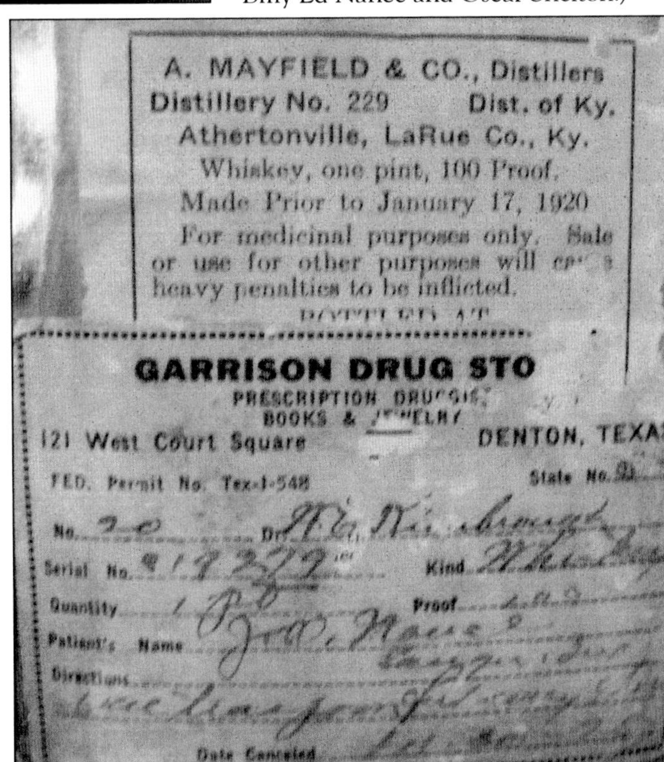

Nine

THE LEARNING

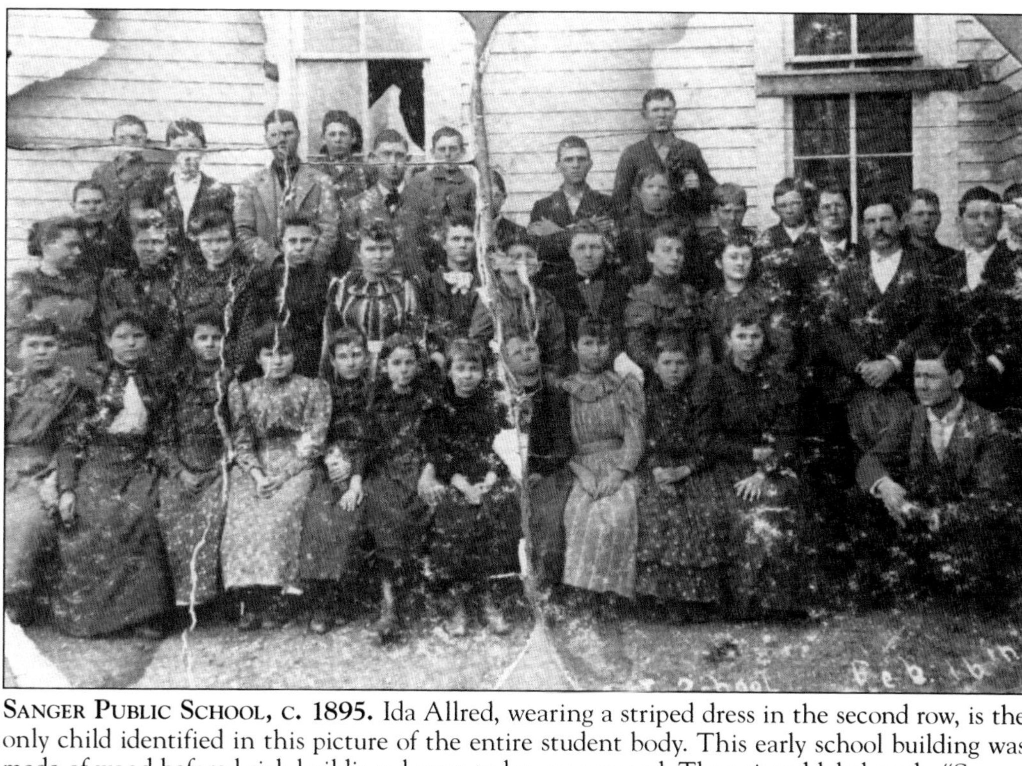

SANGER PUBLIC SCHOOL, C. 1895. Ida Allred, wearing a striped dress in the second row, is the only child identified in this picture of the entire student body. This early school building was made of wood before brick buildings began to be constructed. The printed label reads, "Sanger School, February 16th." Note the broken window. (TWU.)

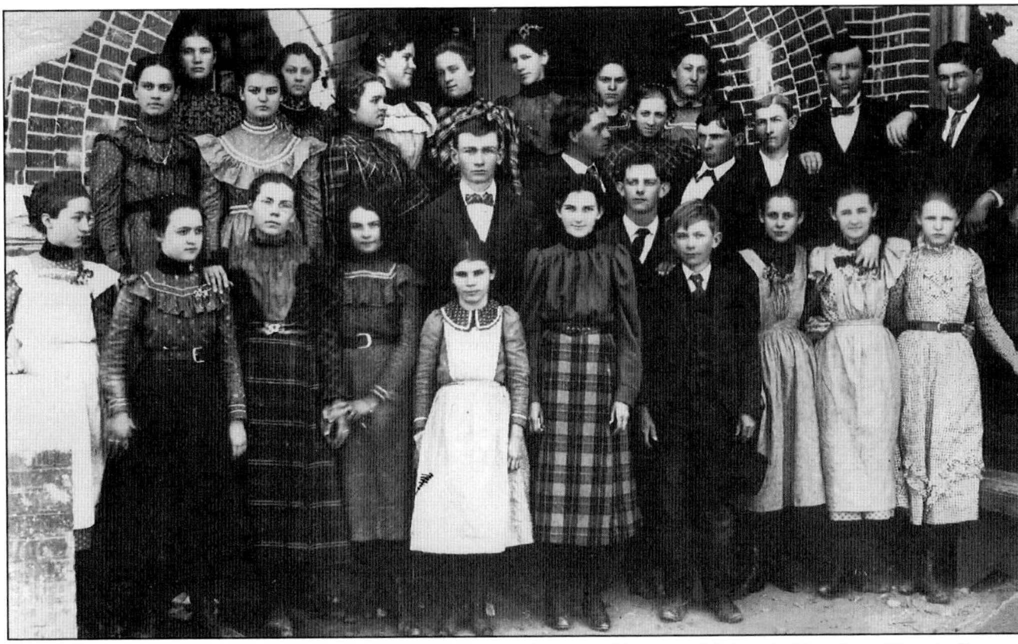

CLASSES OF 1899. Identified above, from left to right, are (first row) Myrtle Partlow, Bessie Bourn, Bettye Sullivan, Adell Hampton, Edna Ready, Matis Gober, Will Taylor, Lon Bowers, Addie Chambers, and Lee Nicholson; (second row) Susie Sluder, ? Mauldin, Alice Davidson, Luther McNeill, Jack Kilgore, Ben Sullivan, Elsie Bourn, Cleburne Warren, Ed McNeill, superintendent, Penny Clark, and Clyde Kay; (third row) Eula Howard, Gena Bowers, Bertha Batis, Carrie Stratton, Annie Kay, Bell Kilgore, and Mae McClellan. (SAHS.)

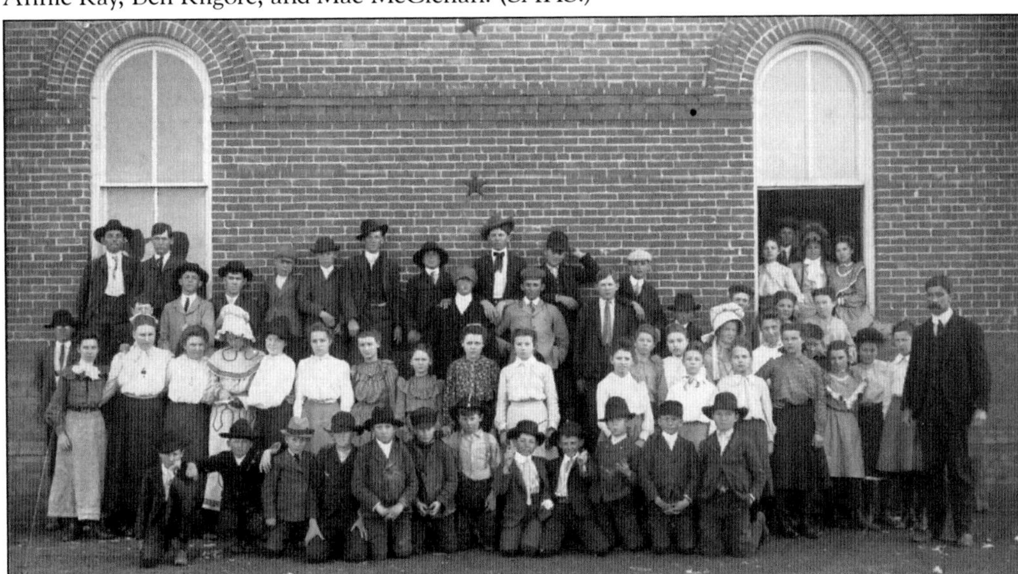

SANGER SCHOOL, C. 1910. A new brick school building had been constructed by 1910. Superintendent J.W. Beatty is on the far right. Almost all of the boys wore hats, but only three girls had bonnets. The picture originally came from the estate of Bessie Kirkland, and her mother's name, "Mrs. Ola Kirkland," is written on the back. The photographer's stamp reads "Hillyer, Sanger, Tex." (TWU.)

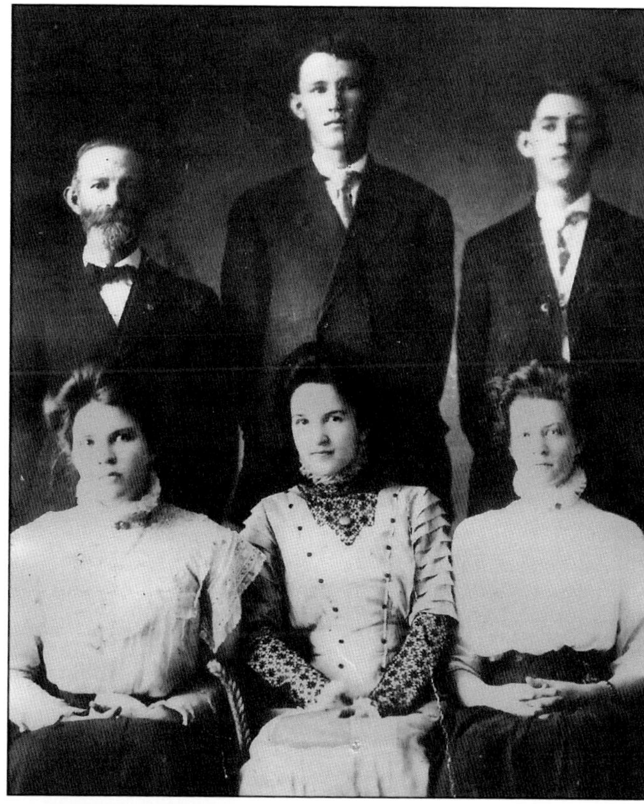

Class of 1906–1907. The first class to graduate from Sanger High School consisted of three students—Ella King, Frankie Lain, and John M. Sullivan. Pictured here is the second graduating class. They are, from left to right, (seated) Jennie Bowers, Alma Lain, and Fay Parker; (standing) superintendent J.W. Parker, Walter Trickey, and W.B. Chambers. Class member Barney Isbell was not present for the picture. (SAHS.)

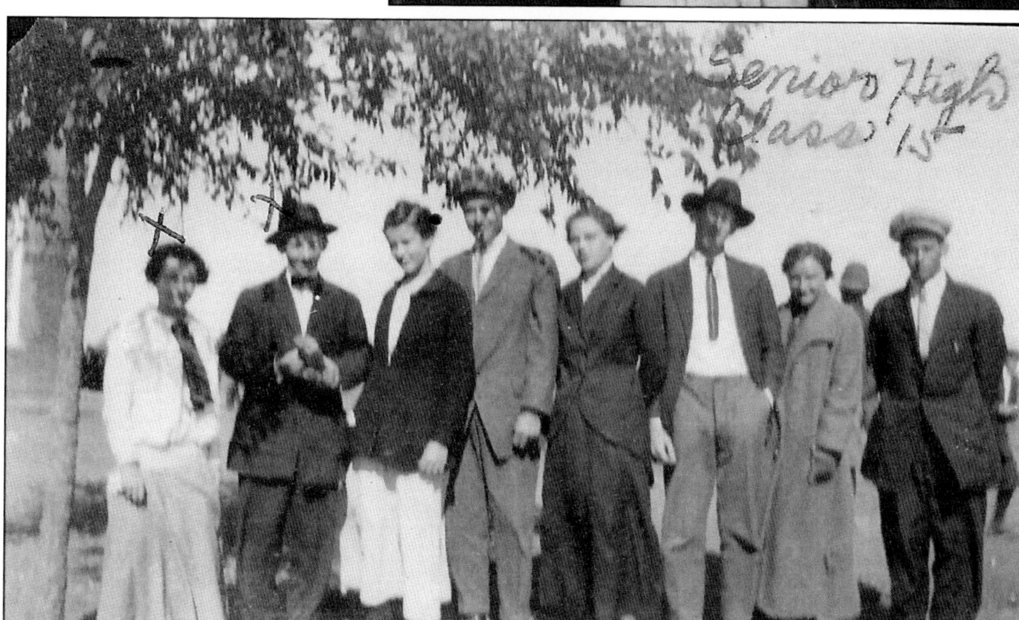

Senior Class, 1915. In the early years of the Sanger school system, the seniors of 1915 were a stylish group. Pictured are teachers Alma (Lain) Chambers and Willie Bush Chambers (on left) with class members including George L. Lain, Joe Trickey, Bill McClellan, Lucille Miller, Foster Robinson, Walter Koons, and Bess Gerlach. (SAHS.)

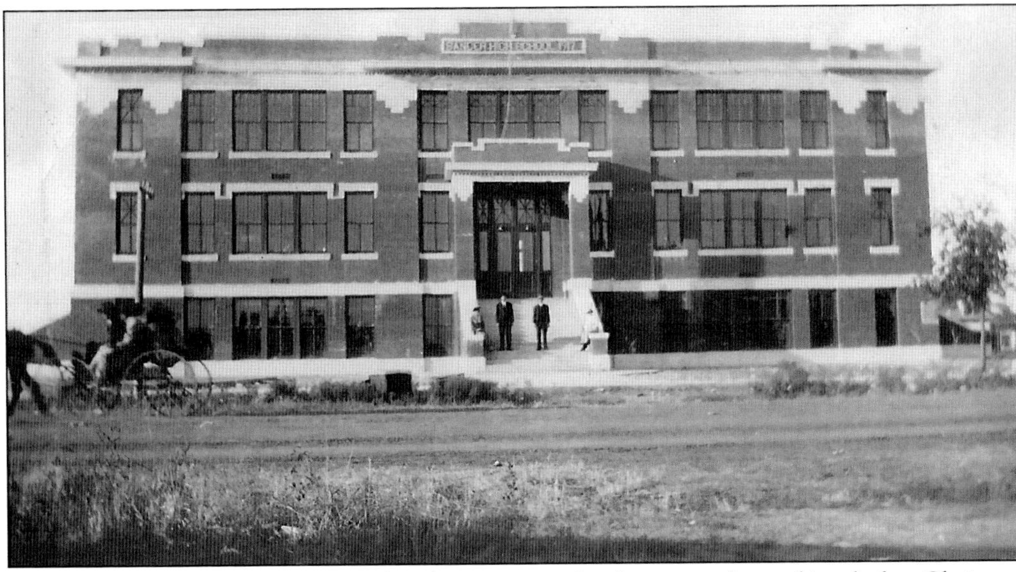

Sanger School Building, 1917. After the previous school structure burned just before Christmas in 1916, this building was erected. The students had to attend classes in the Opera House, the Dunn Building, or various church buildings while it was under construction. It opened in September 1917. In 1948, the building was remodeled, but it later burned in 1984. (SAHS.)

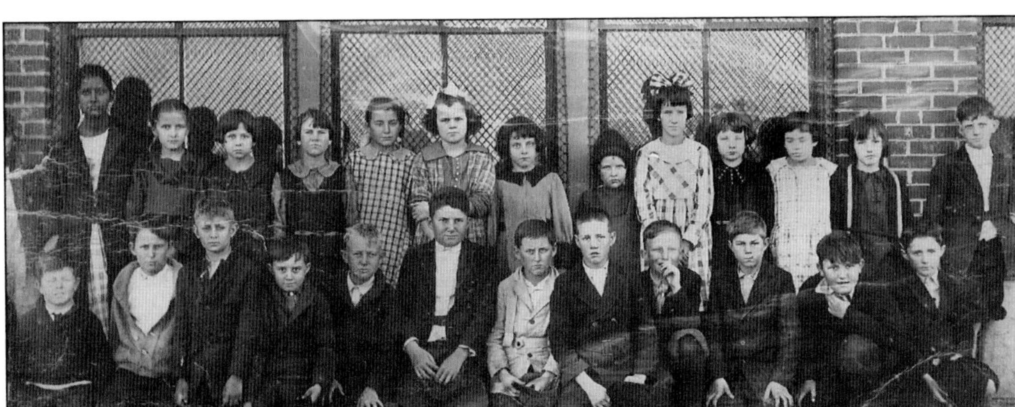

Third Grade, 1920–1921. In the image above, from left to right, are (first row) unidentified, Calvin Kline, Bennie Hughes, Howard Carrico, Bill Burroughs, Tommy McDaniel, Gyp Gibson, J.P. Hampton, Grady Woods, Willard Ashley, Frank Burchard, and unidentified; (second row) Ruby Pearl Odom, Erminia Perez, Alyne Seal, Alta Mae Crandall, Ida Pearl Nance, Faye McClendon, Pauline Carson, Nell Thomas, unidentified, Mildred Touchstone, Oveleta Smith, Mary Sue Lusk, Pauline Burchard, and unidentified. (SAHS.)

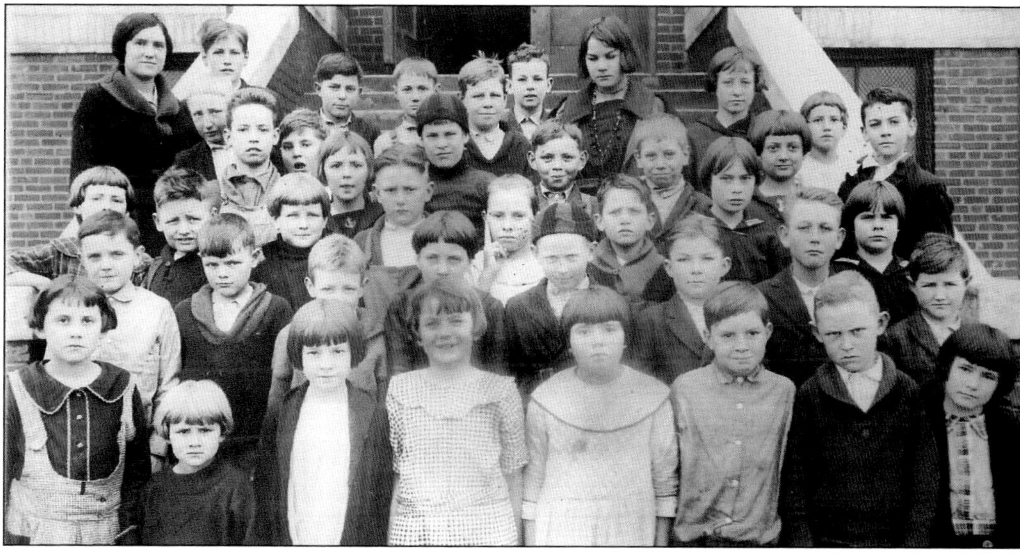

THIRD GRADE, 1923. Classmates from the class of 1931 included Mary Lou LeGear, Beatrice Jones, Ruby Lee McClendon, Warren Jones, Alyne Mallow, Ted Cherry, T.H. Pritchett, J.C. Landers, Essie Vandever, Joe Batis, Joe Bill Rogers, Royce Michaels, J.T. McClellen, Richard Hoehn, H.M. Horst, Edward Spratt, Thomas Moore, Christene Hoehn, and teacher Winnie Minick. (Courtesy of Elleece (Sullivan) Calvert.)

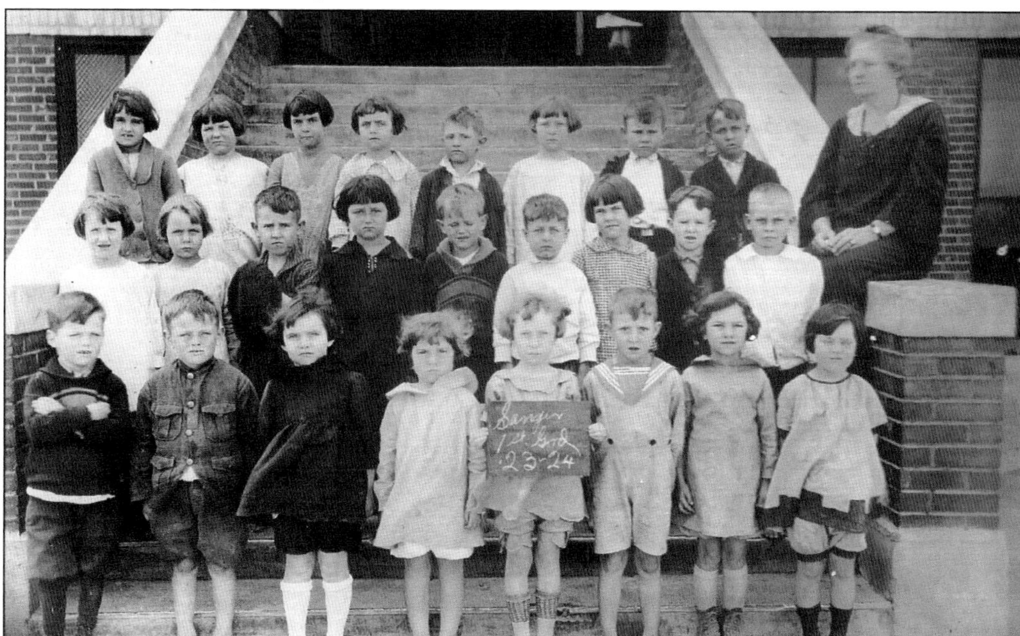

FIRST GRADE, 1924. Pictured above is the class of 1934. They are, from left to right, (first row) John Lewis Sullivan, Henry Sullivan, Laverne Sullivan, Mary Ready, Dorothy Forrest, Rex Moore, Wilma Atkins, and Margaret Brown; (second row) Marguerite Neal, Eloise Echols, Rob Chambers, Alyne Burkholder, ? Yarbrough, James Ready, Mary Jane Batis, Jesse Seal, and ? Duncan; (third row) Clif Wilson, Virginia Pritchett, Ben Sullivan, Abbie Lee Gentle, Ernest Hopkins, unidentified, Newton Stone, R.T. Martindale, and teacher Lina B. Koons. (SAHS.)

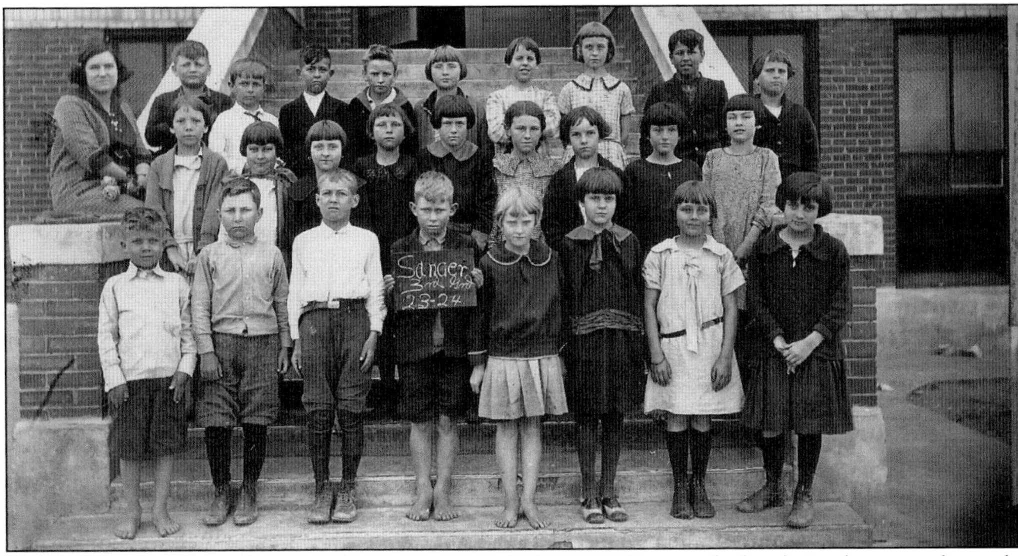

THIRD GRADE, 1924. Students from the class of 1932 standing ready for their photograph on the steps of the school building included Ocie Isbell, Jessie Isbell, Alma Cowling, Florence Horst, Jessie Hopkins, T.H. Pritchett, Hugh Wilfong, Maedell Isbell, Bessie Brown, Gale Draper, Alma McClendon, and teacher Winnie Minick. (SAHS.)

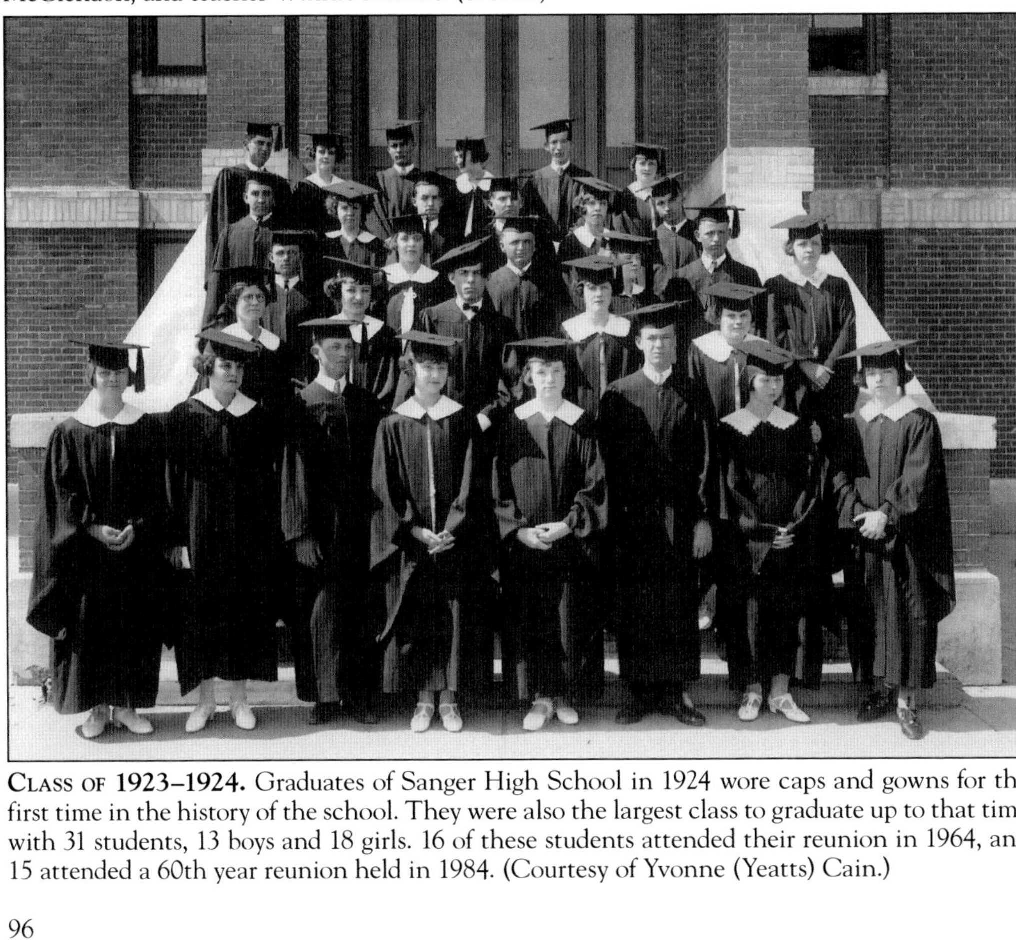

CLASS OF 1923–1924. Graduates of Sanger High School in 1924 wore caps and gowns for the first time in the history of the school. They were also the largest class to graduate up to that time with 31 students, 13 boys and 18 girls. 16 of these students attended their reunion in 1964, and 15 attended a 60th year reunion held in 1984. (Courtesy of Yvonne (Yeatts) Cain.)

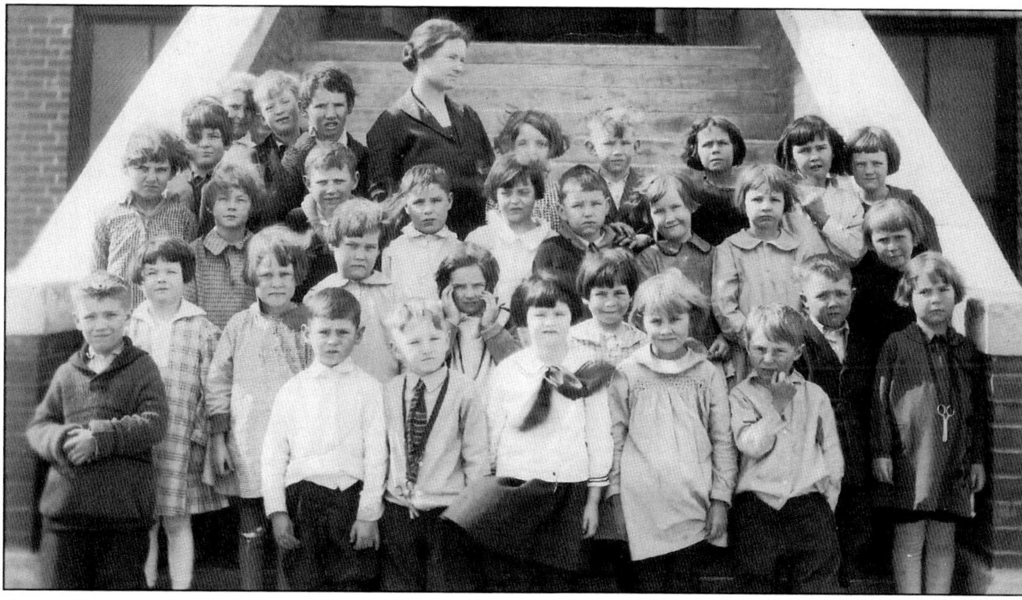

First Grade, 1925. Classmates from the class of 1935 included Floyd Frizzell, Jack Burkholder, J.M. Atkins, Josephine Tyson, Joe LeGear, Cleo Williams, Theda Cherry, Verdie Horst, Buford Chestnut, Mary Ready, Eloise Echols, Clyde Mundy, Floy Ezell Jr., Joyce Spratt, Morris Anderson, Robert Ashley, Esta Caves, Ruby Duncan, Ernestine Hicks, Opal Kerr, Frankie LeGear, Edna Lewis, Limble Lewis, Opal Marion, Katie McClendon, Waymond Miller, Virginia Pritchett, and Evelene Rice. Their teacher was Pearl Boydstun. (SAHS.)

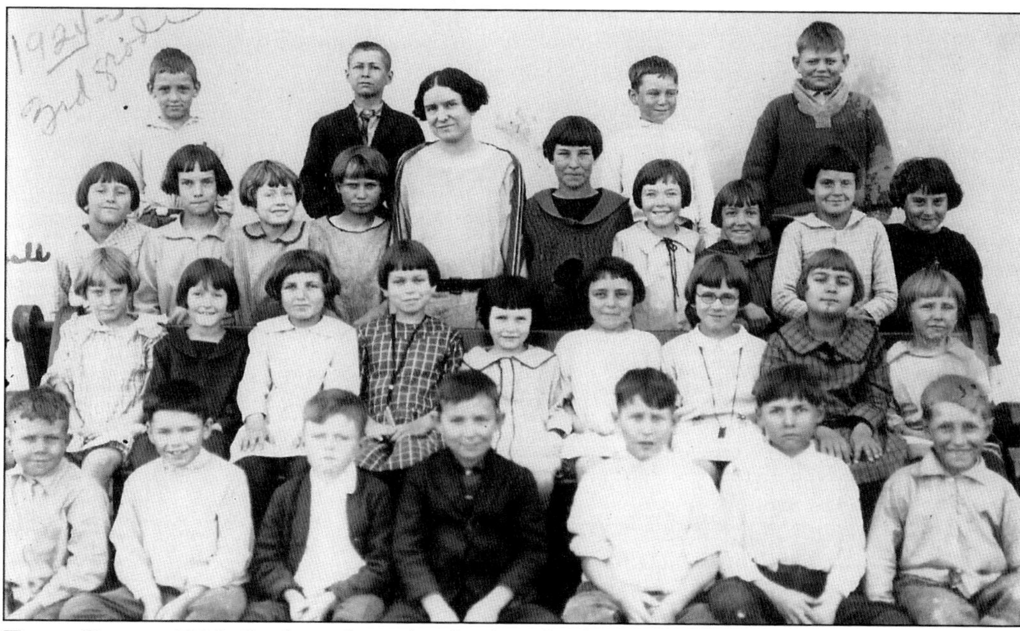

Third Grade, 1925. Students from the third grade class are shown with their teacher, Winnie (Mallow) Minick, who graduated from Sanger High School, attended Decatur Baptist College, and graduated from North Texas State Teachers College. Affectionately known as "Ms. Winnie," she began her career in 1921, taught many generations of students in Sanger, and retired in 1972 after 43 years of service. Pictured above is the class of 1933. (Courtesy of Keta (Prater) Keith.)

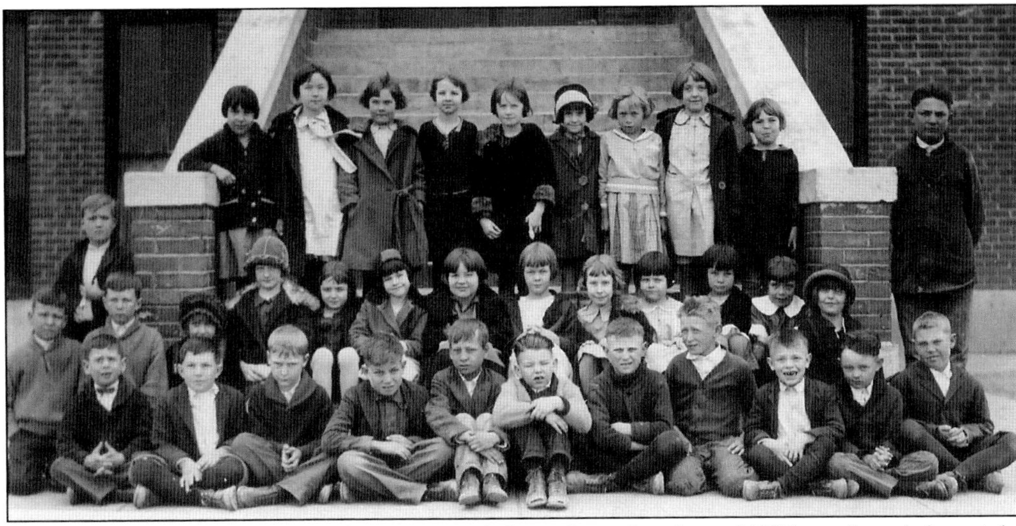

SECOND GRADE, 1926. The students pictured above from the class of 1935 are, from left to right, (first row) Bruce Hampton, Sidney Hampton, Jack Burkholder, Leland Newton, Waymon Miller, Clyde White, Ancil Hardaway, Floy Ezell, Clyde Mundy, L.N. Landers, A. Jones, Alton Dickens, and Burton ?; (second row) Theda Cherry, Esta Caves, Josephine Tyson, Virginia Pritchett, Eloise Echols, Dorothy Forrest, Ruby Duncan, Doyce ?, Mary Miller, and Evelyne Rice; (third row) ? Gadberry, Elizabeth Collins, Verdie Horst, Joyce Spratt, Margarette Neal, Hattie Harwell, Lenora Williams, Earnesteen Hicks, and Mary Ready with teacher Fay Wade. (SAHS.)

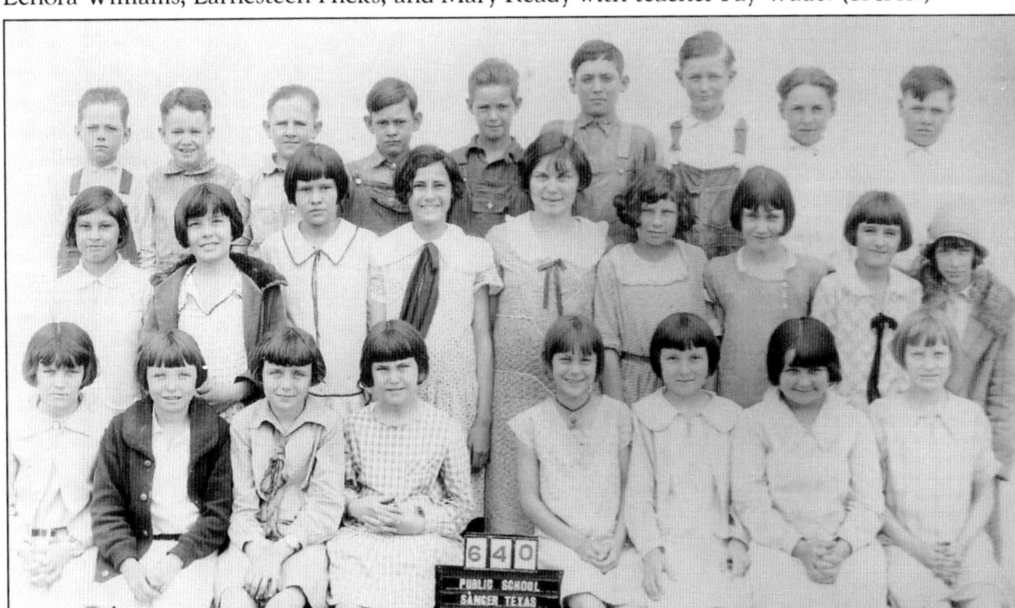

FIFTH GRADE, 1927. Seen here is the class of 1934. They are, from left to right, (first row) Pearl Hollingsworth, Pauline Galbreath, Abbie Lee Gentle, Mary Jane Batis, Maggie Brackney, unidentified, Alyne Burkholder, and Welda Thompson; (second row) Earline Hagler, Jimmy Lusk, Alta Wood, Lula McReynolds, teacher Mrs. Gladden, Ruth Pennington, Mattie McClendon, and Clif Wilson; (third row) John Lewis Sullivan, Jesse Seal, Rob Chambers, Marvin Hagler, Nancy Burton, Roy Winstead, Milford Cates, Ruben Williams, and Frank Carnal. (SAHS.)

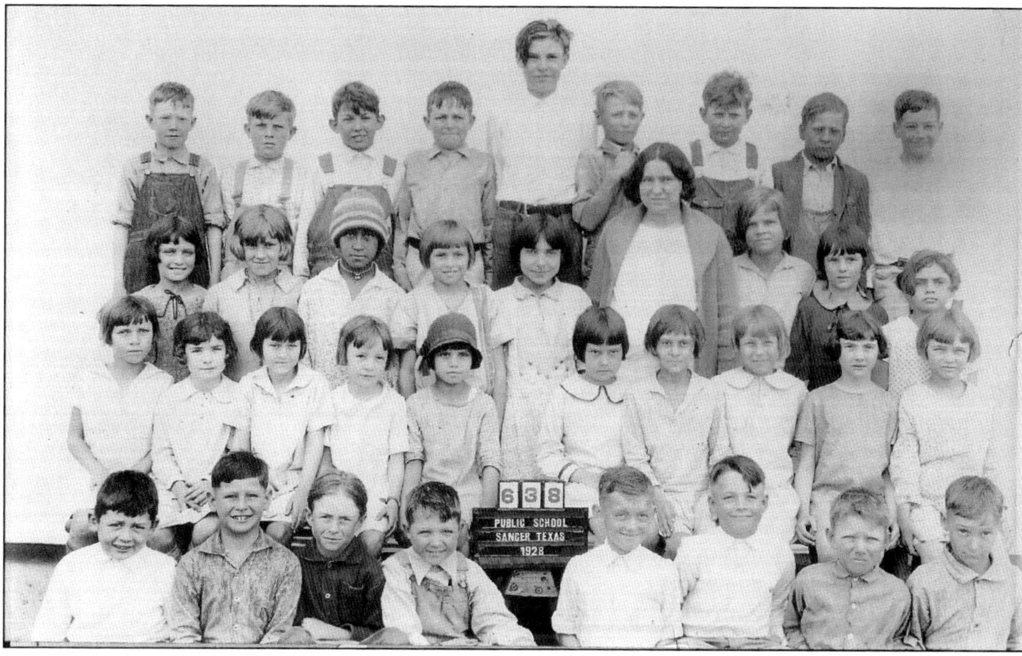

THIRD GRADE, 1928. Noting the short hairstyles of the young ladies in third grade and future class of 1936, classmates included Harry Lyons Jr., Jimmy Williams, Buford Chestnut, Hugh Pate, Guy Herd, Betty Rector, Anita Hicks, Louise Brackney, Edna Mae Sims, Irene McCracken, and Olita Ezell. Their teacher was Winnie Minick. (SAHS.)

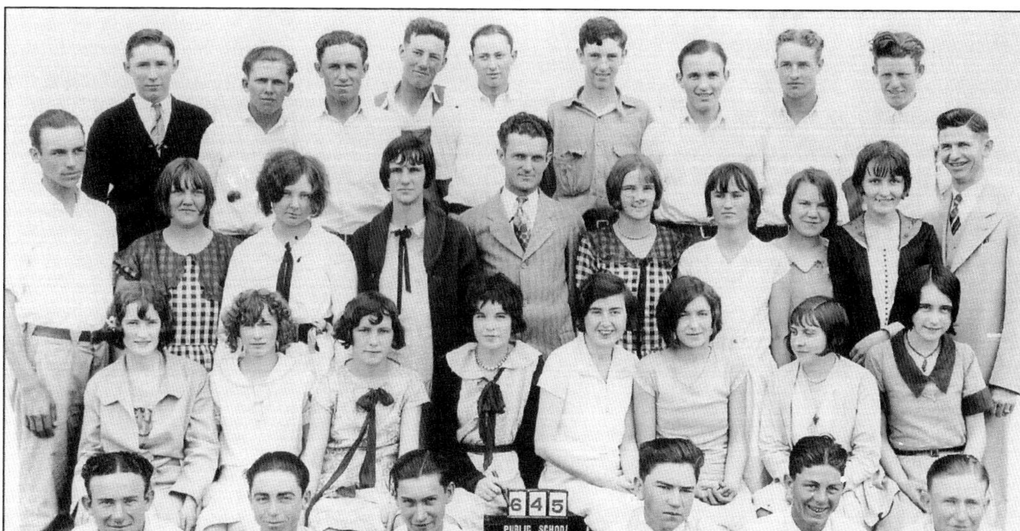

SENIOR CLASS, 1929. In this photograph are, from left to right, (first row) Arlon Newton, Keno Lusk, Lawrence Horst, Clinton Enlow, Willard Ashley, and Grady Woods; (second row) Lucille Miller, Linnie Draper, Frances Jackson, Mary Lusk, Faye McClendon, unidentified, Marybell Montgomery, and Jennie Bronaugh; (third row) Oran Campbell, Clarabell Bentley, unidentified, Mildred Touchstone, C.O. Mitchell, Linnie Melton, unidentified, Ida Pearl Nance, Alyne Seal, and superintendent L.I. Samuel; (fourth row) Jess Schmidt, John Ezell, Harris Brewer, J.P. Hampton, unidentified, J.B. Harper, Frank Burchard, Carl Ganzer, and Claude Allred. (SAHS.)

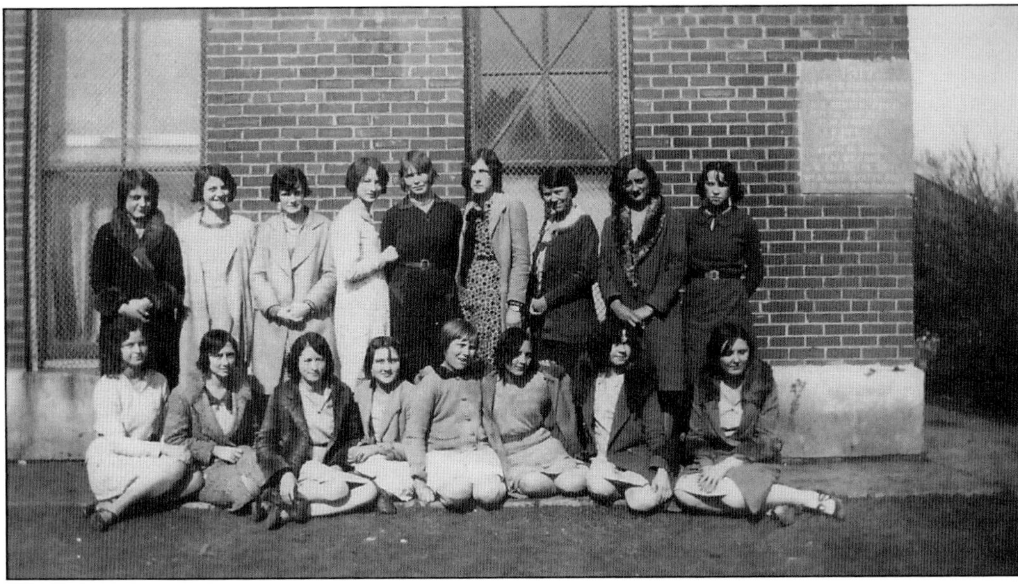

School Cornerstone, 1917. A group of girls taught in Mrs. Jackson's clothing class pose outside the school building in 1929. Those who have been identified are Mildred Brewer (third from left in the front row) and Harriet and Helen Hicks (back left). Above and to the right is the cornerstone of the school building. This cornerstone is now located on school grounds near the administration building. On one side, it offers the names of the members of the school board, the superintendent, the architect, and the contractor. The inscription on the other side shows a Masonic emblem and reads, "Laid by Bolivar Lodge, No. 418, Sept. 27, 1917." (Above, SAHS; below, photograph by Cindy (Mays) Bounds.)

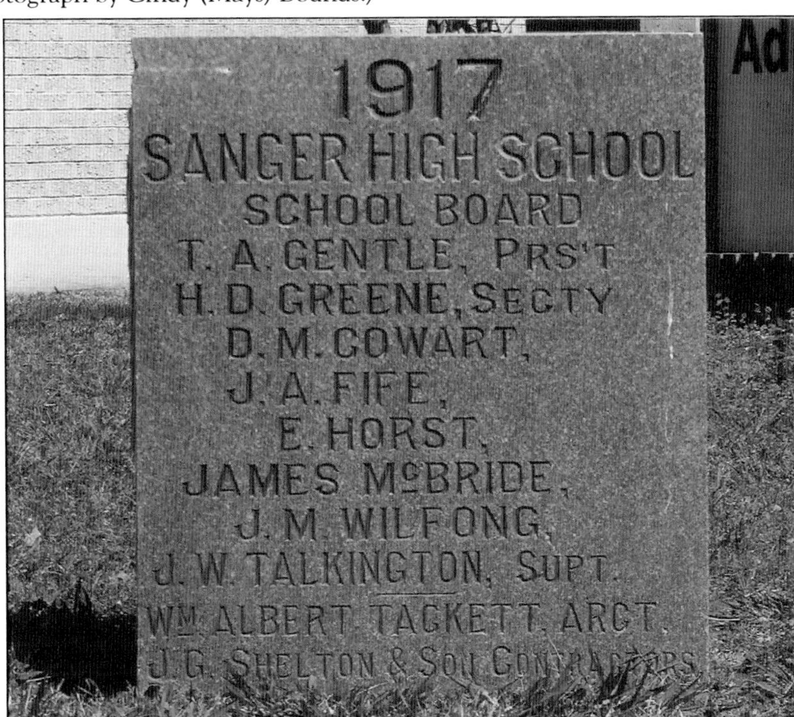

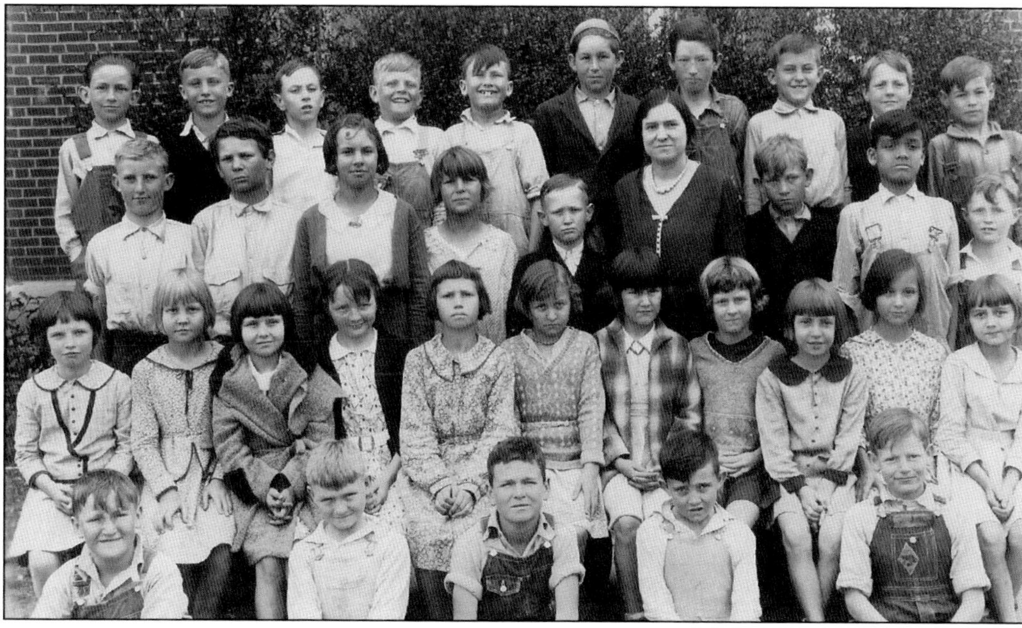

Third Grade, 1929–1930. The people identified in this image, from left to right, are (first row) James Giles, Douglas Tippen, Don Hampton, Wayne Dickens, and Troy Strickland; (second row) Cynthia Crowson, Catherine Flowers, ? Sims, Rebecca Batis, Alta Williams, Idaleene Scheu, and Ouida Holt; (third row) Woody Marion, ? Marion, Franklin Landers, teacher Winnie Minick, and Walter Jones; (fourth row) Frank Terrell, LeRoy Brown, ? Belcher, Ralph Brewer, Billy Gentle, Dick Ready, and Harold Sims. (SAHS.)

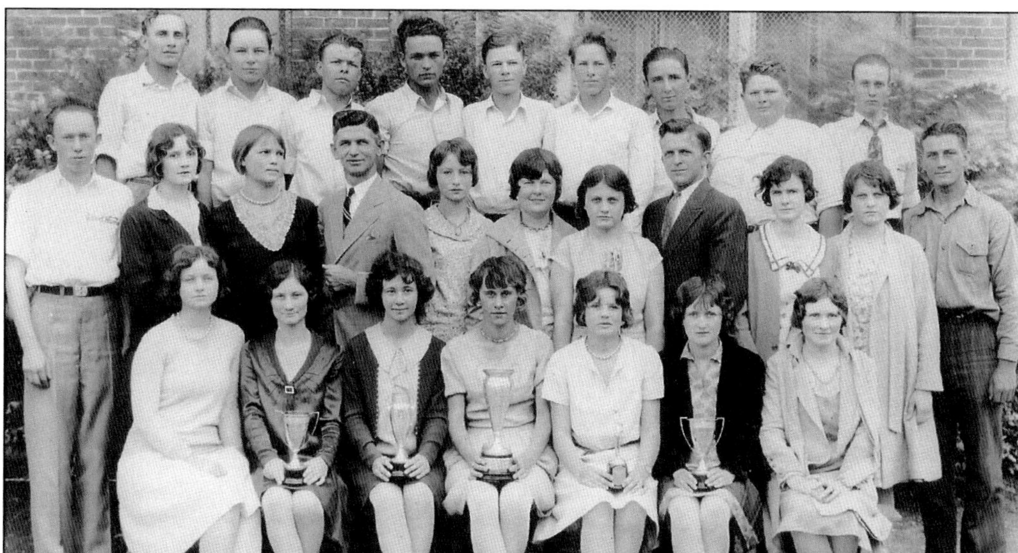

Senior Class, 1930. The students of the class of 1930 are, from left to right, (first row) Effie Sullivan, Velma Stubbs, Winnell Tarver, Hazel Brackney, Euceline Gibson, and Ruth Tippen; (second row) Joe Nathan Wiggins, Ethel Pace, Luellen Meek, superintendent L.I. Samuel, Pauline Harper, Ruth Wylie, Harriett Hicks, Mr. Williams, Emogene Touchstone, Helen Hicks, and Buster Skinner; (third row) Raymond Tippen, Ray Crawford, J.M. Wilfong Jr., Ben Campbell, Ray Enlow, Luther Melton, Ancil Cearley, Rankin Isbell, and Eldridge Sinclair. (SAHS.)

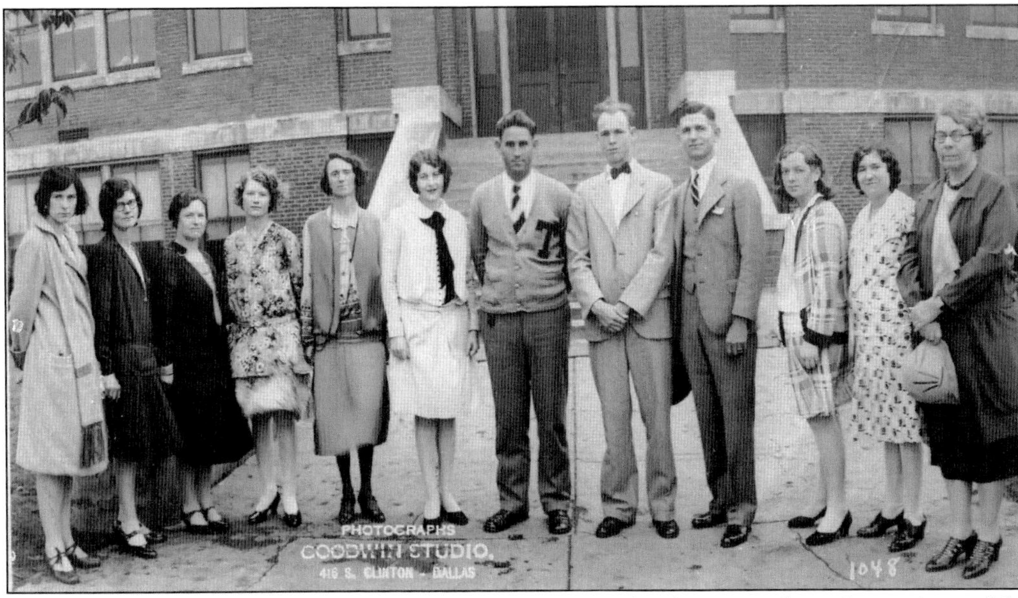

EARLY SANGER SCHOOL FACULTY. The faculty for the entire school is pictured standing in front of the school building that was constructed in 1917. It included, from left to right, Mina Cross, Ruby Seal, Pearl Boydston, ? Williams, Charlotte (Gambill) Sullivan, Dixie Crockett, Bill Crawford, ? Williams, L.I. Samuel, Genevieve (Rice) Stubbs, Winnie (Mallow) Minick, and Mamie (Jones) Sullivan. (TWU.)

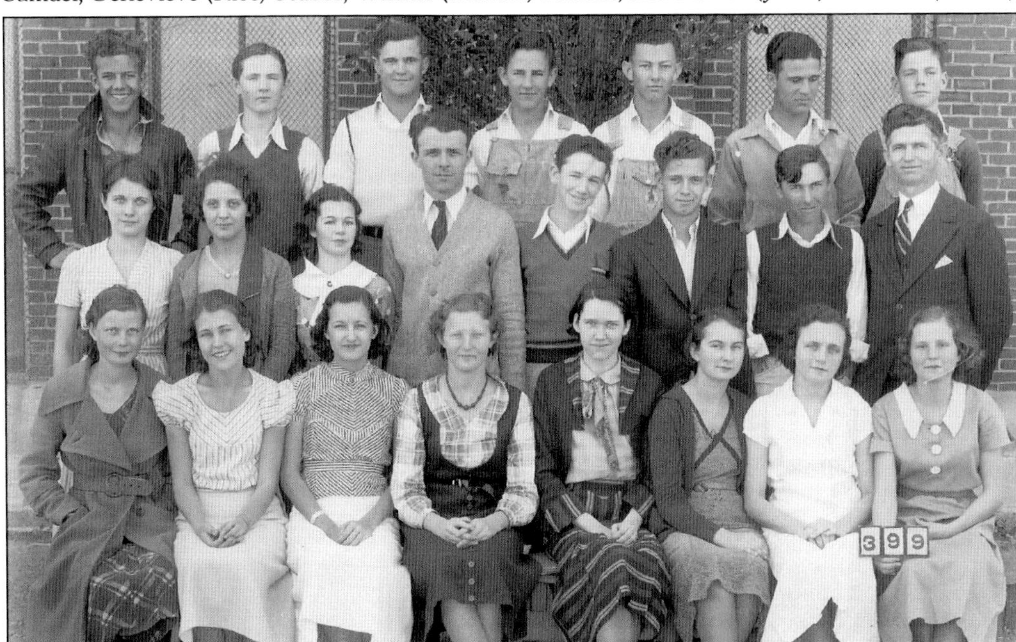

TENTH GRADE, 1932. The class of 1934 included, from left to right (first row) Lucille Fowler, Mary Jane Batis, Clif Wilson, Jeanette McClendon, Mattie Bell McClellan, Polly Jo Bronough, Abbie Lee Gentle, and Margaret Giles; (second row) Williace Reynolds, Bertha Hicks, Mildred Roberts, teacher Walton Wilfong, Jesse Earl Seal, Nancy Burton, Reuben Williams, and superintendent L.I. Samuel; (third row) Lanier Chestnut, J.Q. Burnett, Harvey Payne, Rob Chambers, Lucian Williams, Jim Foster, and John Lewis Sullivan. (SAHS.)

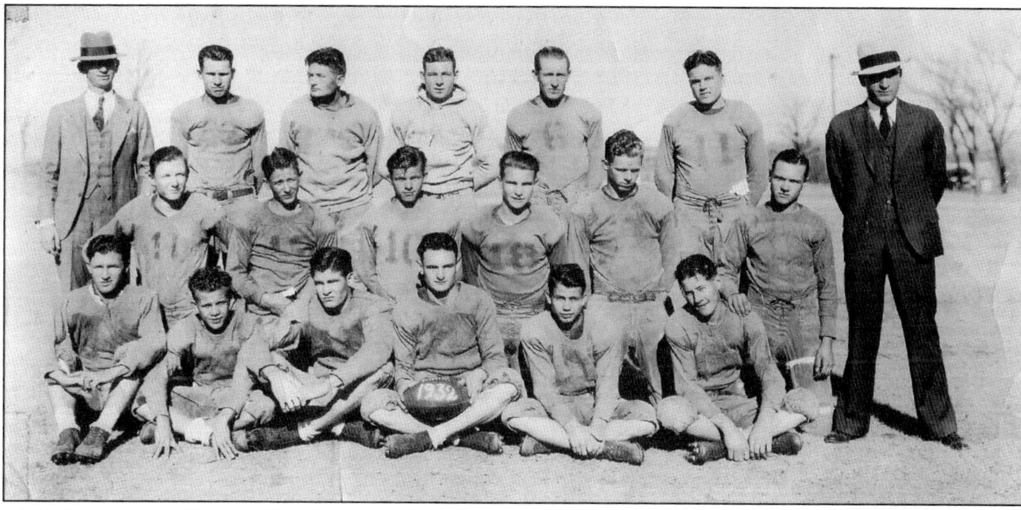

1932 Football Team. The Sanger High football team had a successful season of six wins, one loss, and one tie game. Led by coach Sam McClure, the players included Tip Allred, T.H. Averitt, Joe Batis, Clyde Berryhill, Lynwood Brewer, Frank Cornell, Leon Caves, Lanier Chestnut, Edwin Ganzer, L.N. Landers, J.F. Mundkowsky, T.H. Pritchett, Marion Newton, Bill Rector, Weldon Roane, Jimmie Tyson, and Edward Spratt. (SAHS.)

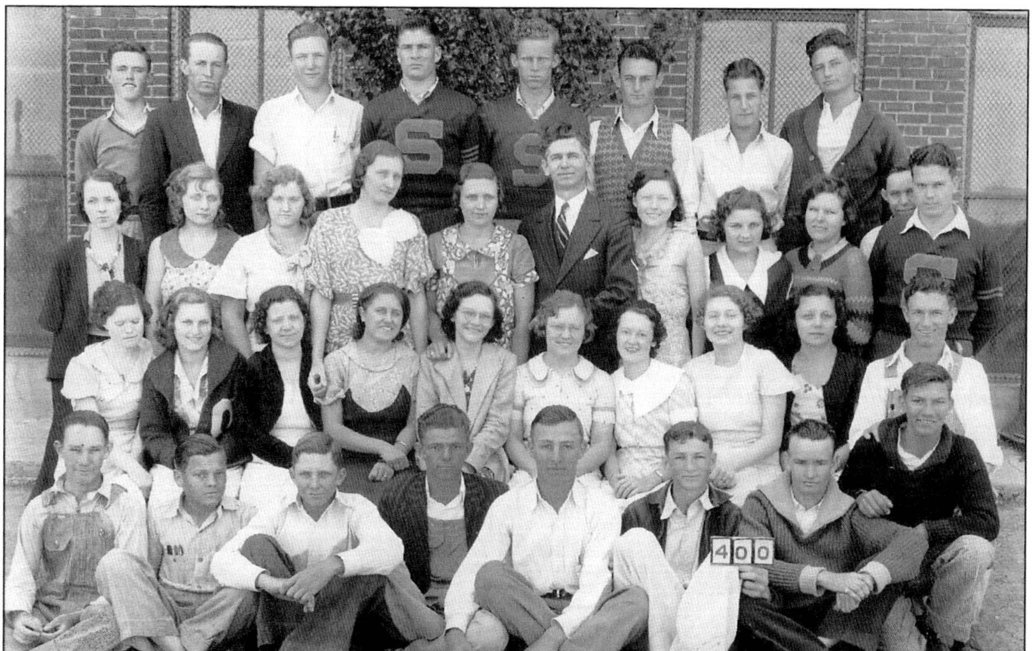

Senior Class, 1933. This class included, from left to right, (first row) John Garrison, Floyd Carson, John Rodgers, Weldon Roane, Raymond Selzer, L.P. Enlow, Gale Draper, and Gilbert Whitehead; (second row) Ollie Davis, Ilma Thompson, Minnie Morris, Estelle Simpson, Juanita Hale, Beulah Robertson, Christine Pate, Marjorie Burroughs, Julia Miller, and Lynwood Brewer; (third row) teacher Miss Rice, Dean Mann, Jessie Isbell, Nina Collins, Helen Enlow, Johnnie Feagan, Clyde Berryhill, and Glenn Mays; (fourth row) Gambill Sullivan, Marion Newton, J.F. Mundkowsky, Joe Batis, Tip Allred, Leon Caves, Bill Rector, and T.H. Pritchett. (SAHS.)

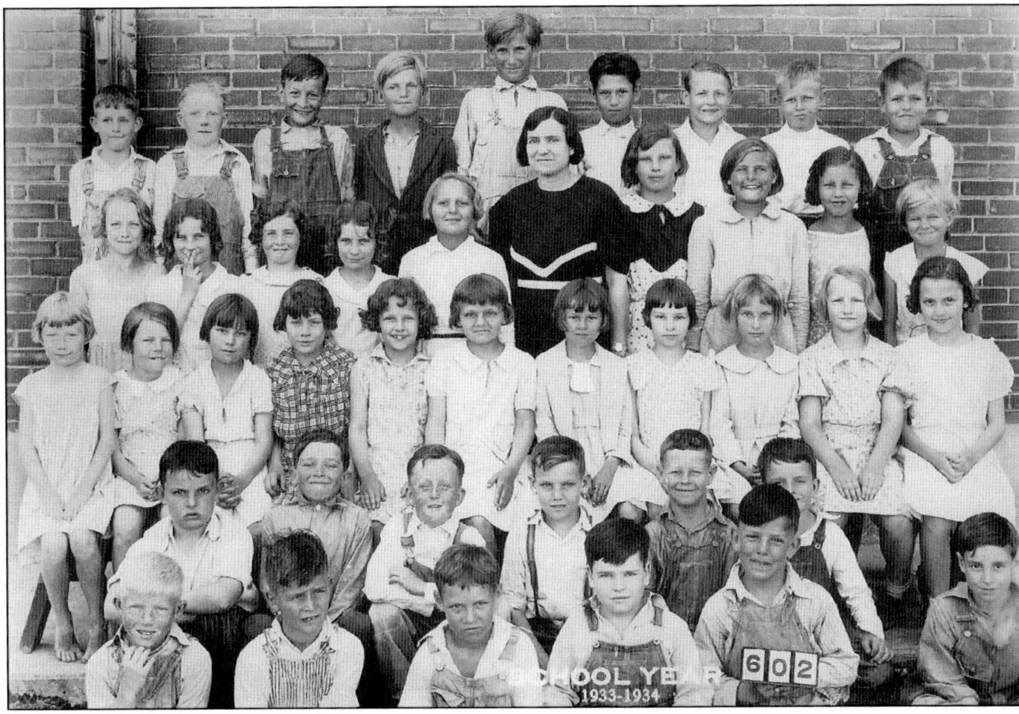

Third Grade, 1933–1934. The last names of students identified in this class are Boydston, Brown, Burk, Burroughs, Carr, Connley, Crier, DeVilla, Echols, Gheen, Hayden, King, Kline, Landers, Marion, McKenzie, Nance, Owens, Robertson, Spratt, Strickland, Stricklin, Summers, Vaughn, Wilson, and Wyatt. Their teacher was Winnie Minick, and many of them graduated in 1942. (SAHS.)

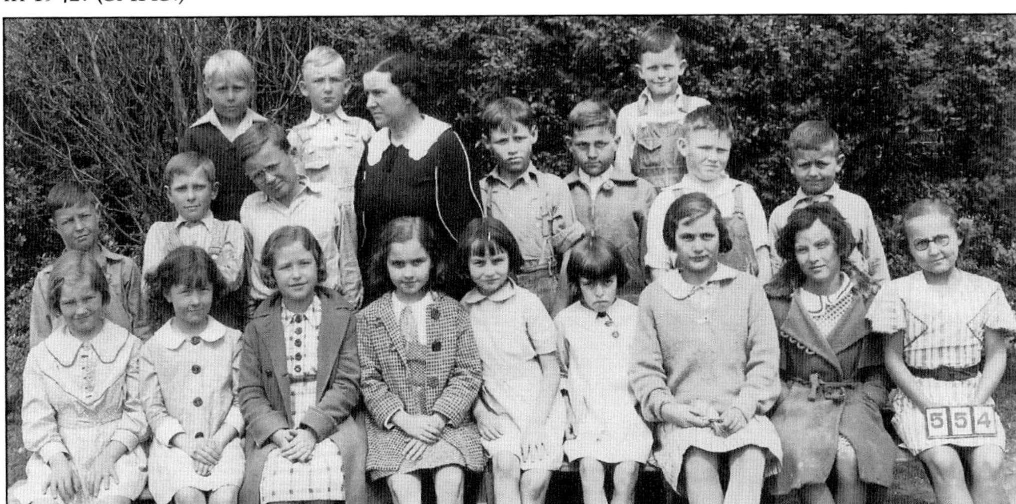

Third Grade, 1934–1935. From left to right are (first row) Sue Wylie, Evelena Baker, Peggy Riley, Sally Ann Gentle, Wanda Jean Waide, Juanita Chastain, Minnie Lee Dial, Pauline Odom, and Ruby Jo Cearley; (second row) J.M. Sims, Dick Klein, Virgil Ward, teacher Winnie Minick, Douglas McKinney, Waylon Vandever, George L. Morrow, and Hugh Young; (third row) Sam Rector, Teddy Wayne Morris, and Billy Jack Tyson. (SAHS.)

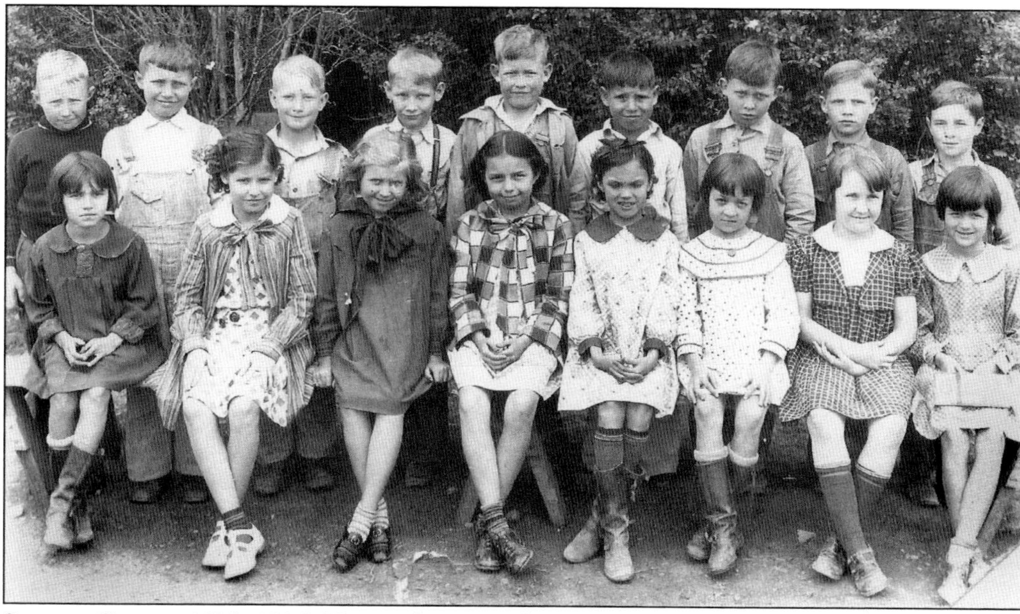

SECOND GRADE, 1935–1936. The students are, from left to right, (first row) Ellen ?, Lois Bucks, Pearl Mullins, Betty Hughes, Japaline Brewer, Betty Rippey, Peggy Vaughan, and Nelda Jo Long; (second row) Clayton Conley, Glenn C. Wilson, Johnny Landers, Walter Wilson, Lewis Bucks, Bobby Daniels, Venard McKinzie, Leo Vandever, and Jimmy Habern. (SAHS.)

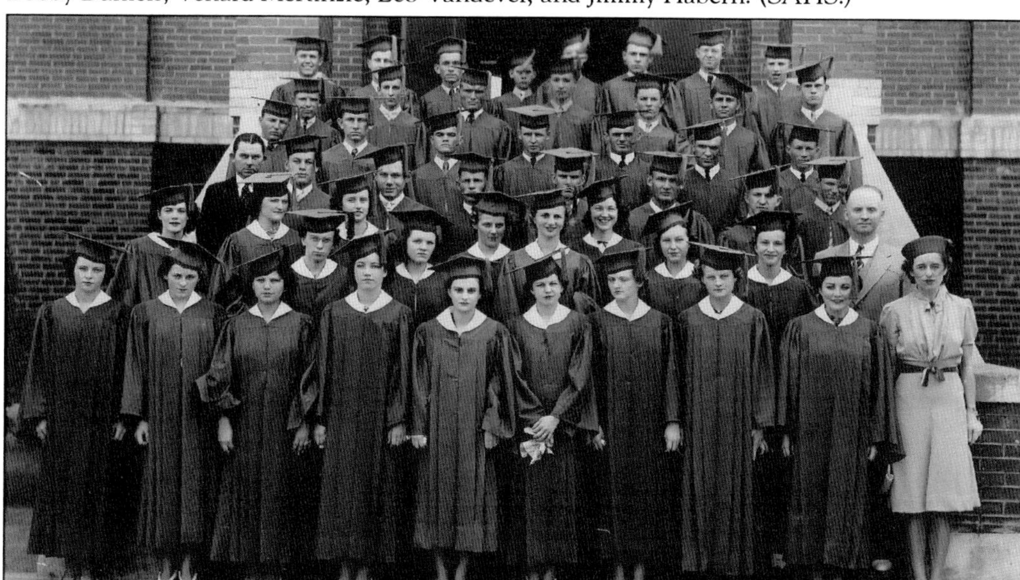

SENIOR CLASS, 1938. The classmates above, identified by last names only, are, from left to right, (first row) Greene, Ramsey, Davila, Michael, Forrest, Nance, Leftwich, McWilliams, Rue, and co-sponsor Bush; (second row) Herd, Harris, Ary, Selzer, Horst, Gober, Bryant, Guyer, King, Lewter, and Superintendent Harris; (third row) room sponsor Lamb, Beeman, Burroughs, Dickens, Robinson, Boydstun, Toon, and Ausband; (fourth row) Landers, Williams, Wagoner, Smith, Selzer, Harris, and Melton; (fifth row) Kline, Wilson, Holder, Brown, Willis, Burkholder, and Brown; (sixth row) Schmitz, Gadberry, Hassenpflug, Hollingsworth, Hughes, Lewis, Anderson, and McNeill. (SAHS.)

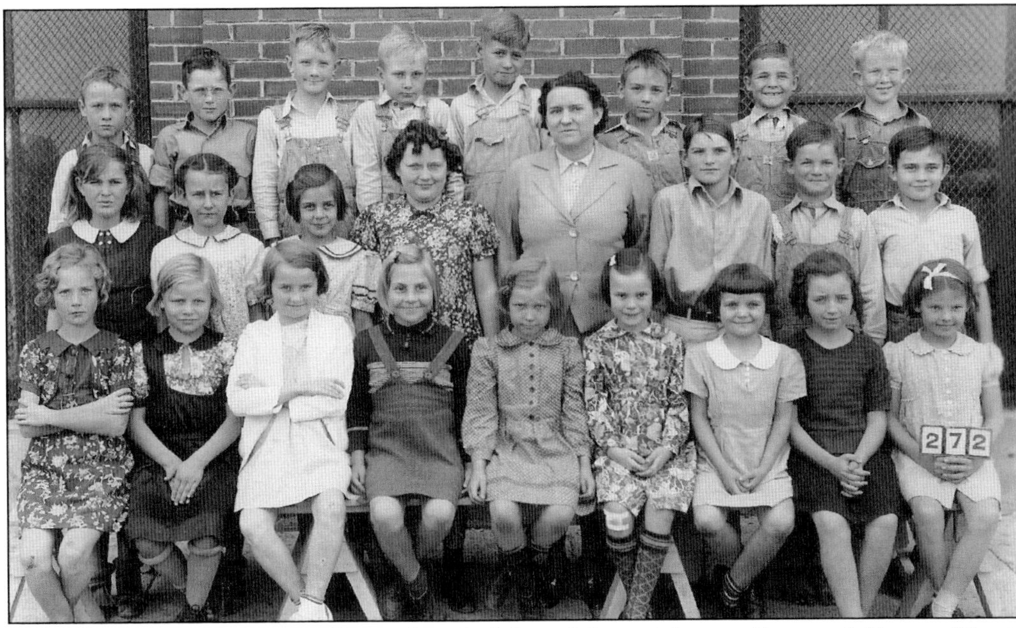

THIRD GRADE, 1938–1939. Those identified from left to right are (first row) Yvonne Harris, Mickie Lewis, Jeannine Wylie, Anna Mae Scott, Dorothy Hix, LaVerne Brown, and Twilla Woods; (second row) Opal Elrod, Mary Kathrine Carr, Patsy Ward, teacher Winnie Minick, and Bobby Strickland; (third row) Dale Cole, LeRoy Kirby, Billy Roy Baker, Jimmy Belcher, John Doyle, and Tom Hood. (SAHS.)

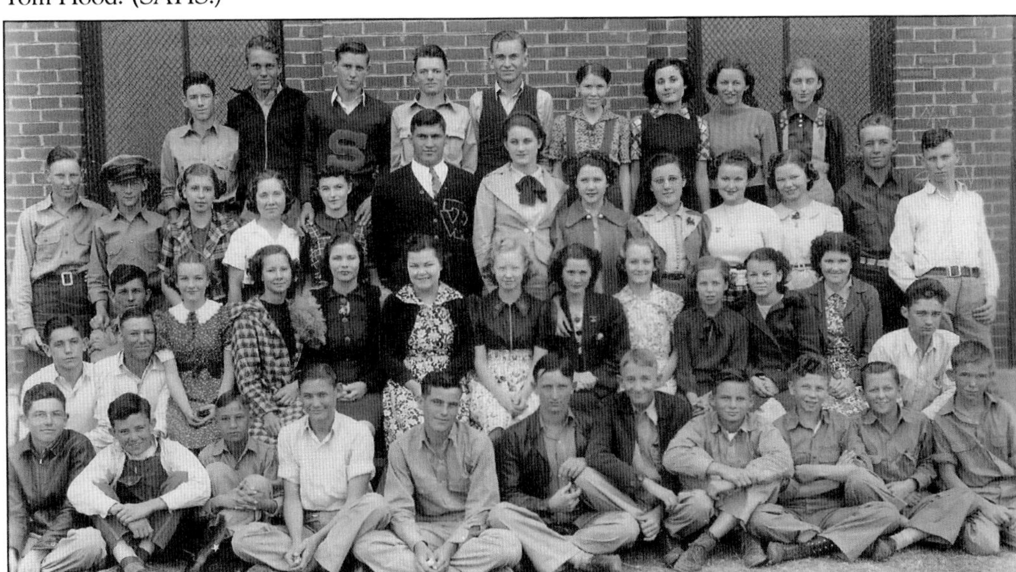

SOPHOMORES, 1938–1939. The last names of the students in this class are Amyx, Anderson, Appleton, Ausband, Barton, Batis, Bilbrey, Bishop, Brown, Christian, Cook, Davis, Dickens, Frizelle, Gentle, Harris, Harvey, Hood, Howerton, Jones, Kelly, King, Lancaster, Lanier, McAfee, McKinney, McReynolds, Melton, Mundy, Newland, Pate, Reynolds, Scheu, Seely, Tarver, Thompson, Toon, Vaughan, Waide, Winfred, and Yarbrough. Also pictured is their sponsor, Coach Randolph, wearing a tie. (SAHS.)

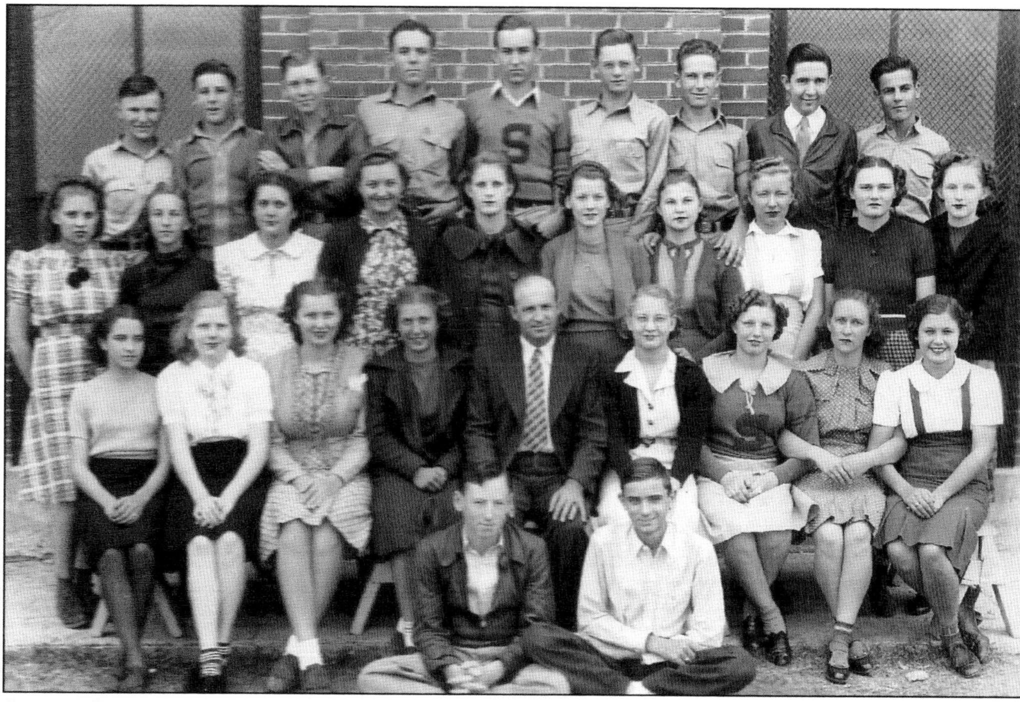

Senior Class, 1939. Pictured above, identified only by their last names, are, from left to right, (first row) Anderson and Anderson; (second row) Sullivan, Gheen, Ary, Simpson, teacher Mr. Brooks, Carruthers, Brandburger, Wilson, and Winstead; (third row) LeGear, Seely, Vandever, Simpson, Brown, Pate, Harberson, Landers, McCraw, and Hood; (fourth row) Terry, Enlow, Gilbert, Beck, Wheeler, Hollingsworth, Kelly, Chambers, and Teel. (Courtesy of Bill Mundy.)

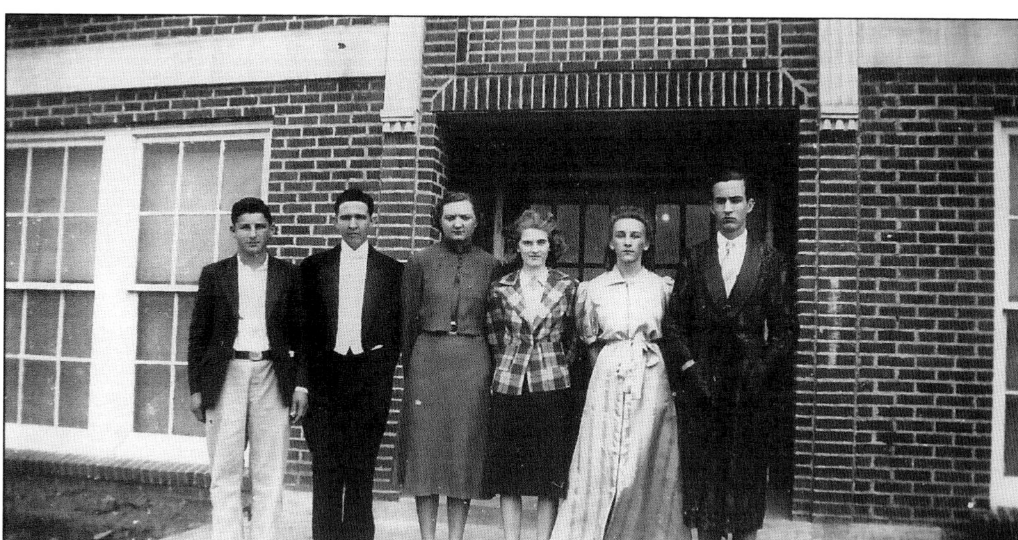

University Interscholastic League (UIL) Play, 1939. A one-act play garnered first place for the Sanger High School drama team at the UIL competition held at Denton High School in 1939. Students participating at the competition seen here are manager Billy Enlow, Johnny Chambers, Beatrice Simpson, speech teacher Lucy Tribble, Helen Seely, and Sonny Wheeler. (SAHS.)

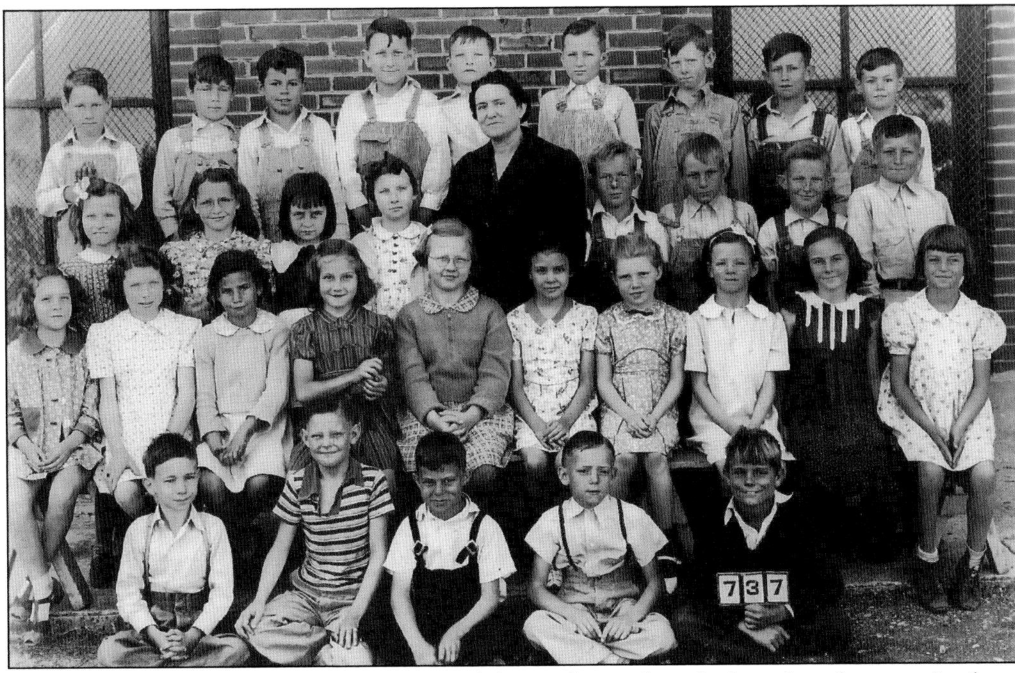

THIRD GRADE, 1939–1940. Last names of the students identified in this class are Anthony, Appleton, Ary, Bowery, Brewer, Cherry, Echols, Enlow, George, Goin, Higgs, Hood, Howard, Kirby, Masten, Rice, Stinson, Tarver, Thomas, Toon, Vaughan, Windle, and Wolfenbarger. Their teacher was Winnie Minick. Many of this class graduated from high school in 1948. (SAHS.)

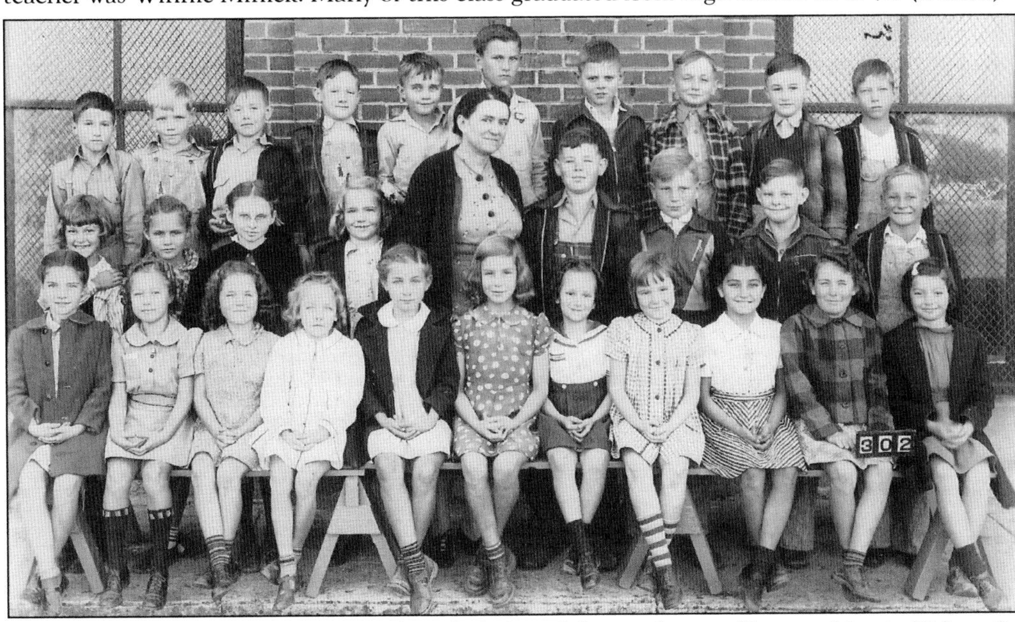

THIRD GRADE, 1940–1941. Those identified, from left to right, are (first row) Jessie Bishop, Joy Rippey, Oma Pennington, Mary George, Clariece Willis, Betty Hood, ? Winstead, Patsy Rector, and Dorothy Jones; (second row) Nelzine Lynch, Bobbie Lewter, teacher Winnie Minick, Albert Hammons, Sid George, and Teddy Wolfenbarger; (third row) Billy Ed Long, Bobby Jim Kline, Tommy Green, Johnny Strickland, Frank Willis, Sammy Spratt, and Troy Miller. (SAHS.)

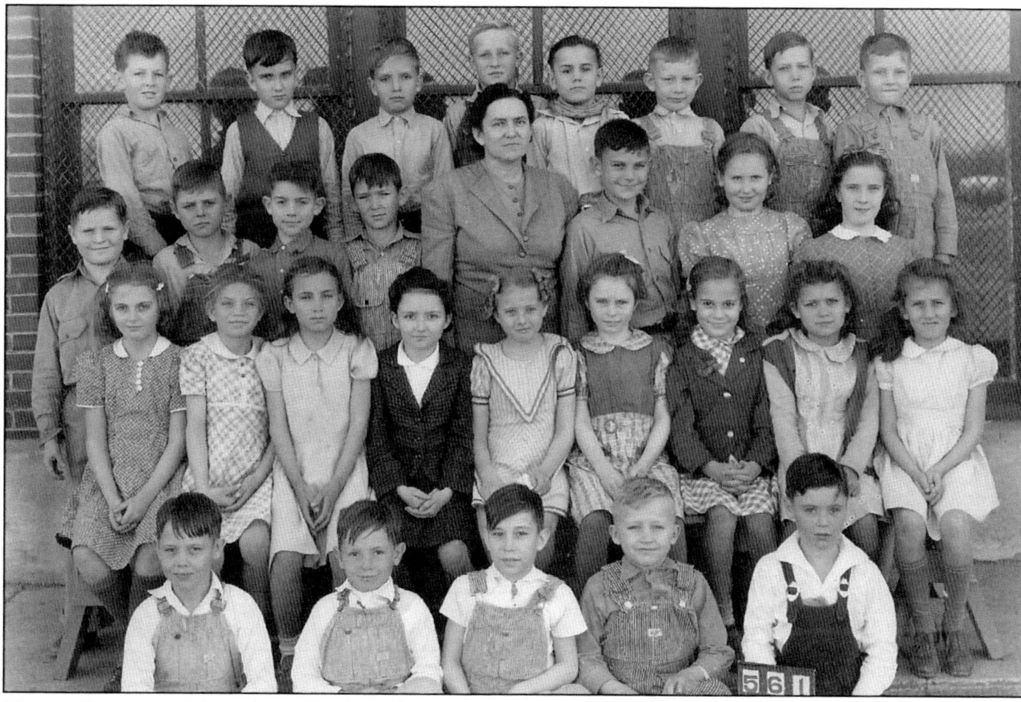

THIRD GRADE, 1941–1942. In this class portrait are, from left to right, (first row) Bobby Lynch, Robert Cashion, Rodney Hobbs, Freddie Harvey, and Young Powell; (second row) Wanda Sullivan, Mary Dennison, Lucille Pennington, Marion Coffey, Oleta Davis, Gladys Cockrell, Patsy Stricklin, Carlene Anthony, and Patsy Sullivan; (third row) Fitzhugh Talbot, George Lynch, Waide Herd, teacher Winnie Minick, Frank Willis, Patsy Ashcraft, and Martha Enis; (fourth row) Homer Cooke, Philip Saltsman, Gene Hollingsworth, Robert Windle, and James Reed. (SAHS.)

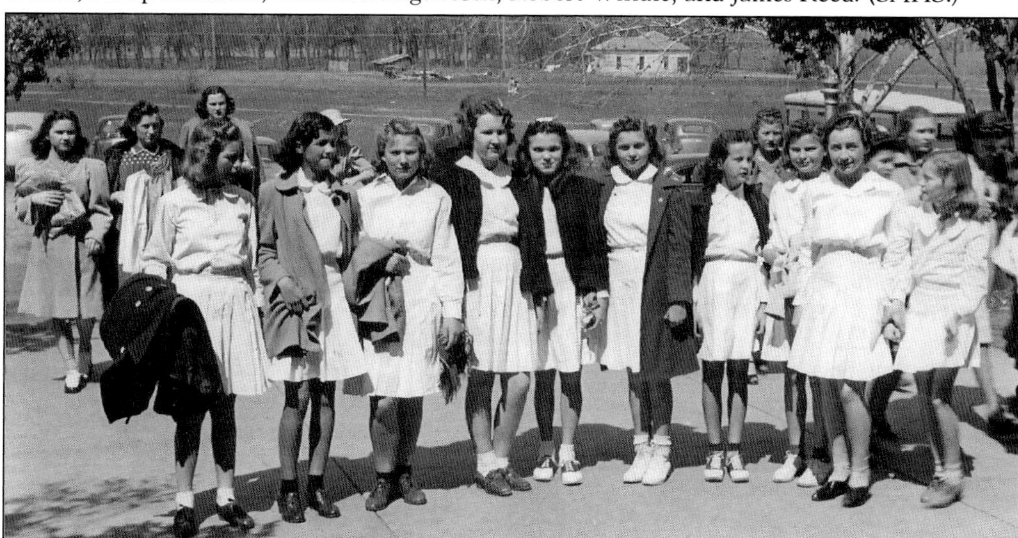

HIGH SCHOOL GIRLS, 1942. From left to right are (first row) unidentified, Nelda Jo Long, Alma Jean Giles, Peggy Vaughan, Japaline Brewer, Minnie Belle Hicks, Carmen Teel, Rachel Toon, LaVerne Brown, and Mona Ruth Quisenberry; (second row) Sally Ann Gentle, Mildred Willis, and four unidentified. Parked cars can be seen in the background. (SAHS.)

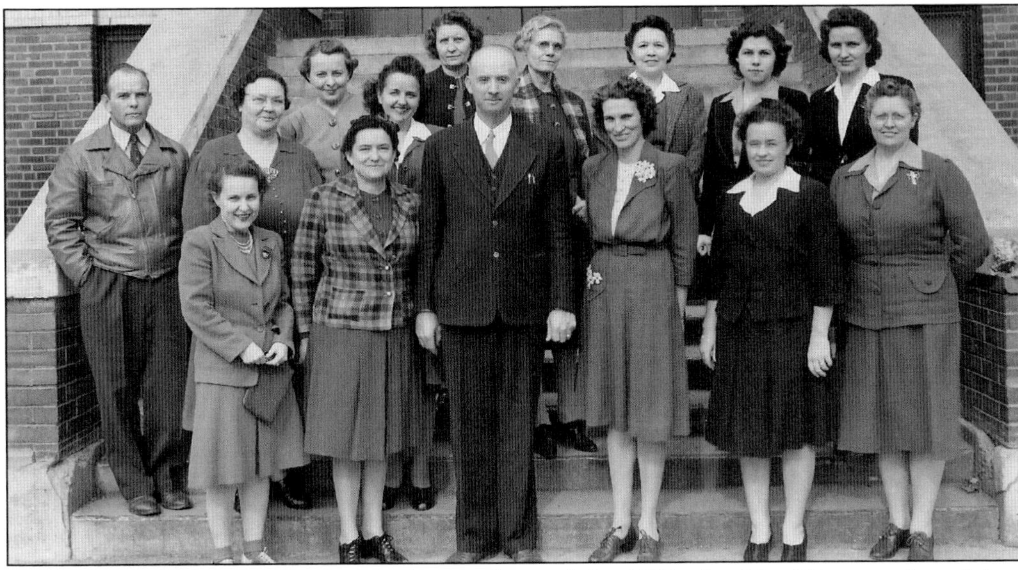

School Faculty, 1943–1944. Standing in front of the 1917 school building are, from left to right, (first row) Louise (Toon) Stinson, Winnie (Mallow) Minick, H.O. Harris, Cathlene Gentle, Hestaline Burroughs, and Virgie George Heffley; (second row) Dale Davis, Callie Miller, and Lorena Simms; (third row) Eunice (Sullivan) Gray, Marguerite (McDaniel) Riggs, Neppie (Bishop) Burroughs, Mary Lou Wright, unidentified, and Alyne Seal. (SAHS.)

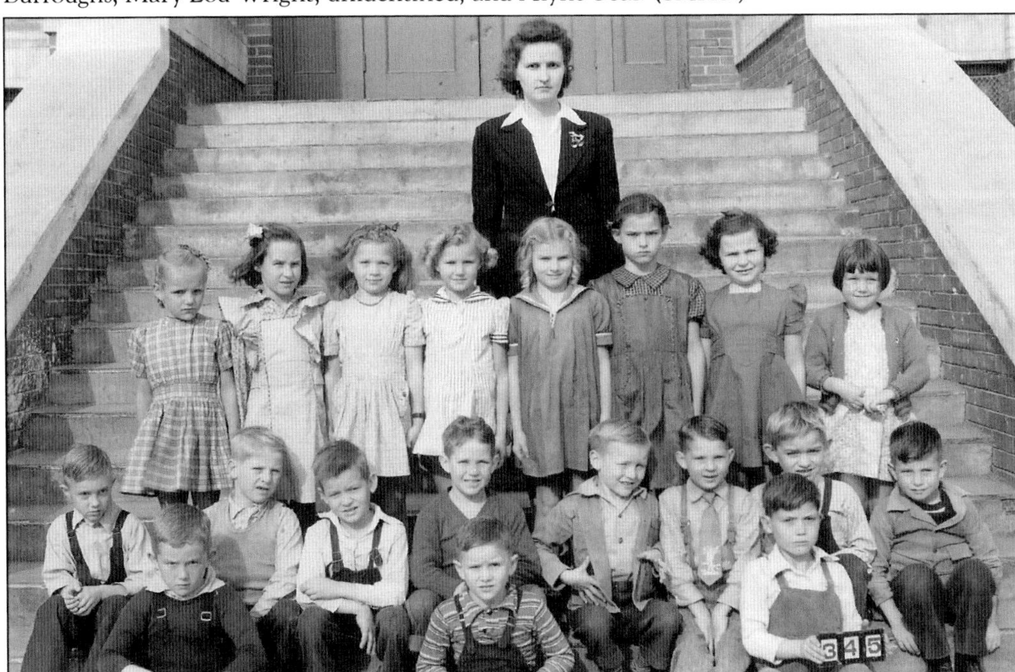

First Grade, 1943–1944. Students from left to right are (first row) Billy Ed Nance, Gene Skipworth, and Billy Bishop; (second row) unidentified, Neal Odom, Lloyd George, Richard Patton, unidentified, Wylie Vaughn, William Saltsman, and unidentified; (third row) Jo Dean Lynch, Gladys Vaughan, Margaret George, JoAnn Priddy, Doris Pennington, Nellie Lynch, Gayla Ann Garrison, and Charlene Hammons. The teacher, Alyne Seal, stands in the back. (SAHS.)

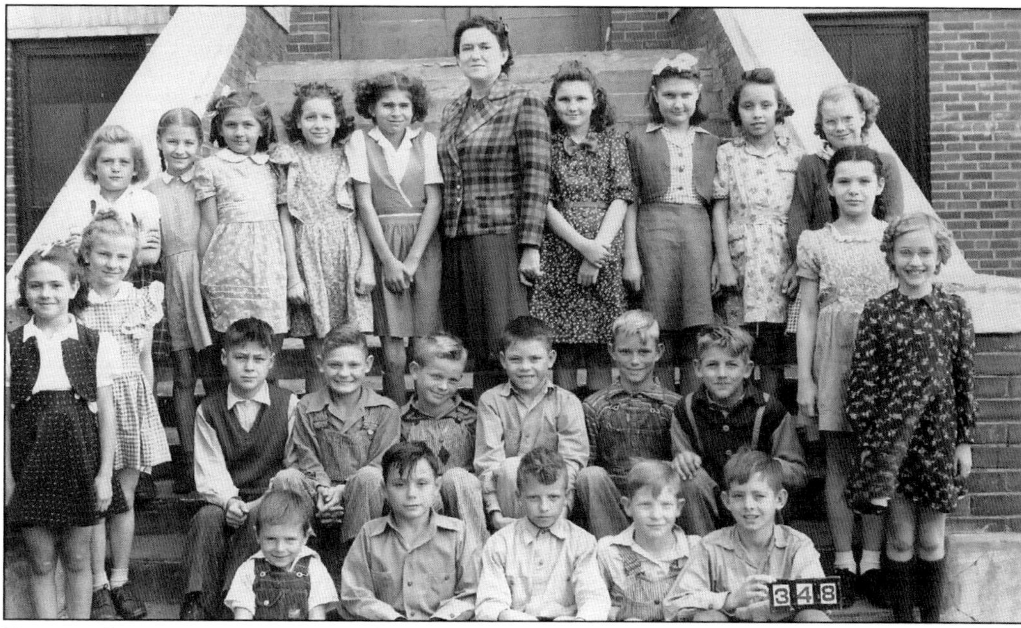

Fourth Grade, 1943–1944. Students identified from left to right are (first row) Alton Lynch, Robert Cudd, and J.B. Howard; (second row) ? Denison, and ? Bishop; (third row) Betty Sue Switzer, Willene Rippey, Anna Frances Hinzman, Mildred Pennington, teacher Winnie Minick, Betty Temple, Jeannie McFarlin, and Betty Burks. (SAHS.)

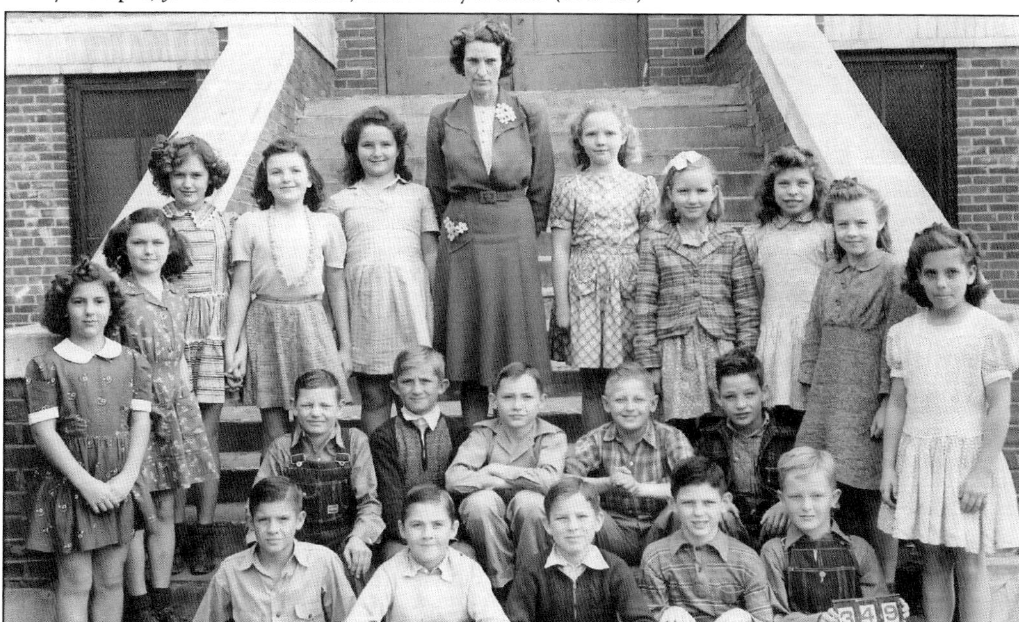

Fifth Grade, 1943–1944. From left to right are (first row) Dean Jones, Earl Pierce, Billy Ezell, Gail Christopher, and J.A. Maughan; (second row) Roy Wayne Harper, Harold Kirby, Walter Warschun, Billy John Golliday, and Martin Cole; (third row) Peggy Ready, Peggy Mosley, Jerriann Cooper, Wanda Bryant, Betty Cearley, teacher Cathlene Gentle, Doreen Kline, Alta Saltsman, Peggy Turpin, Opal Johnson, and Bobbie Jo King. (SAHS.)

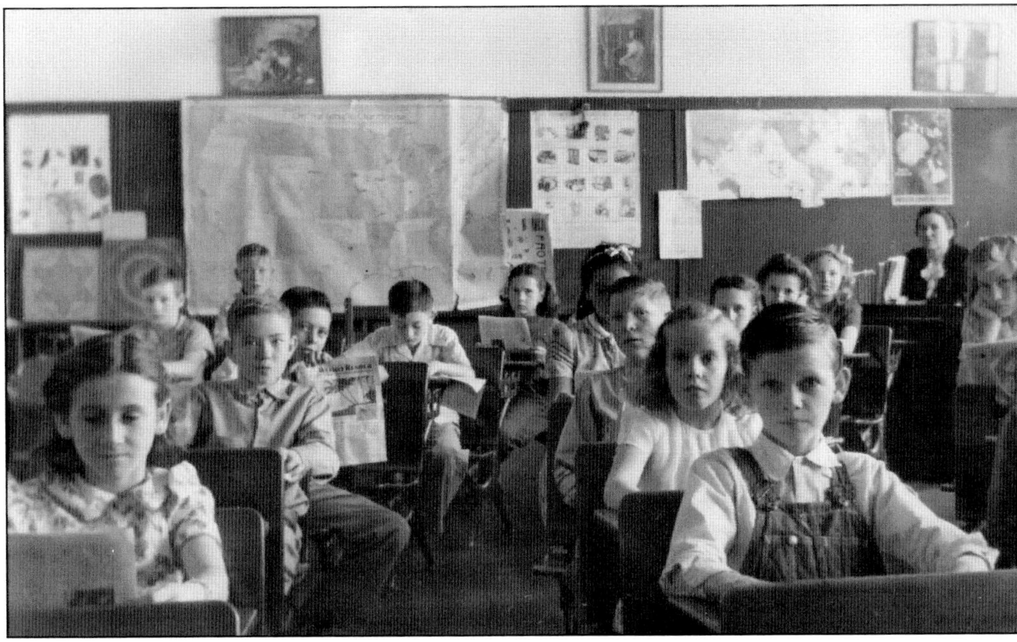

FOURTH GRADE, 1944–1945. Students who have been identified above include, from left to right, (first row) Betty Jo Kirby; (third row) Red Howard; (fourth row) Virgie Mary Reed; (fifth row) Elaine Baker and Elizabeth Belcher; (sixth row) Betty Britt; (seventh row) Alice Sullivan. Below, are, from left to right, (first row) Carrol Moore and Robert Cudd; (second row) LaWanda Christian, Charles Warfield, and Bobby Mosley; (third row) Jackie Nell Odom and Billy George Draper; (fourth row) Greta Gene Hughes and Donna Bess Harwell. Their teacher, Winnie Minick, is seated at her desk. Notice the chalkboards lining the wall and maps hanging above them. The students are enjoying their *Weekly Reader*, an age-appropriate newspaper for students. (SAHS.)

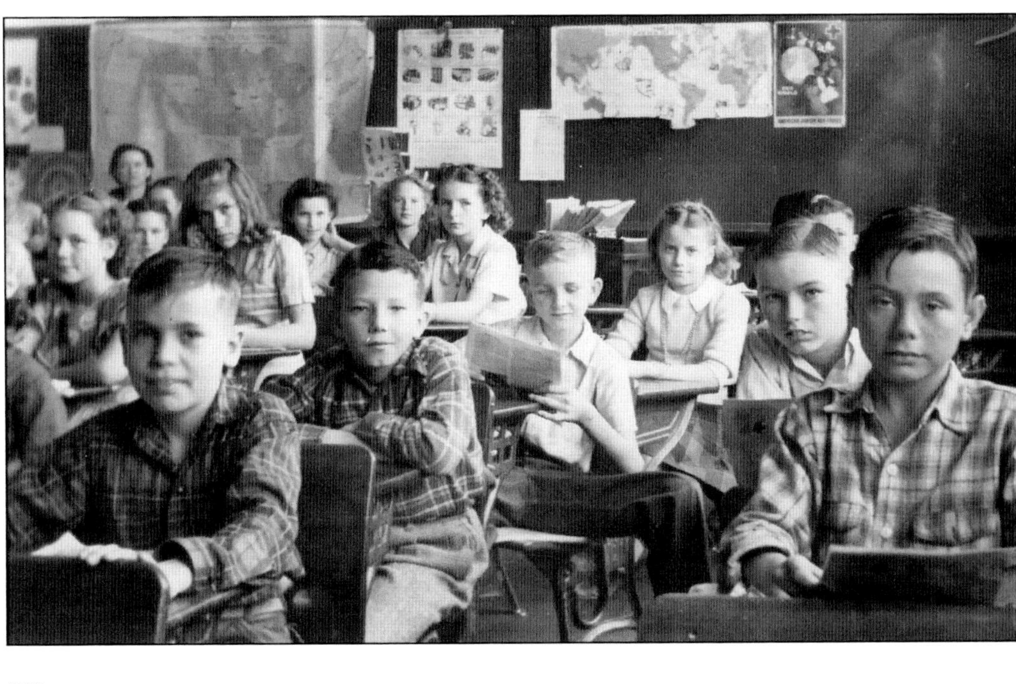

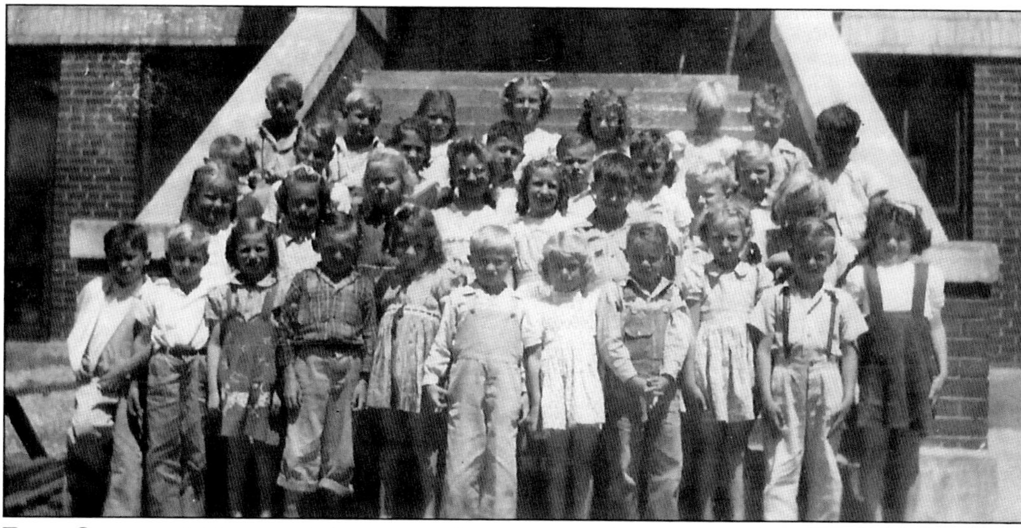

First Grade, 1945–1946. Those identified are, from left to right, (first row) Grady Bishop, Yvonne Yeatts, Bobby Ramsey, Billy Burroughs, Betty Lou Burns, Marquieta Prater, and Tivy Lewis; (second row) JoAnn Dyer, Rosene Amyx, and Elizabeth Gillum; (third row) Johnny Charles Odom, Verdie Horst, Charles Weeks, and Nelda Chisam; (fourth row) Bobby George, Billy George, Ann Morris, Barbara Landers, Clara Pennington, and George Morris. Their teacher was Alyne Seal. (SAHS.)

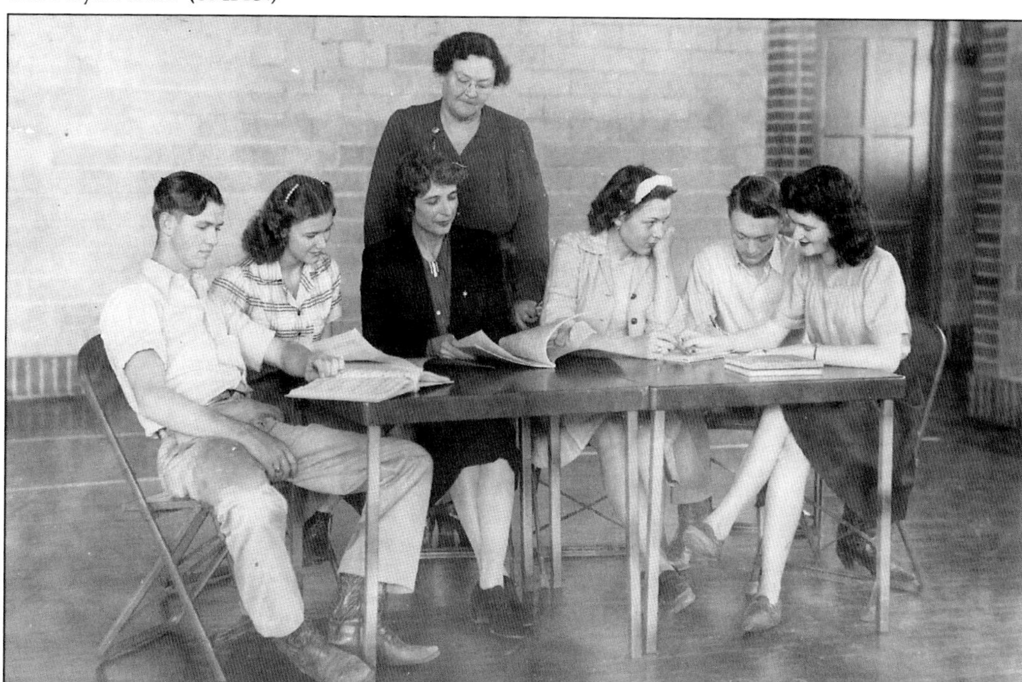

Annual Staff, 1946. Working on the yearbook *The Sanger Indians* were, from left to right, Burns Ashley, Betty Jo King, sponsors Hilda Cunningham and Callie Miller, Dee Schertz, Billy Doyle, and Anne Acker. The book included pictures of first- through twelfth-grade students. This was the first annual published after World War II. Printing of annuals had been suspended during the war years. (Courtesy of Haleigh CeBallos and Betty (Marshall) Wylie.)

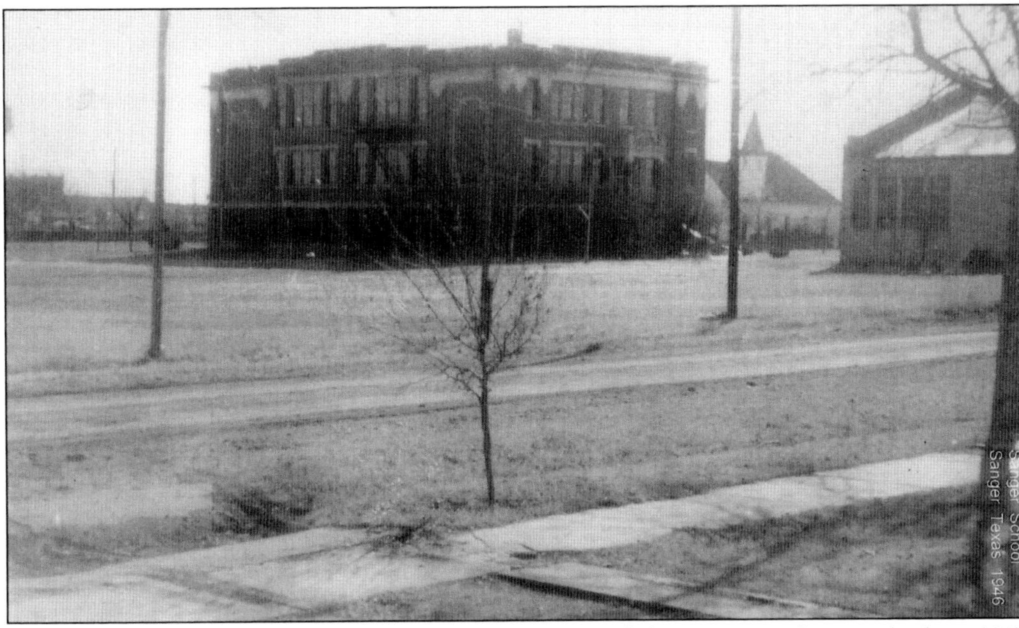

REAR VIEW OF SCHOOL, 1946. Looking southeast toward the structure that was built in 1917, the separate gymnasium can be seen on the right, and near the center is the Landmark Baptist Church, which was across the street. To the left, the downtown business district is visible with the water tower in the far background. The football field was located behind this school building. (Courtesy of Oscar Shelton.)

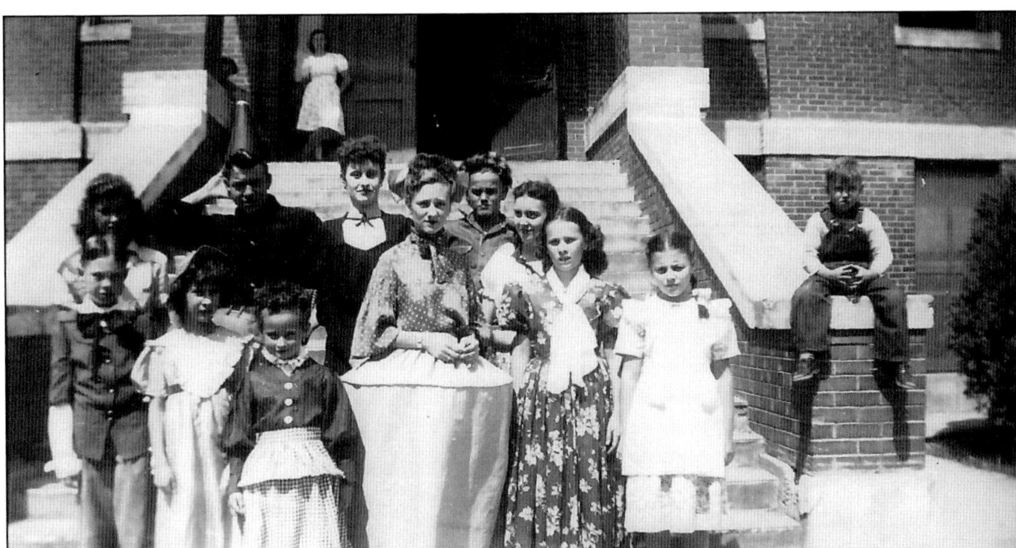

FLOAT RIDERS, 1946. Denton County was created from Fannin County in 1846. Sanger sponsored a float 100 years later depicting a one-room pioneer school in a Denton parade. Participating students, from left to right, are (first row) Verdie Horst, Nancy Campbell, Clariece Willis, Elaine Baker, and Karla Crawford; (second row) Buddy Wright and LaVerne Masten; (third row) Jeannine Wylie, Weldon Fellers, "teacher" Merle Ary, and Gene Hollingsworth. (Courtesy of Nancy (Campbell) Smith.)

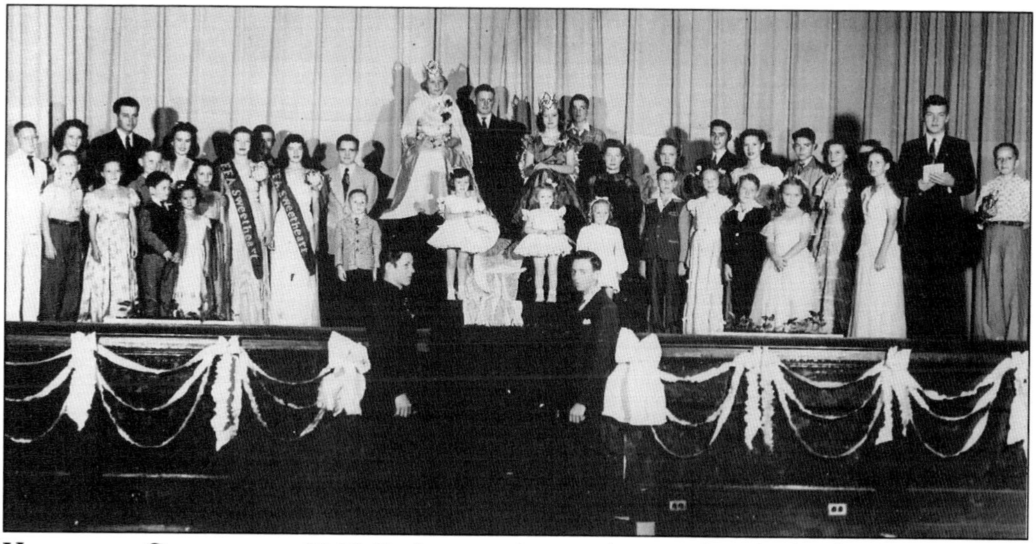

Halloween Coronation, 1946. Each year, a king and queen from high school and a prince and princess from elementary school were chosen for this event. Each grade was represented by a boy and girl in the formal affair. Other students also participated. The coronation was held in the gymnasium until it burned in 1948. The next year, it was held in the city park. (Courtesy of Jerriann (Cooper) Shepard.)

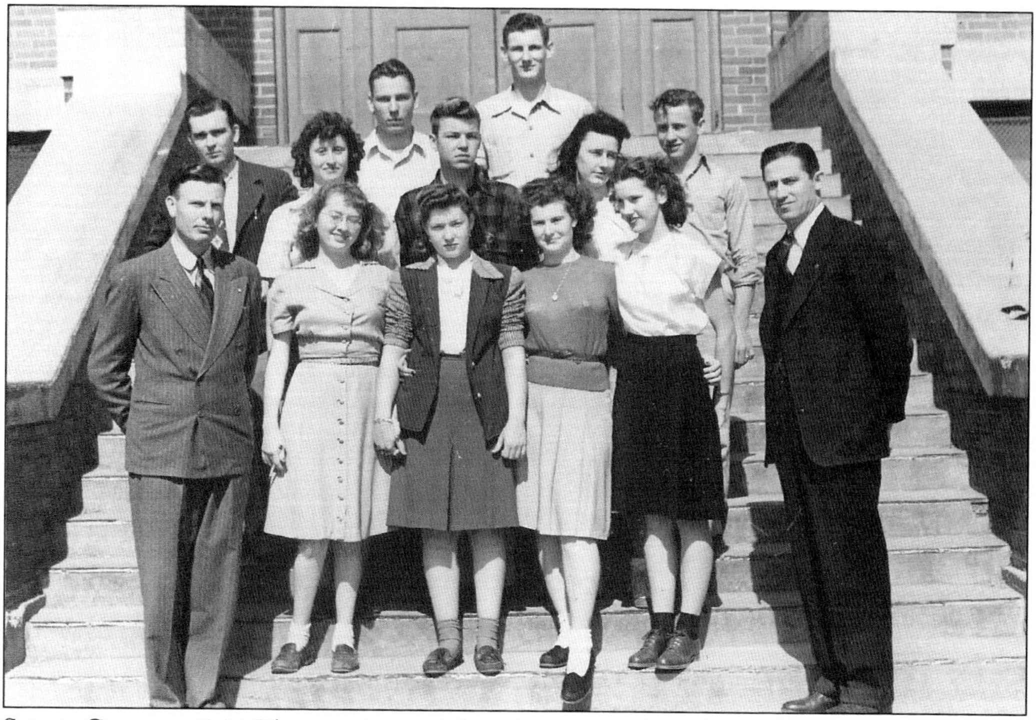

Senior Class of 1947. These seniors and three faculty members, from left to right, are (first row) sponsor E.C. McMurray, Yvonne Harris, Jeannine Wylie, Juanita Hammons, Betty Marshall, and superintendent C.D. Allen; (second row) coach Nash Keel, Merle Ary, Weldon Fellers, Opal Elrod, and Dale Cole; (third row) Benny Belz, and Bobby Joe Willis. (Courtesy of Haleigh CeBallos and Betty (Marshall) Wylie.)

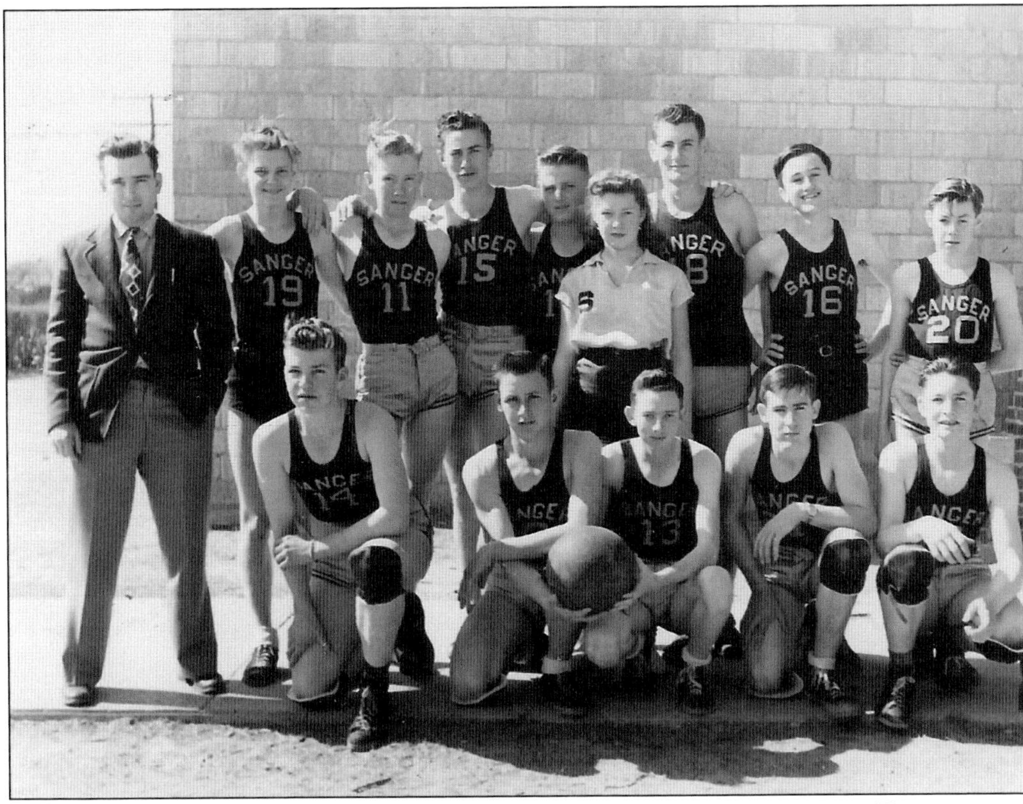

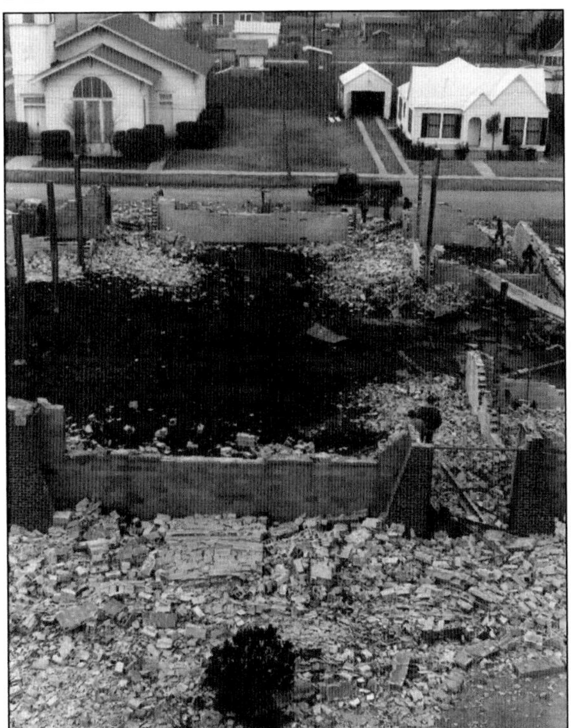

Basketball Boys, 1947. Teammates of this Sanger High basketball team, from left to right, are (first row) Weldon Fellers, J.D. Jones, Junior Davis, W.H. Hammons, and Nick Cherry; (second row) coach Nash Keel, Teddy Joe Wolfenbarger, G.W. Crunk, Marvin Priddy, J.R. Lovell, Bobby Joe Willis, Troy Miller, and Bruce Anthony. Basketball queen Jeannine Wylie is in the center. (Courtesy of Haleigh CeBallos and Betty (Marshall) Wylie.)

Sanger Gymnasium, 1948. Construction of the school gymnasium was started in late 1935 using Works Progress Administration funds. It was separate from the main building. The gymnasium, which also featured a stage, was used for many school activities until it burned in January 1948. The loss was estimated at $60,000. A new gymnasium and stage were in the upper story of the renovated school building that opened in the fall. (SAHS.)

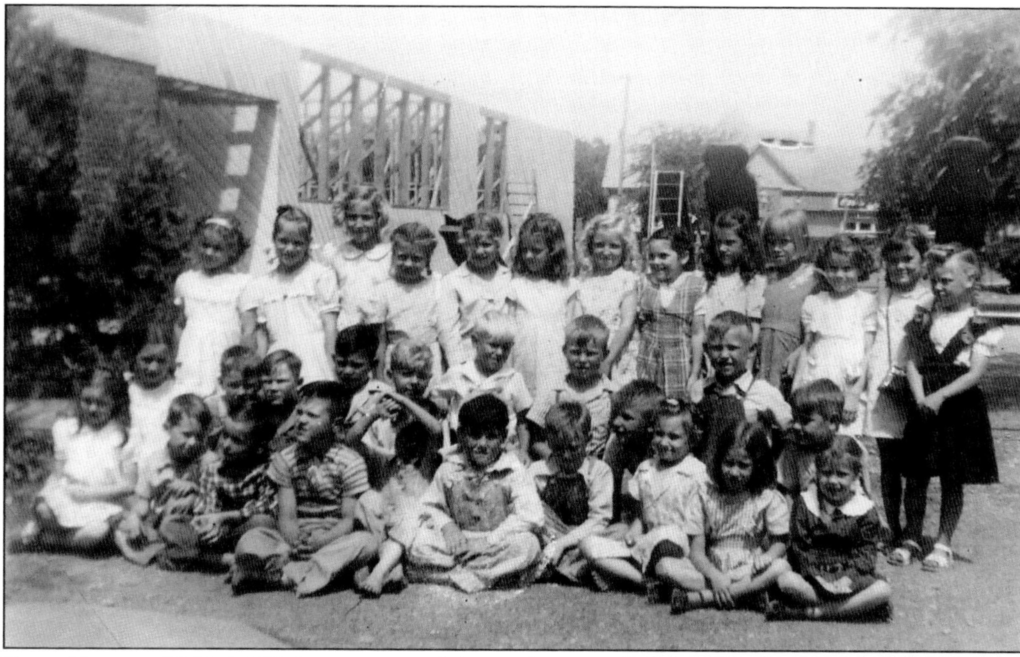

First Grade, 1947–1948. Last names of the students in this class are Amyx, Anthony, Blevins, Carter, Coffey, Coy, Elliot, Enlow, Galbreath, George, Goin, Harberson, Harvey, Howard, Landers, Lynch, Massengale, Mays, Murrell, Ramsey, Reed, Saltsman, Schertz, Scott, Springer, Sullivan, Vaughan, Wade, and Yeatts. Notice the construction on the east wing of the school building in the background. Across the street is Fellers' Cafe. (SAHS.)

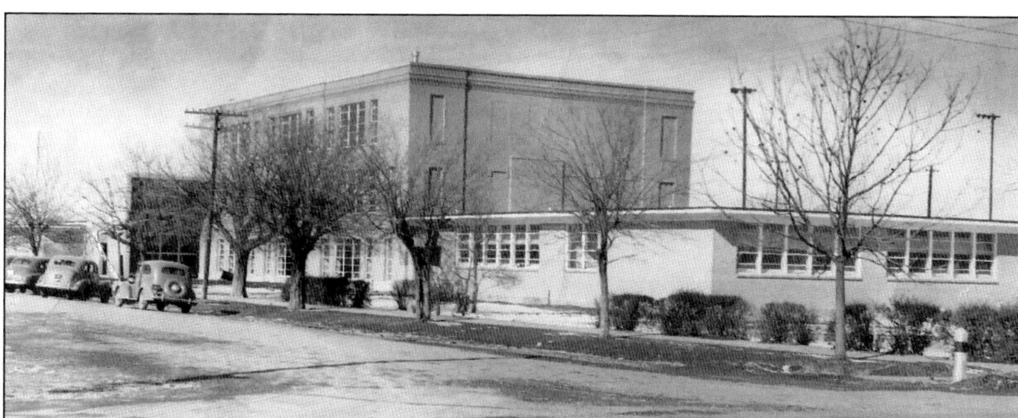

Sanger School Building, 1948. For many years, there was only one school building at a time in Sanger that housed all grades. This picture is of the renovated building, which was ready in the fall of 1948. Extensions had been added to both ends of the existing building to meet the demands of a growing population. The school administration office is all that remains of this structure. (SAHS)

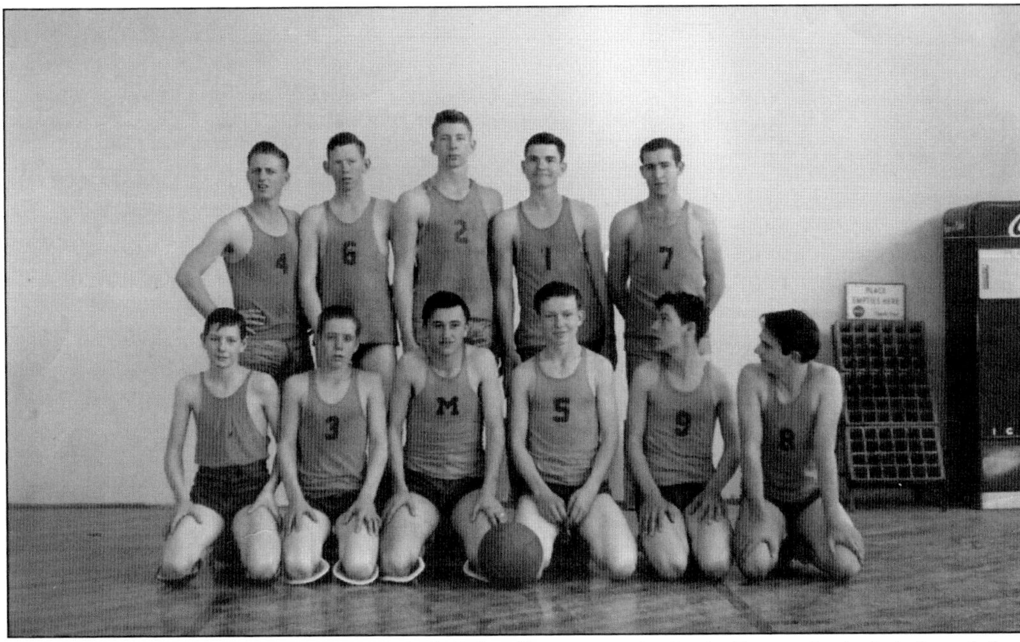

DISTRICT CHAMPIONS, 1949. Sanger High School's winning basketball team included, from left to right, (first row) Roy Wayne Harper, Bobby Jim Kline, Troy Miller, Robert Windle, Martin Cole, and Thomas Amyx; (second row) J.R. Lovell, Billy Jack Higgs, Melvin Chapman, Jerry Lovell, and W.H. Hammons. (Courtesy of Robert Windle.)

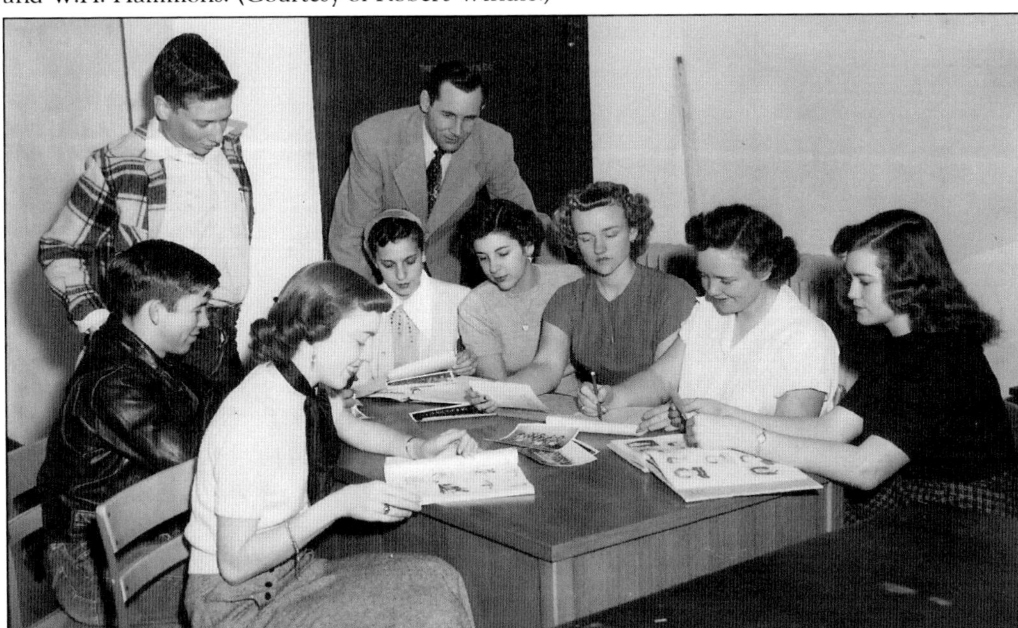

ANNUAL STAFF, 1951. In the image above, from left to right, Claudette Sullivan (business manager), Billy Ezell (sports editor), Bobby Waide (assistant editor), Jim Kearns (sponsor), Bobbie Jo King (sports editor), Peggy Ready (advertising manager), Betty Sullivan (editor in chief), Doreen Kline (snapshot editor), and Jerriann Cooper (art editor) are working on the *Prairie Smoke*. (Courtesy of Jerriann (Cooper) Shepherd.)

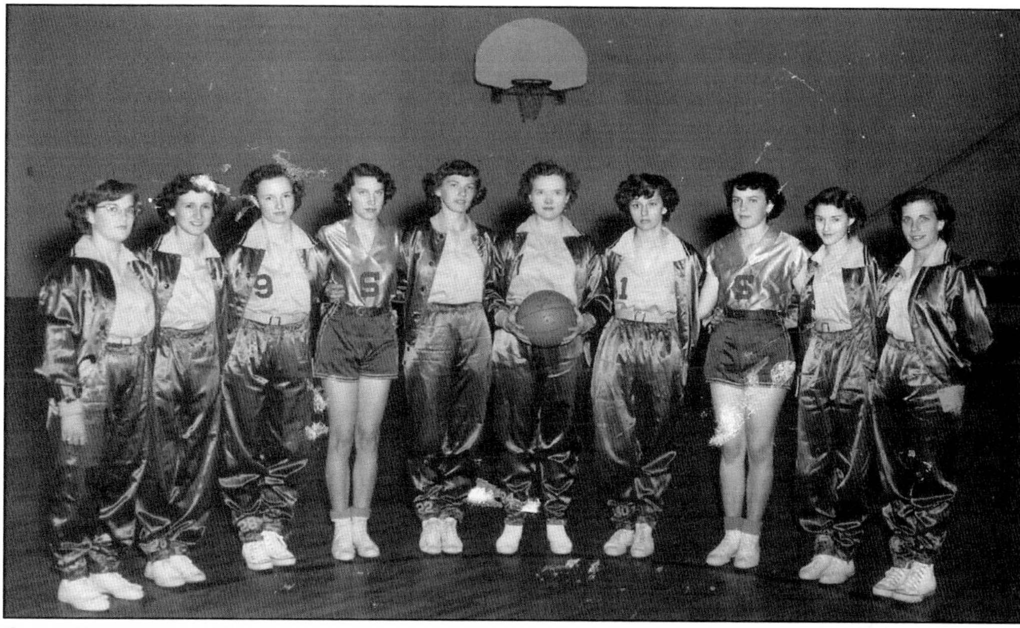

Girls Basketball Team, 1950–1951. This basketball team won all of its games. From left to right are Willene Rippey, Betty Jo Kirby, Emillee Horst, Sarah Horst, Anna Frances Hinzman, Doreen Kline, Alta Mae Holder, Shirley Moseley, Geneva Davis, and Bobbie Jo (King) Oden. Their scorekeeper was Claudette Sullivan. Girls' basketball was played with forwards on one end of the court and guards on the other, each with their opposing team's players. (SAHS.)

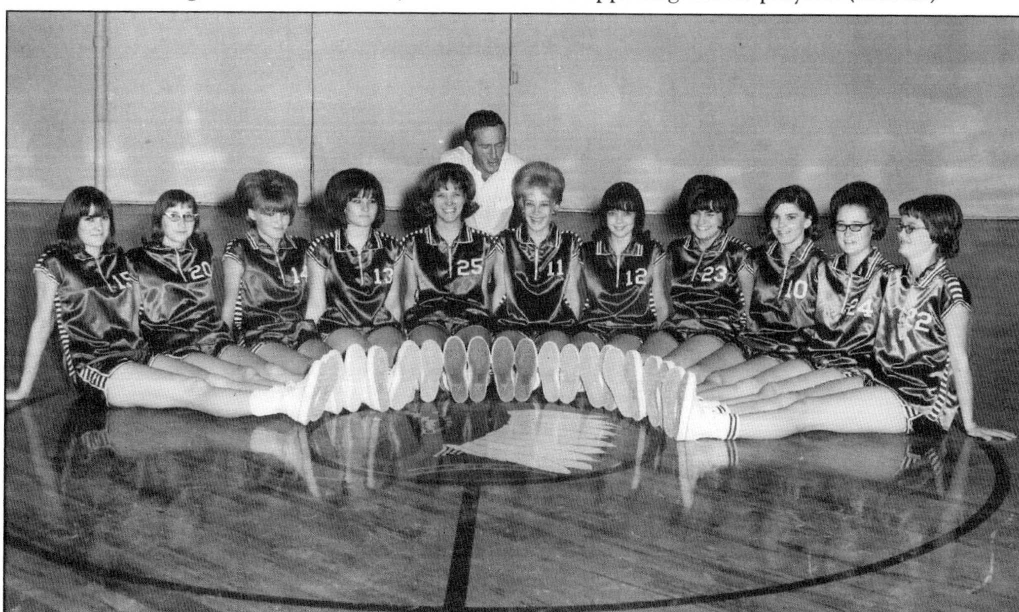

Sanger High Girls' Basketball Team, 1965–1966. This photograph, taken in the high school second floor gymnasium, includes the girls' basketball team members, from left to right, Melinda LeGear, Beverly Romines, Kathy Howard, Carolyn Harberson, Myrl Yeary, coach Billy Ed Nance, Teresa Klein, Beverly McReynolds, Linda Harvey, Tona Batis, Ann Williams, and Brenda Holder. (Courtesy of Myrl (Yeary) Webb.)

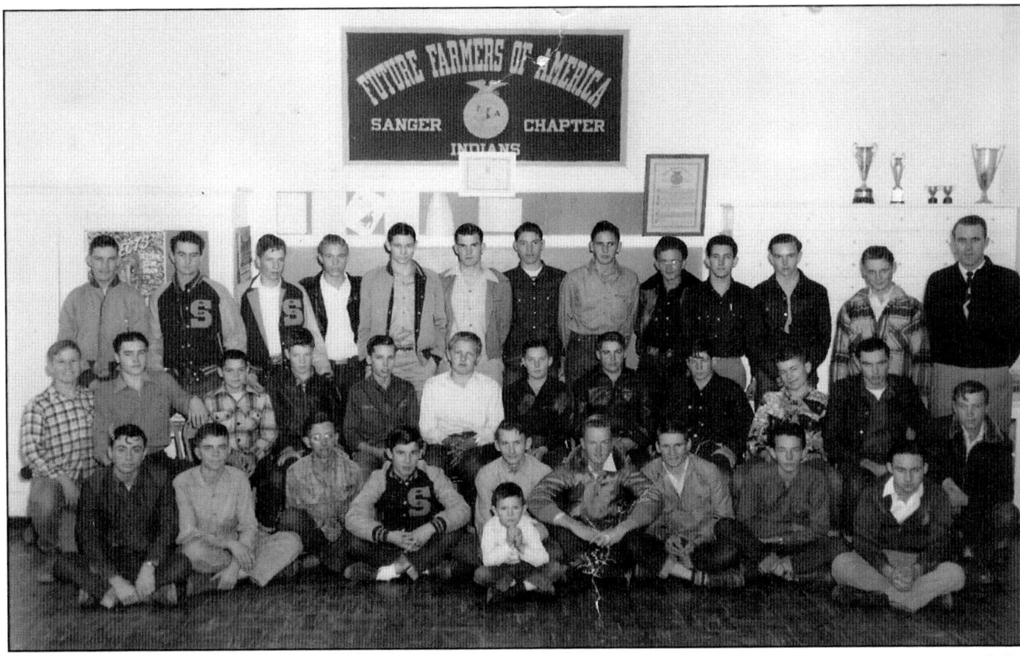

Future Farmers of America, 1950–1951. Most of the high school boys were members of the Future Farmers of America and also took agriculture taught by Will Curtis (back row, far right). The officers were, from left to right, (first row) Billy Ezell (reporter), Jimmy Cole (third vice president), and Charles Lambert (vice president); (second row) Arlon Scoggins (parliamentarian) and Carrol Moore (secretary); (third row) Martin Cole (second vice president), Thomas Amyx (sentinel), Bobby Waide (president), Roy Wayne Harper (song leader), and Jerry Lovell (treasurer). (SAHS.)

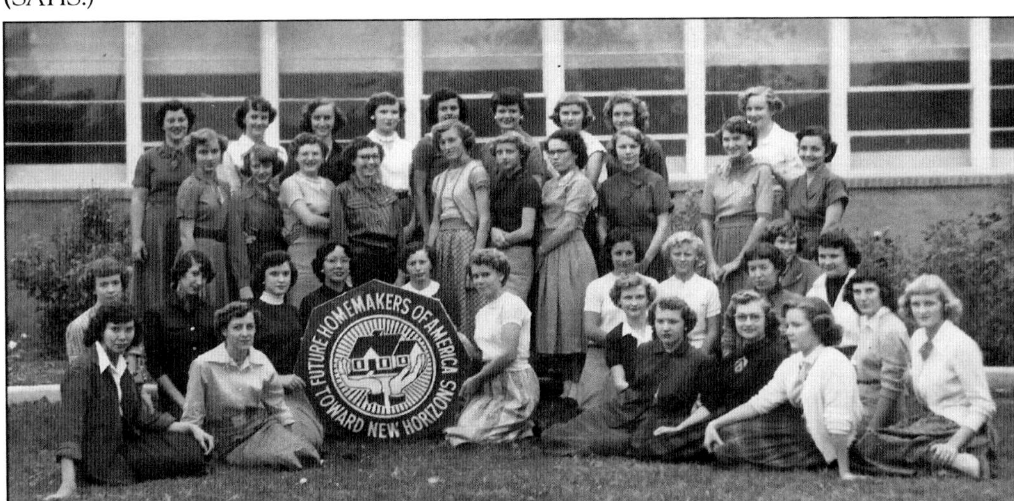

Future Homemakers of America, 1953–1954. Corresponding to the boys' activities, most high school girls were members of Future Homemakers of America and took the homemaking class taught by Mary Nichols (third row, far right). This year's officers were, from left to right, (first row) Mary Jo Golliday and Jane Crider; (second row) Mary Cooke and Ruth Tumlison; (third row) Doris Pennington and Connie Voss; (fourth row) Virginia Anderson, Bunny Thomas, and Maribelle Ward. (SAHS.)

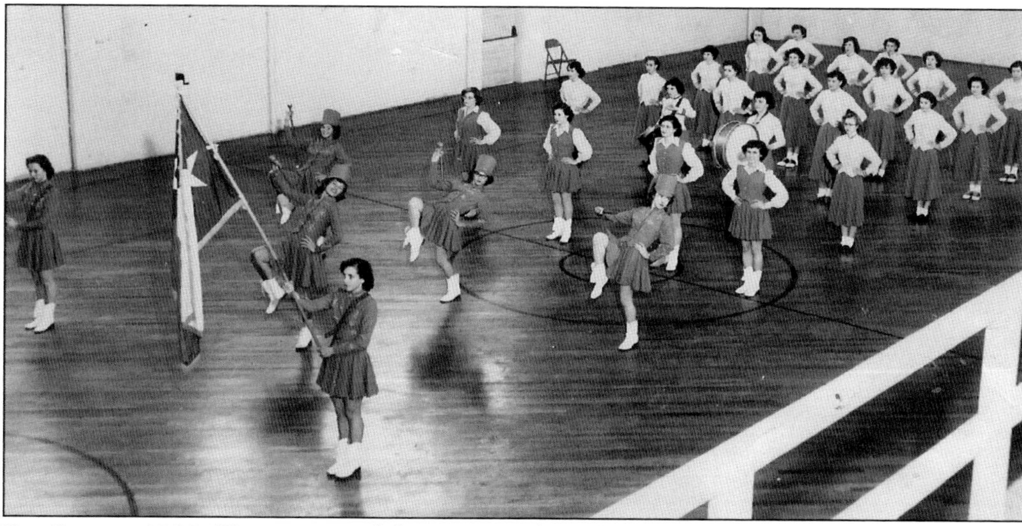

Pep Squad, 1950. This picture of the pep squad on the basketball court was taken from the bleachers in the gymnasium. From left to right are (first row) flagbearers Emillee Horst and Bobbie Jo (King) Oden; (second row) head majorette Anna Hinzman; (third row) majorettes Betty Sue Switzer, Claudette Sullivan, and Elaine Baker; (fourth row) cheerleaders Willene Rippey, Betty Jo Kirby, Peggy Mosley, and Ethelyn Ready. (SAHS.)

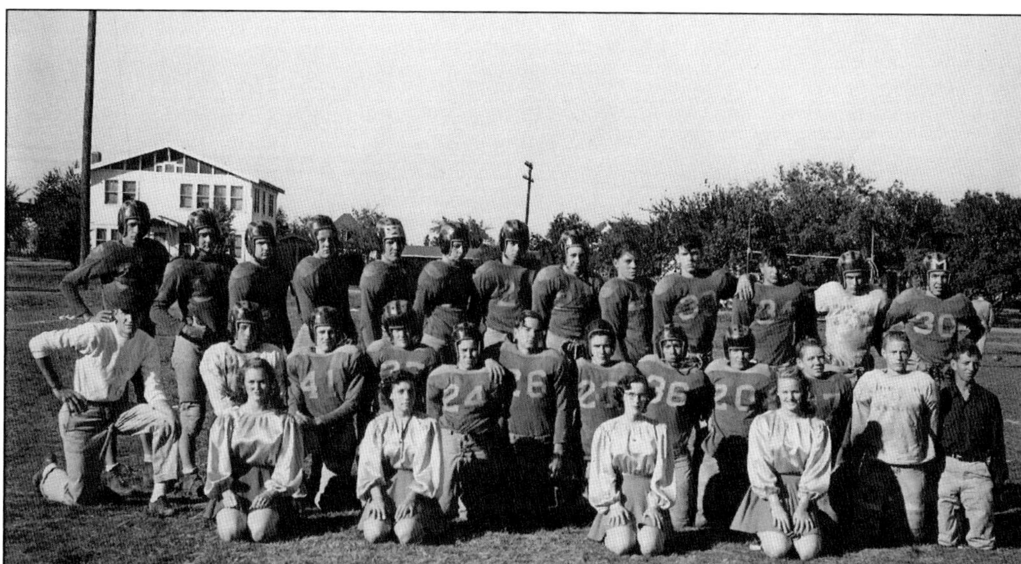

Cheerleaders and Football Team, 1949. The cheerleaders, from left to right, are Jerriann Cooper, Bobbie King, Martha Enis, and Dorothy Stanford. The last names of football players are, from left to right, (first row) Warfield, Harvey, Maughan, Ezell, Pace, Reed, Draper, Kline, Stanford, and manager Phillips with coach Ken Kearns on the far left; (second row) Wicker, Amyx, Davis, Windle, Cole, Harper, Herd, Warschun, Bishop, Cobler, Curtsinger, Moseley, and Marshall. (SAHS.)

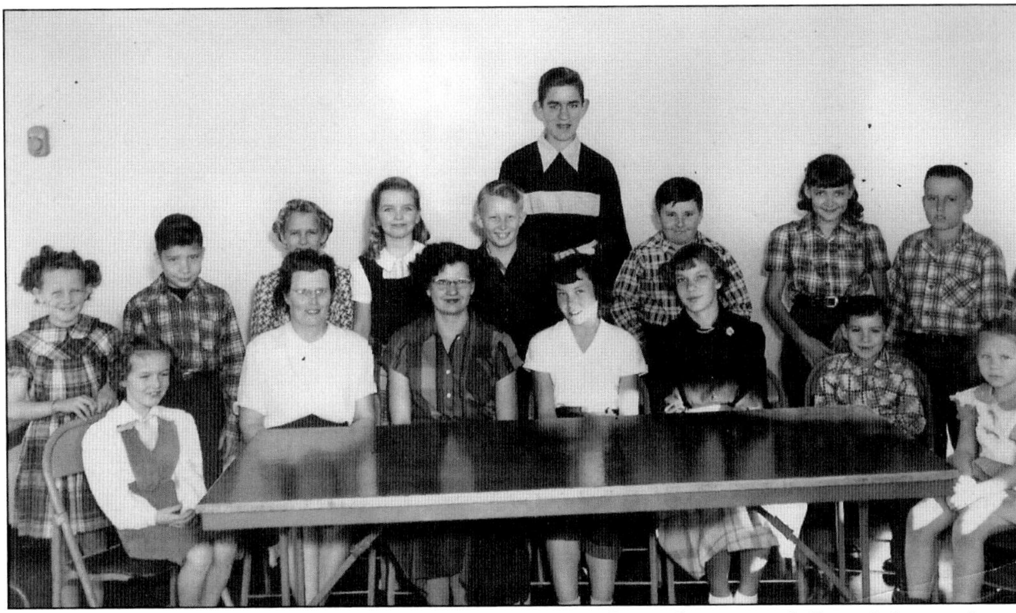

HEALTH COUNCIL, 1951–1952. Elementary students made up this council. From left to right are (seated) Snowflake Belcher, sponsor Cleo Lockhart, Maribelle Ward, Wilma Cudd, Patsy Cole, Johnny Forest, and Shirley George; (standing) unidentified, Bill Hewlett, Darrelene Ramsey, Diane Hughes, Tommy Chapman, William Saltsman, Tommy William McDaniel, Sue Bentley, and Gerald Ramsey. (SAHS.)

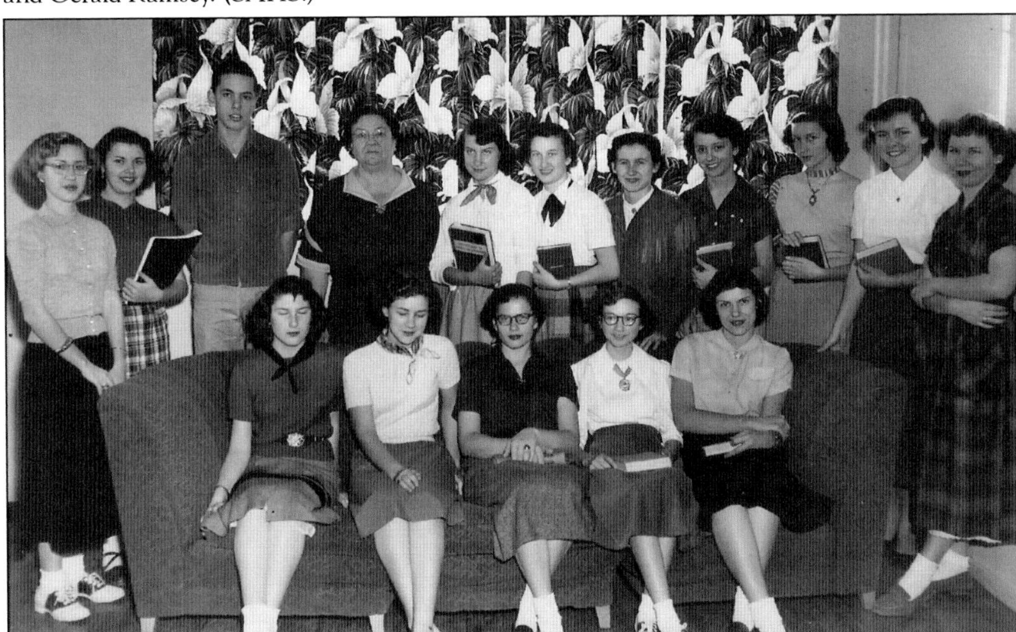

NATIONAL HONOR SOCIETY, 1951–1952. Members of the honor society are, from left to right, (seated) Louroyce Jones, secretary-historian Ethelyn Ready, president Elaine Baker, Billie Jean Coffey, and Jackie Nell Odom; (standing) Betty Ann Burks, Barbara Cole, Carrol Moore, sponsor Callie Miller, Sarah Horst, Elizabeth Belcher, vice president Betty Jo Kirby, Alta Holder, Patricia Harberson, reporter Greta Miller, and Georgia Blakely. (SAHS.)

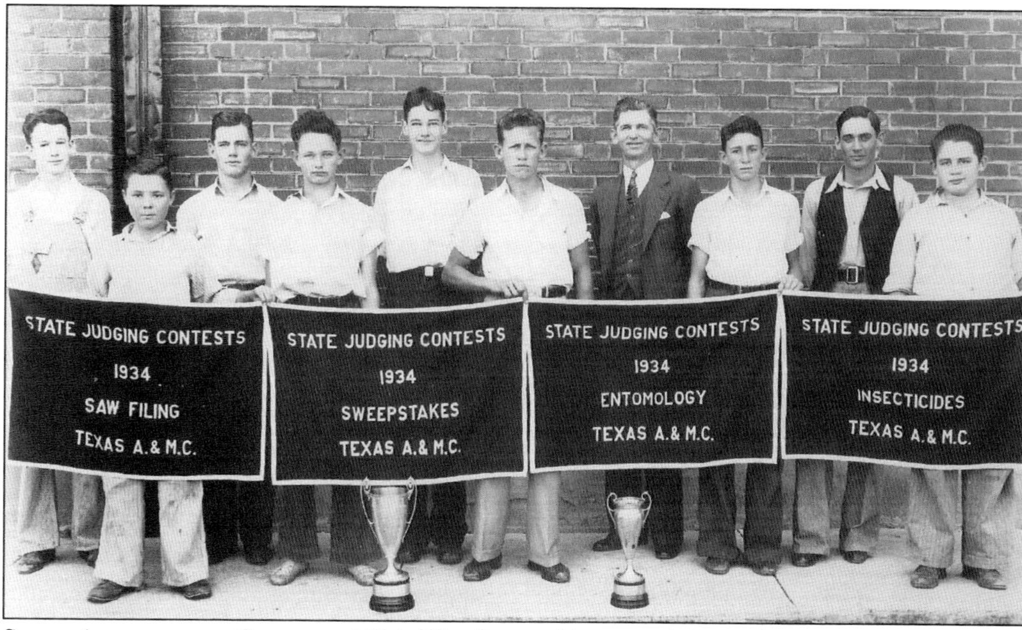

State Agriculture Contest, 1934. The Sanger Vocational Agriculture students' trip to the annual state competition at Texas A&M College was well rewarded with four trophies. From left to right are Jesse Earl Seal, Marshall Cearley, John Lewis Sullivan, Alton Dickens, Gober McClellan, Francis "Holly" Hollingsworth, teacher L.I. Samuel, Rex Moore, Roy Winstead, and Harry "Tubby" Lyons. (SAHS.)

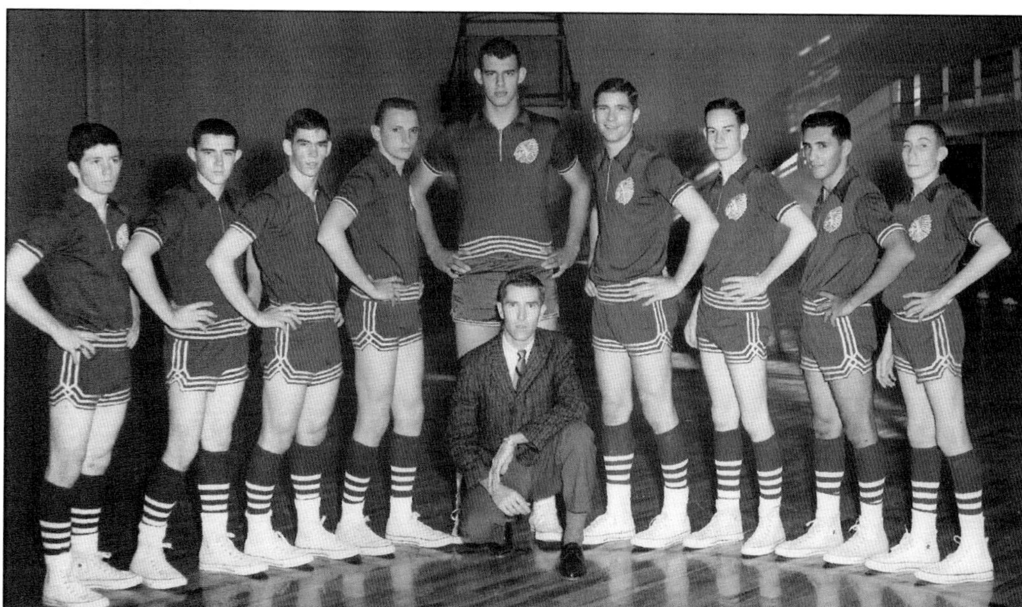

Sanger High Boys' Basketball Team, 1965–1966. In this photograph, taken in the high school second-floor gymnasium, the boys' basketball team members are, from left to right, Bobby Payne, Billy Tidwell, Larry Campbell, V.B. Atchison, Jerry Dale Ashcraft, Ed Yeary, Kenny Cook, Arnold Garza, and Keith Cook with coach John Lowery in the bottom center. (Courtesy of Myrl (Yeary) Webb.)

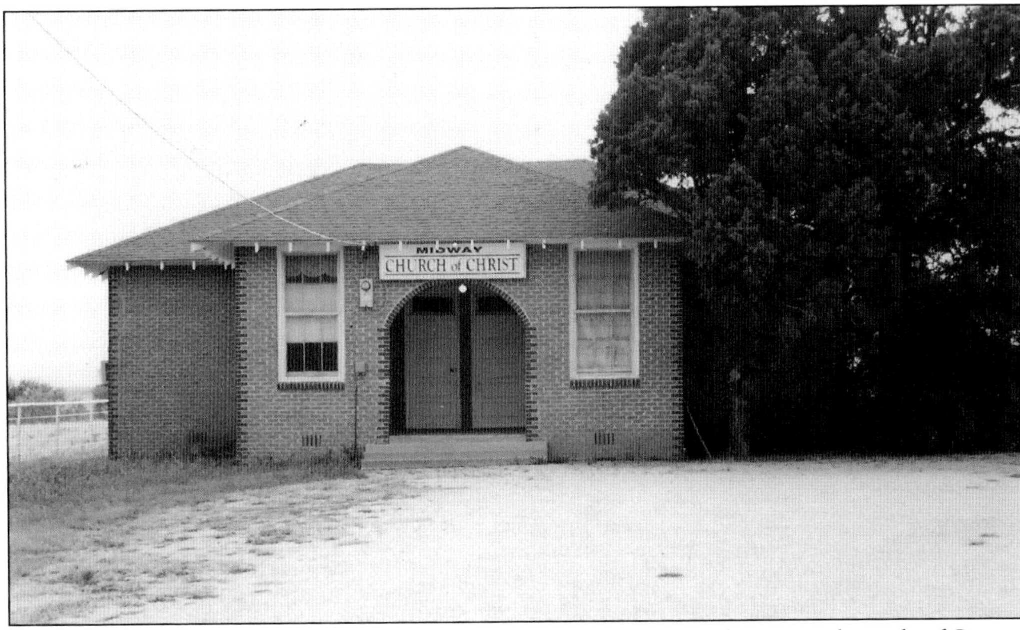

Blue Mound School, 1884. The school for the community of Blue Mound, south of Sanger, was established prior to World War I. This brick building, constructed in the 1930s, was used until the school consolidated with Sanger Independent School District in 1949. It has also served as a community center. The building on Interstate 35 is now the home of the Midway Church of Christ. (SAHS.)

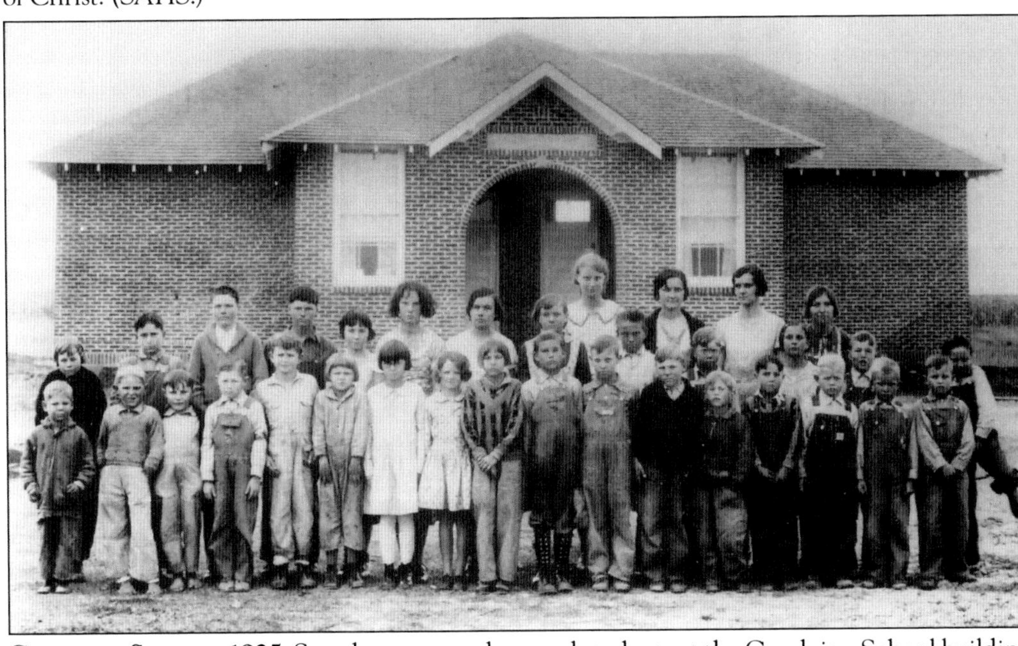

Goodview School, 1925. Seen here are teachers and students at the Goodview School building located on the southeast corner of Metz and View Roads, north of Sanger, where it still stands today. The building is very similar in design to the Blue Mound Schoolhouse on Interstate 35, south of Sanger. In later years, the brick Goodview Schoolhouse was the home of Joe and Esta Ashcraft. (SAHS).

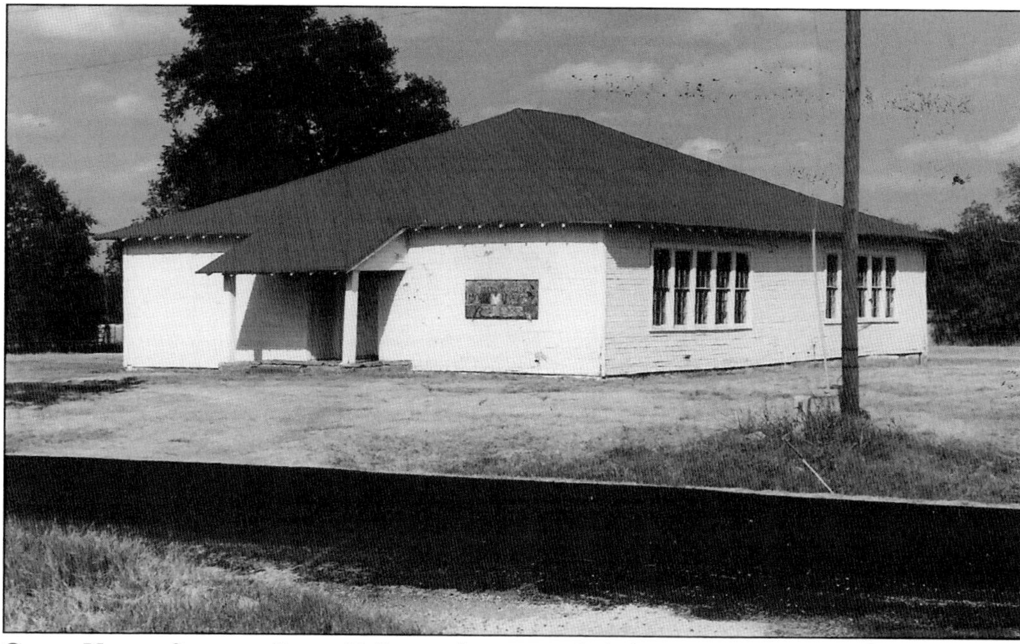

GREEN VALLEY SCHOOL. Green Valley students attended classes in a vacant farmhouse in 1878. In 1884, the school district was organized in a one-room schoolhouse that burned in 1894, so a four-room building was constructed in 1919. In 1935, the high school students were transferred to Denton, resulting in the school closing in 1949. The schoolhouse was later converted to a community center and awarded a Texas Historical Marker in 2001. (SAHS.)

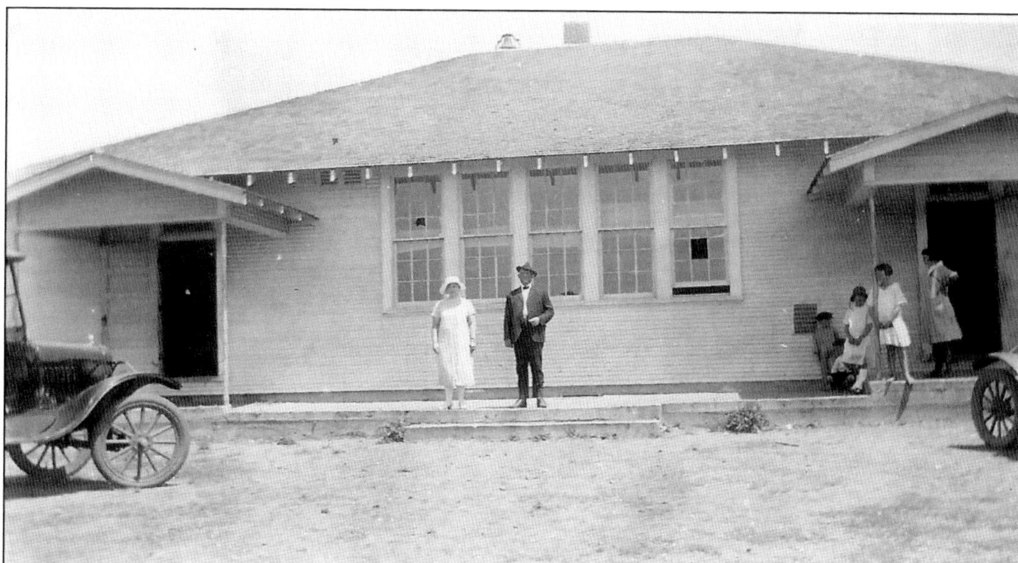

UNION HILL SCHOOL, 1884. The school was also known as Pond Creek. The Union Hill community, located northeast of Sanger, used this building to house a school and a Baptist church. The school was consolidated with Sanger Independent School District in 1947. In the 1960s, the building was remodeled into a home for Billy Earl and Gwen (Harris) Switzer. It was later destroyed by fire. (Courtesy of Elleece (Sullivan) Calvert.)

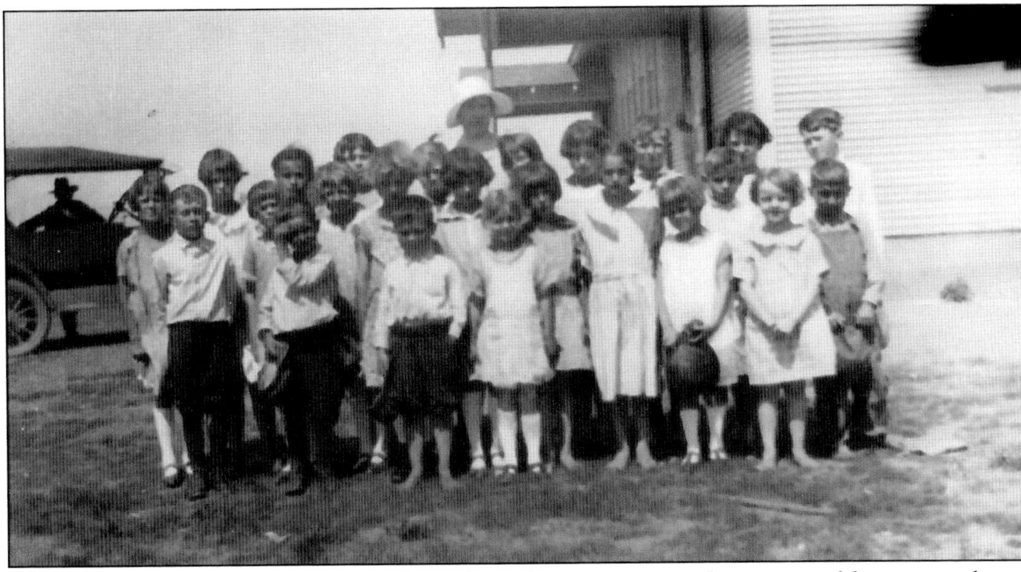

Union Hill Students. Above, teacher Alma Newton poses with a group of first, second, and third grade students from the Union Hill community. Students who have been identified include J.F., Bertie, and Garrison Mundkowsky; Ollie and Harvey Davis; Estelle and Ouanita Sullivan; George Anderson; Marshall Cearly; Pearl Spindle; and J. D. Ford. The picture below shows high school students who later transferred to other schools to graduate. Many of them graduated from Sanger High School. Pictured from left to right are (first row) teacher Mr. Stubbs, Ollie Davis, Ruby McKinney, Opal Spindle, Lillie Belle Melton, Clara Bell Sullivan, Vergie Jones, and Jimmie Campbell; (second row) Alyne Michael, Alton Sullivan, Herman Sullivan, Guy Michael, J.T. Sullivan, Alva Campbell, Harvey Davis, and Claudie Sullivan. (Above, courtesy of Elleece (Sullivan) Calvert; below, courtesy of Marlene Harper.)

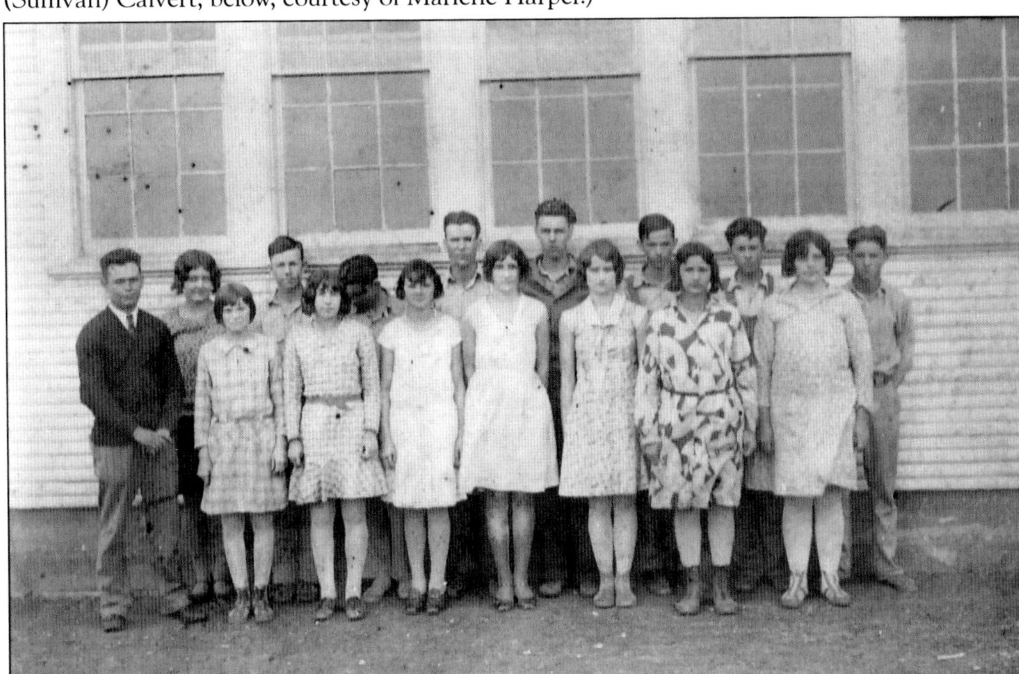

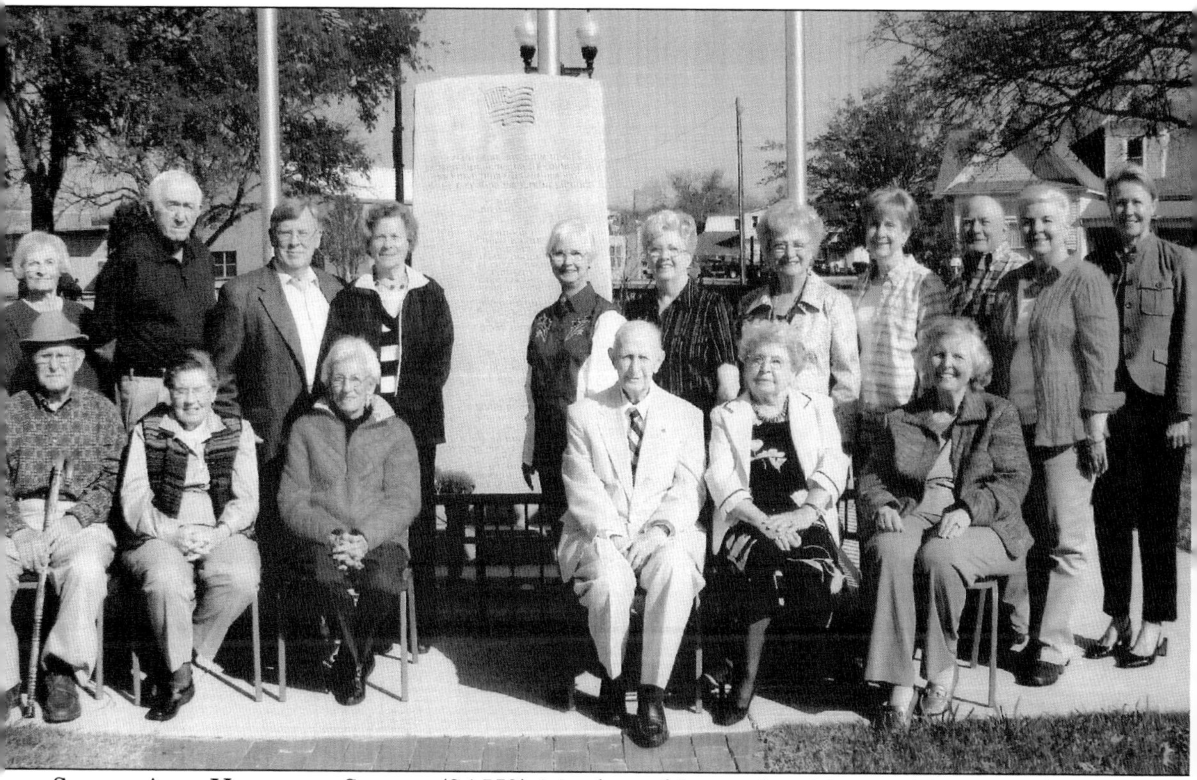

Sanger Area Historical Society (SAHS). Members of Sanger Area Historical Society gather in the Sanger city park in April 2011 by the War Memorial. The society, established in 1999, has sponsored the restoration of the Presbyterian church, Christmas Tour of Homes, school programs, historical markers, genealogy short courses, Sanger Area Historical Driving Tour brochure, Christmas Around the Piano, Sanger Public Library newspaper archiving, Memorial Day memorabilia display, and homecoming parade participation. The society continues to focus on promoting historic preservation for the community with informative programs for the general public. This pictorial book was published to capture the photographs of our history for future generations and those who hold memories of Sanger. From left to right are (seated) Jack and Nel Armstrong, Helen Bounds, John Chambers, Idaleene Fuqua, and Greta Miller; (standing) Jane and Billy Ed Nance, Billy and Virginia Ezell, Nancy Smith, Pat Kerby, Elizabeth Higgs, Rosene Sebastian, Bobby and Tona Payne, and Carolyn Briner. Not pictured are Richard Briner, Joe Higgs, Troy Miller, Richard Muir, Thomas and Kay Trietsch, and Mary Walling. (Photograph by Millard Smith.)